MOTHER'S INTENTION:
HOW BELIEF SHAPES BIRTH

Harbor
& Hill

MOTHER'S INTENTION:
HOW BELIEF SHAPES BIRTH

A Commonsense Guide to
Safe, Comfortable Guilt-free
Birth

BY

KIM WILDNER, CCE, CHT, HBCE

Harbor & Hill Publishing
United States

Harbor
& Hill

Disclaimer:
This book has been written in the attempt to help women make their own best choices regarding their births. The whole point of the book is for women to research their options and initiate dialog with their care providers about their options. No action should be taken without consultation with a qualified health care professional. Mother's Intention is not meant to replace the advice of any health care professional.
Persons following any course of action as a result of this book do so of their own free will and do not hold the author or publisher responsible for any problems encountered as a result of said action. The reader assumes all responsibility for their own health and care during their pregnancy, birth and postpartum period.
Do not use as a substitute for childbirth education classes, but as an enhancement. Great effort has been made to assure compatibility with all independent classes centering around evidence-based care and informed consumerism.
Personal accounts are either composites of many situations with identifying core material altered, or the parties involved have given permission for inclusion. Any resemblance to people, living or deceased, is purely coincidental.

Harbor & Hill Publishing, P.O. Box 265, Ludington, MI 49431

Cover and Logo designs: Kim Wildner

Colophon:
Manuscript written in Microsoft Word 2000
Original typesetting and layout in Microsoft Word
Type font: High Tower Text
Chapter Headings and title page in Copperplate Gothic Lt

What people are saying about this revolutionary work:

"In <u>Mother's Intention</u> Wildner has given to all women who are pregnant and to all who wish to be pregnant an honest, accurate and clearly marked roadmap for their journey toward achieving safe and comfortable birthing. It is a must read!"
Marie F. Mongan, Founder HypnoBirthing® Institute
www.hypnobirthing.com

"If everyone were to read this book and honestly venture into their own beliefs regarding pregnancy, birth and parenthood, great things would happen! Our country's infant mortality rate would drastically decline, women would fully embrace the power of their femininity, and best of all, the act of birth would no longer be feared. It would be anticipated with joy, engaged in totally, and treasured as the miracle it is!"
Lynette M. Prentice A.A.H.C.C.
Birth Instructor and Mother of three

"This book provides pregnant families with an opportunity to explore their beliefs and feelings around pregnancy and birth. Opportunities for contemplation and journaling thread throughout the book, helping families clarify their own thoughts and feelings with a fresh perspective."
Pat Sonnenstuhl, CNM, HBCE, CPPI
http://home.attbi.com/~prebirthhealth/

"It's time to quit the whining, and take our births back. No more "I didn't know", "Where were you when I had my baby", "Nobody told me". Here it is. It IS possible for birth to be a peak experience, and it's worth working for. Ms. Wildner provides both theory and tools to help women shape this amazing event. So read the book, do the thinking, and create the framework for the experience you want for yourself, your baby and your life."
Kip Kozlowski, RN, CNM, CHt.
Director, Greenhouse Birth Center

"Wildner has a very special way of putting down information that is not agenda based or negative. Her work will be used in training doulas as well as expectant mothers. You will have a new outlook on life and birth when you are done with this book."
*Dee Nipper, Doula and Executive producer and host of **The Real Side of Birth**, A positive radio show about birth and your choices.*
www.realsideofbirth.com

This work is dedicated to my loving husband, Dave, whose unwavering faith made this book possible and to my gorgeous daughter, Chelsea Raine, whose gentle birth inspired me to use my life toward improving the world she will inherit. I love you both.

I am also grateful for the many parents who have expanded my horizons. I've learned innumerable lessons from their joy...and pain. I would specifically like to thank Shelley and Alan for believing in me more than I believed in myself, and Rebecca, for showing me how strong women really are.

To the many professionals within the birthing community, working diligently for better birth, I thank you. My own 'fairytale' birth, possible through the efforts of those who have ceaselessly poured their hearts into improving birth outcomes for the last 30 or more years, empowered me. My passion for better birth is a direct result, this book, the manifestation of the passion. My paradigm shift regarding pain and birth could not have happened without Mickey. My introduction to HypnoBirthing® planted the seed that became a garden.

I'd like to thank Yolanda, for first suggesting that maybe the Universe was trying to steer me toward writing and education.

Trish also suggested I collect my thoughts and share them. I didn't listen to her at first either! I am grateful for those that kept trying to point out my strengths and helped me refine them.

My best friend Diane lifted me through frustrations and shared my epiphanies at all hours of the day and night, all while nursing two boys through babyhood. I am grateful for her stamina and the unique ability she has to nourish my soul.

Last, but not least, I would like to thank Kip for helping me sort out my thoughts...for her seemingly endless reservoir of support and encouragement as well as her expertise. Without her help this work truly would not have ever come to fruition. Her wisdom kept me in line, her humor kept me laughing and her affection kept my spirits up.

CONTENTS

FOREWORD   9
INTRODUCTION   13

PART ONE-INSPIRATION   17
*KNOWING THAT 'FAIRY-TALE' BIRTHS ARE CREATED, NOT
ENCOUNTERED IS THE FIRST STEP TOWARD MAKING IT HAPPEN.*
    CHAPTER 1: CLEARING THE WAY   19
    CHAPTER 2: BIRTH BELIEFS   55
    CHAPTER 3: MOTHER GUILT   69

PART TWO-MOTIVATION   91
*NOW THAT YOU KNOW BIRTH CAN BE SAFE <u>AND</u> COMFORTABLE
YOU NEED TO KNOW HOW TO MAKE IT HAPPEN.*
    CHAPTER 4: (PRO) CREATION   93
    CHAPTER 5: HUMAN NATURE   115
    CHAPTER 6: MOTHER NATURE   143

PART THREE-INTERNALIZATION   167
*YOU'VE BEEN INSPIRED TO REACH HIGHER, YOU WANT IT TO
HAPPEN...NOW YOU MUST BELIEVE IT INTO BEING.*
    CHAPTER 7: BIRTH RITE   169
    CHAPTER 8: INTENTIONS AND EXPECTATIONS   183
    CHAPTER 9: AGONY OR ECSTASY   201

PART FOUR-EXTERNALIZATION   227
*MAKING BETTER BIRTH **YOUR** REALITY MEANS TAKING ACTION.*
    CHAPTER 10: VARIABLES AND OUTCOMES   229
    CHAPTER 11: SAFETY FIRST?   247
    CHAPTER 12: TO FORGIVE (NOT FORGET) 267

PART FIVE-REALIZATION   283
*THE BIRTH OF A MOTHER-BABY...CHANGING THE WORLD, ONE
BIRTH AT A TIME.*
    CHAPTER 13: IN CONTROL   285
    CHAPTER 14: DREAM IT, DO IT   307
AFTERWORD   325
SELECTED BIBLIOGRAPHY   331
WEB RESOURCES   333
ORDER FORM   335

FOREWORD

We have this saying in the doula world. KNOWLEDGE IS POWER.

The most important thing you can do for yourself and your baby is to take away all the misinformation provided by friends and family. All you tend to hear are horror stories everywhere you turn. I feel that this happens because they didn't feel like they had the right to question or dream of that beautiful birth.

Well, beautiful births happen all the time and I know this because I am at those births with my clients. They come in all different ways. Some of my clients use midwives but most of them are in a hospital and they choose a place and a doctor that have the same belief system and are open to what the mom feels is the right way for her and her baby to deliver. It really comes down to what you feel is right for you.

Kim has written a book that I call a map to your birth. When you are going to take a trip in a car some where, you pull out a map and you look for all the ways to get there.

Let's say you are going to grandmas house and you haven't been there since you were a kid. Grandma hasn't left her house in 4 years and she has not left her town for 30 years. You call her and she starts telling you how to get there. She tells you that it will take about 10 hours. She then starts telling you that you will need to bring chains for your tires because the snow can be really deep at the pass. She also tells you that you need to bring extra gas because if the snow is to deep the one gas station might be closed. She then says that you need extra food in case you get stuck or if they close the pass, and to bring blankets and an extra radio with batteries. She then tells you that you might want to get extra car insurance because she remembers that a lot of cars seem to get really damaged on this road. You say goodbye to her and hang up the phone and you start thinking that there has got to be a better way there. So, you get your map and start looking and see that there are a lot of different ways to get to Grandma's house. There are roads that are completely paved and roads that go by beautiful streams and waterfalls. There are roads that have a lot of historic meaning that you could stop and appreciate. And then, you notice that on every road there are forks that you can take at any time to change your direction or length of your trip. You notice that you never have to go over that pass that causes so much of the problem. You feel relieved and so glad that there are maps to make this trip something to be excited about.

This book is YOUR map to your birth. It is a map of all the different ways to have your baby with all the information of every way so that you can take the road you want and when you have forks in the road you'll know which one to take because you'll know what each road and fork offers you and the outcomes it delivers.

Thank you, Kim for putting this in a form that all can understand. There are no agendas here. There is no shame here if you pick a birth that is not "natural".

This is a training book for many if not all things in your life. You will be changed after reading this book and on the road to a healthy and beautiful birth with no regrets or questions unanswered.

Dee Nipper, Doula and Executive producer and host of The Real Side of Birth, A positive radio show about birth and your choices www.realsideofbirth.com

A few years ago, I began a journey to empower moms and dads during birth.

It started after several of the couples from my class went into a downward tailspin after a prenatal visit. Sometimes they were told that the baby was going to be too big, that they didn't have enough amniotic fluid, that the due date was changing again or that they couldn't have the birth they wanted for any number of other reasons.

I felt helpless. I wanted to help but, moms and dads could not get past the belief that birth was flawed. What I saw over, and over again, were moms who were completely panicked and fearful before the birth, and very angry after the birth.

Once in a while I would see a couple who would ask the provider question after question and do their own research until they were fully educated on the matter. If they met resistance from a care giver about having the birth their way, these clients would usually hunt for a new doctor who could meet their high expectations. They had fabulous births.

Some couples had providers who were verbally abusive before the birth. They did not bother to find a better care provider. During the birth the care provider was still abusive. The couple did not enjoy the birth of their baby and they had quite a bit of anger that lasted for months, if not years.

I prayed for a tool that could help them. I even started producing and co-hosting a radio show called "The Real Side of Birth" with the purpose of better educating the couples as early as possible.

I didn't think it was possible that someone in another part of the country would not only feel the same way as I did but would find away of explaining so eloquently how these challenges could be resolved.

When I read the book, *Mother's Intention*, I cried. My tears were of sadness for the many women who didn't have this resource before having their babies and tears of joy that I was privy to one of the most amazing books that I'd ever read. I was glued to the book for two days. I found the answers that I had been searching for. I finally had a resource that my clients could read that would change the course of their birth. This resource would guide them through the medical system. As I read each chapter, I was startled by all of the new information I learned about birthing. There were things I never thought about questioning before, that now were so obvious.

I hope that this will be the first book that women will read when they discover that they are pregnant. I'm sure that you will find this book to be one of the most helpful of all guides in your journey to have a wonderful and happy birthing day.

SheriMenelli
Certified HypnoBirthing Educator and Certified Hypnotherapist
Producer and Co-Host of The Real Side of Birth

INTRODUCTION

Before I even begin to explain who I am and how this book came about, I feel it may be helpful to the reader if I explain the motivation for writing it.

Childbirth books are plentiful. Many on gentle birth have been dismissed out-of-hand by the very persons who need them most, with amazing rationalizations.

How and why have some women dismissed books that held the key to better birth?

One way is that even though women *want* gentle birth, many do not *believe* it's really possible. Avoiding concepts that challenge core beliefs is a coping mechanism. Therefore, experts in natural childbirth have been labeled 'naturalists' or 'alarmists', which makes them easy to write off. Some women insist that to suggest birth can be joyful or comfortable is to be deceitful; to suggest our current system has flaws is seen as nearly heretical, or at the very least a negative thing. This is, basically, 'shooting the messenger'.

This book puts forth some very concrete and positive steps to creating the best birth possible for the reader. In order to implement these steps, the rationale for them needs to be established. This means it's imperative to first acknowledge, then define, the problems that currently exist so that the solutions make sense. I have struggled with how to do this in the most positive way, and what I have come up with is to simply rely on the results—scientific evidence--to speak to the success or failure of what is currently considered the 'norm' and let the individual decide what makes sense.

To a reader who has been tempted to disregard other works, I would ask "What would be the ulterior motive behind the 'breast is best' or 'natural birth is preferable' message? I have actually read articles, full of animosity, declare that breastfeeding advocates are 'nipple-nazis' with an agenda. What would that be, exactly? I implore the readers of this book to consider that maybe, just maybe, there is truth in these messages. Act 'as if' there might be legitimacy to the idea that nature has a plan that allows you to have your cake and eat it too, so to speak. If, after you are finished with the book and actually done the work, you still don't believe that birth can be wonderful, that's fine. I have no problem in agreeing to disagree. It's your birth to do your way. However, I would speculate that you've picked up this book to help you create a better birth. That goal is attainable if you go into this with a willing heart.

My childbearing days are done, so that fact that childbirth options are eroding at an appalling pace is of no personal concern to me. Stop. Did you inwardly scoff at the thought that women currently don't have control over their births? Were you tempted to reject the very idea? Was your first reaction to rationalize that maybe other women don't have options, but *you* certainly do? Then you need this book. Or, did you nod your head in agreement that certainly, you have no choice but to do whatever your care-provider tells you, even if it's contrary to common sense? Then you need this book *more*.

Why do I passionately advocate for gentle birth? Believe me, I ask myself that question on a regular basis! Why have I put the time and energy into your babies by writing, lecturing, and teaching? There's always a pay-off. What's mine? I don't own a breast-milk bank. I don't hold stock in endorphins or prolactin (a couple of the body's natural 'feel good' hormones). The fact that my husband calls this my 'expensive hobby' may indicate what the financial reward has been. I don't get a fiscal incentive for 'converting' someone to a midwife-attended birth, nor am I rewarded with expensive gifts for support of holistic doctors (though, hey, I'm open to the possibility). I am very proud of the parenting decisions we've made, confident that they were right for us, so there is no emotional motivation in the 'bad company is better than no company' sort of way. I will admit to living vicariously through mothers who glowingly rave about the birth they originally thought impossible. I experience again the wonderment of my own birth. I also like being around these gently born children who exhibit impulse control, compassion and empathy, just as scientists researching undisturbed brain development suggested they would. I feel good knowing these kids will impact my world, and the world my child inherits, in a positive way.

Every time I've been ready to just tap out, someone has told me I helped them change their life. Someone told me the day I sat down to write this introduction. When I know that someone's birth was an act of empowerment that helped a family bond into a beautiful thing, because of something I shared, it keeps me going.

My objective is to reduce *irrational* fear so that women can have the best birth they can have. A fear that is disproportionate to the actual risk is irrational. Fear of birth is completely out of proportion, as you will see if you do the journal exercises in this book, agreeing to keep an open mind about the facts you will read.

They may seem implausible with the current thinking of the average parent-to-be, but by the end of the book you should be seeing the possibilities that are available to you in a whole new light.

Entire chapters are devoted to issues of fear, guilt and motivation behind many controversies within the 'birthing community'. I ask that the reader move through the book sequentially, taking a few days to mull over what they've read in each chapter and to do the work. The material is nothing new, but it may be new to you. It asks, for your own health and well-being and that of your baby, that you entertain thoughts you may never have considered. Some thoughts are contrary to popular belief. I will ask you to look deeply into *beliefs* you may currently hold as self-evident truths.

You can take control of what is controllable in birth, which is a great deal. This is how guilt is avoided...by being secure in the knowledge that you've made decisions based on all of the information available and with the best of intent. If you want a great birth, do what those who tell great births stories do. If you want to be one of the ones telling horror stories, do what everyone else does. It's that simple.

During pregnancy and in the early years of parenting, if you don't become knowledgeable it could affect your life in a big way. When you are knowledgeable, no one can take advantage of you. It's much easier to do the work ahead of time. By reading this book you won't be one of the increasing numbers of women asking, "Why didn't anyone tell me?" I'm telling you, right now.

The question is, are you willing to listen?

PART ONE
INSPIRATION

ARE YOUR BELIEFS ABOUT BIRTH CONSTRUCTED OF PERCEPTUAL REALITY OR FACTUAL REALITY? HOW DO YOU KNOW THE DIFFERENCE? HOW DOES WHAT YOU BELIEVE ABOUT BIRTH AFFECT YOUR BIRTH? WHAT CAN YOU DO TO BRING YOUR BELIEFS IN LINE WITH SCIENCE SO THAT YOU MIGHT BE INSPIRED TO REACH HIGHER? IS IT POSSIBLE TO ENJOY GIVING BIRTH?

CLEARING THE WAY

We all have a common objective...healthy, happy mother-babies. Used to it's highest good, this book can save you time, effort, money, embarrassment, injury and maybe even a life.

Clear communication is essential if the reader is to maximally benefit from this work, so I would like to clarify some terminology that's often tossed about quite casually.

Because it is human nature to assume others are like ourselves, we talk about birth with the assumption that we are all talking about the same experience. Differing birth philosophies mean we may not be, making for emotionally charged exchanges if we don't first take this step.

Even though the majority of birth professionals go out of their way to use neutral language, inevitably miscommunication develops around such personal issues if terminology is not defined. It's human nature to become defensive if a dearly held belief is being challenged. Nowhere are our beliefs held as deeply as those relating to childbirth and childrearing.

Certain terms are inappropriately applied to natural birth advocates on a regular basis. This misuse of language has even spawned new, judgmental terminology, which is interesting, because they stem from the charge that natural birth advocates are 'judgmental'.

I offer the following dictionary definitions for a few of the most common of these characterizations, with discussion of the misapplication of each.

balanced: to make two parts exactly equal; a means of judging or deciding; counter balancing with force or influence; to equalize in weight, number or proportion; weigh; to bring into harmony or proportion. Common use regarding childbirth and parenting information: *"I chose the hospital class because they provide balanced information"*.

biased: to give a bias to; prejudice. (prejudice: preconceived judgment or opinion; a favoring or dislike of something without just grounds or before sufficient knowledge; an irrational attitude or hostility directed at an individual, a group or race; to cause or have prejudice: bias.) Common use regarding childbirth and parenting information: *"I didn't find that book useful because it was so biased"*

judge/judgment/judgmental: to form an authoritative opinion by discerning or comparing; an opinion so formed; the capacity for judging; discernment. Common use: *"Women on the natural childbirth message boards are so judgmental! What a bunch of birth nazis (or "naturalists" or other, ironically, judgmental labels)"*.

natural: born in or with one; innate; being such by nature; existing or used in or produced by nature; having or showing qualities held to part of the nature of man; conforming to the laws of nature; not made or altered by man; marked by simplicity or sincerity; not affected. Common debate: *What constitutes 'natural childbirth'?*

objective: existing outside and independent of the mind; treating or dealing with facts without distortion by personal feeling or prejudice. *"I would like objective information about my birthing options."*

Which words accurately describe natural birth and parenting advocates? More importantly, which apply to the information about to be presented in this book? How are these words used in heated debate and who does it harm?

Let us look at *"balanced"* first..."*to make two parts exactly equal.*" What if the two parts are <u>not</u> equal? What if a parent will be making decisions that will affect her and her baby with both short and long term consequences. Is it fair to distort reality so that the information she has to choose from seems 'equal', even though it really isn't? Why would a parent want information that *appears* balanced, but isn't *factual*?

"a means of judging or deciding; counter balancing with force or influence; to equalize in weight, number or proportion; weigh; to bring into harmony or proportion" Using this definition, it would be reasonable to find the following in the hands of those that claim to seek "balance":

<u>Gentle Birth Choices</u>, by Barbara Harper (which gives equal time to all options)
<u>Five Standards for Safe Childbearing</u>, by Stewert (which weighs all existing data on what makes birth safe)
<u>The Thinking Woman's Guide to Better Birth</u> or <u>Obstetric Myths versus Research Realities</u>, by Henci Goer (both weigh current practice against the scientific literature)

However, that's not usually the case. The books most often found maintain the status quo and are not supported by one bit of evidence...do not give "equal force or influence to" proven safe options such as homebirth or freestanding birth centers. By "informing" women that they can *expect* substandard care, women *accept* substandard care.

If asked why they chose a childbirth class at the hospital instead of an independent class, parents maintain it's more "balanced".

Consider this:

In a hospital class the childbirth educator (CBE) is an employee of the hospital. She may only teach pre-approved material. She may not be able to fully answer questions posed by parents if the response contradicts the protocols of the hospital, or even one doctor, no matter if she can provide scientific evidence for her answer and the doctor cannot. An instructor in an institution cannot give unbiased, balanced information that includes any providers other than those who sign her checks. Think about it from the hospital's point of view...would you hire someone who would provide information that might help parents take their dollars elsewhere? As a doctor, would you send your patients to a class where they might learn there are other caregivers who practice under safer guidelines?

Classes in the hospital are actually more affordable because of the bias under which they operate. Formula and drug companies often subsidize these classes. The content of the class can be determined in large part by how involved other parties are. The 'free' gifts are not always 'free'.

An independent instructor is not subsidized. Her passion for birth usually happened one of two ways—either she had such a horrible birth experience she went on a mission to discover what went wrong and now wants to spare you her anguish, *or* she had such a wonderful birth experience she wants to share the steps to better birth she used. I'm the latter, in case you wondered.

With an independent instructor, you sign her paycheck. She can fully, and honestly, answer any question you ask. She works as a CBE because she wants to make a difference, not because she's grudgingly been assigned the task on top of her long OB nursing shift.

In fact, she may not even be a nurse, which is to your advantage. Nursing is a highly skilled profession requiring an enormous amount of knowledge from pediatrics to geriatrics; surgical to pharmaceutical. Normal labor and birth are a very small part of what they learn in their extensive training, and an even smaller part of their experience if the only births they ever witness are medically managed.

An independent CBE is an autonomous practitioner who only studies pregnancy, birth and (sometimes) early parenting. Because her specialty is quite narrow, she knows more about what *you* <u>need</u> to know. Her education likely included study of all birth options, as does her continuing education.

An independent instructor has compared and contrasted *every* option available to pregnant mothers. Having done so, her classes are most likely 'natural childbirth' classes.

Parents often <u>think</u> that's what their hospital class is. If it's called a 'prepared childbirth' class or an 'expectant parent' class, it's not. Even a class billed 'natural childbirth' may not be what it seems. There is confusion over what 'natural childbirth' means, which is why I included it in the list of terms to clarify. We can't have a discussion about birth if we are not on the same page, so to speak.

There is a trend deeming any vaginal birth 'natural'. Going back to our dictionary definition, *"born in or with one; innate; being such by nature; existing or used in or produced by nature; having or showing qualities held to part of the nature of man; conforming to the laws of nature; not made or altered by man; marked by simplicity or sincerity; not affected"*, what can logically be called 'natural'?

"born in or with one; innate; being such by nature; existing or used in or produced by nature" could include a vaginal birth with **natural** (*produced by nature*) interventions such as nipple stimulation, herbs, positional changes or relaxation techniques that trigger the "relaxation response", an innate biological state of being that counters the affects of the 'fight or flight response', which inhibits natural labor.

Is pitocin made by nature? No. Does it affect the natural process of birth? Yes. Are drugs such as stadol, nubain or Demerol made in nature? No. Do they affect the natural process? Yes. Are epidural drugs made by nature? No. Do they affect normal labor progression. Yes.

It would stand to reason then, that while a *vaginal* birth is possible with such alterations of the birth process, *natural* birth is not.

Please note that restoring the term 'natural childbirth' to it's actual meaning does not 'take' anything away from anyone who wishes to reframe their experience. It simply brings the term back into compliance with the definition of 'natural' for the sake of clear communication. Perception is reality. Some prefer to call surgical births 'natural', which is their prerogative. I am choosing to use natural in the literal sense.

Also note that in doing so, no judgment has been implied. Distinction of *natural* birth, *vaginal* birth and *surgical* birth simply means they are dissimilar. There is no doubt that they are different experiences. Not better or worse, just different.

Even having taken great pains to use neutral language and explicitly state that different only means different, I know from experience that there will be a few people who will read 'better/worse, good/bad, always/never' where it does not exist. If your initial reaction is to do so, please take a moment to consider why. Is there a subconscious need to claim this rite of passage? Is there underlying self-doubt or low self-esteem issues? Is there inner conflict over the intent behind past decisions?

Birth does not place us in competition with other women. We do that to ourselves. Birth is the most singular experience with our true self that we can have. In the following examples, see how removal of the personal element by using a different experience shifts perception, thus reality.

Weight loss is very hard for some. One person may entirely change their diet and exercise twice a day to reach their goal. One person may take prescription drugs. Another may choose herbal, over-the-counter assistance. Yet another might have gastric by-pass surgery to achieve the same goal.

Each person reaches their goal, but they all have different experiences. We don't define them with judgment words of 'better' or 'worse', nor do we judge the people themselves. What if we decided to call all of these experiences 'natural weight loss programs'? Does deciding it make them so?

How about if we take it out of the medical realm? Since birth is not a medical event or illness, it may be more appropriate to use an example of marathon participants, where the objective is to test one's endurance, finishing the race, but not necessarily first. Pride comes from the accomplishment of working hard to achieve a goal. There are no losers.

- One person trained hard all year, eating well and exercising daily.
- One person does the same, with the addition that he requires insulin for a diabetic condition (or any medication for any medical condition).
- One person does the same, aided by a prosthesis replacing a lost limb.
- One person does the same from a wheel chair due to paraplegia.
- One sort of prepares, but decides part way through the race that it's too hard, and so catches a ride to the finish line.

All the same experience? No. There is no shame in finishing a race assisted by modern medicine when necessary. Indeed, those people must overcome obstacles others never even face. Should the person who *could not* have functioned without assistance of wheels be viewed the same as someone who *chose* them? How fair is it to the person who worked so hard to be put in the same category as someone who makes the decision *not* to? If the only goal is to cross the finish line, who is to judge how one gets there? The only opinion that matters is the participant's. Who is to determine how a participant should *feel*? Who decides who will be allowed to say they did it 'on their own'? Must we all agree on a definition of 'success', or is reality wholly the participant's perception?

It's obvious that 'natural childbirth' is a coveted experience, but how did it come-to-pass that the definition of 'natural' included the very antithesis of 'natural'?

Intentionally. By manipulating language, we manipulate experience. 'Natural' **should** mean 'normal'. By calling the obstetrically managed experience 'normal' despite the many non-medially indicated, inappropriately applied interventions used, those interventions then come to be seen as 'natural'. This is the progression of how flat-on-the-back births with IVs, drugs, inductions and episiotomies came to be accepted as 'normal'. Birth has been re-conceptualized, re-labeled and remarketed. It's up to mothers to reclaim natural birth.

In order to do that, mothers have to stop arguing over what is 'natural'. I propose the following commonsense definitions:

- Natural birth-Birth not made or altered by man; being such by nature.
- Vaginal birth-Birth wherein the baby passes though the birth passage, regardless of interventions used. A natural birth is a vaginal birth, but a vaginal birth may not be a natural birth.
- Surgical birth-Birth wherein the baby is surgically removed from the mother's uterus.

All terms use the word 'birth'; no term is inflammatory or derogatory; all are accurate and honest.

Honesty is frequently (and erroneously) called 'judgmental' when the subject is birth or parenting. There are two important components to this identity crisis.

One must first ask, "Was the intent malicious or benevolent?" then "Did the language *actually* contain judgment words, or did I hear judgment words?" and finally "If no judgment was intended or implied, why did I hear it? Is there self-judgment, or am I projecting judgment?"

Actual 'judgmental attitudes', the negative meaning usually ascribed to the term, are easy to spot and quite different from simple honesty when the two are compared and contrasted. I don't know a childbirth professional who would ever make judgmental comments to any mother like those found in the second group that follows, though I know many who have been accused of saying those things when what actually they said was something similar to the neutral comments first presented. I won't claim that no one, professional or not, ever passes judgment in a negative way, only that the accusation is most often unfounded.

Judgmental statements use judgmental words and blanket statements...bad, good, crazy, idiot, horrible, selfish, always, never. Shoot, just typing them made me feel bad. Please be aware that I do <u>not</u> hold the opinions given as 'judgmental'! I do not know anyone who does. I have heard them mistaken for the *honest* statements, which is why I chose to use them as examples!

<u>Honest phrases:</u>

- There is no medical reason for routine circumcision.
- There is no artificial mother's milk substitute that is good for babies.

- Epidurals have short and long-term negative effects on both mother and baby.
- Natural birth means "as nature intended."

Judgmental phrases:

- Genital mutilation is never justified.
- Women who don't breastfeed are selfish.
- Mothers who need epidurals are wimps.
- It's idiotic to call an induced or epidural birth "natural".

Who talks to other people that way? Not many, though, countless *give themselves* such harsh assessments.

Judgments are based on opinion and therefore cannot be substantiated. *Anyone* who hears them would be offended. Honest statements, on-the-other-hand, are made with neutral language. They contain verifiable truth. Honest statements do not hold judgment, though the judgmental may hold some truth, which is where people may get confused.

Honest statements may be heard as judgmental by someone who *is* judgmental, but not by everyone. An objective bystander hearing an honest statement might wonder why it would upset anyone.

An objective bystander would be hard to find, though, since we <u>all</u> see the world through the lens of our personal experience. We all form opinions from the time we begin absorbing our environment. Some of our opinions we have formulated on our own through experience, some we have inherited. This colors incoming messages. If we hear malice or judgment where it does not exist, it is the lens we currently use that distorts what we allow into our reality construct.

What if there *is* malice intended? What if a truly vicious person makes a comment with the sole intent of making another person feel badly for no reason?

It's still all about the malicious person holding the judgment, whose reality is created by the lens that distorts *their* perception. Their judgment has nothing to do with anyone but them. Even if the judgment is directed at me, I know the person holding the judgment feels that way about everyone, all the time. If I don't take it personally, it doesn't have to hurt me. I can choose to ignore it, realizing it has nothing to do with me. Only you can decide if you will choose to let it mean anything to you.

Do you care what a stranger thinks about your birth? Do you care what *anyone* thinks about your choices? Why? How liberating it is to be able to step back and not take someone else's perception of reality personally. It takes an awful lot of energy to be offended by comments with no offense behind them, and isn't it also a little arrogant to think that the choices we make regarding birth are of concern to anyone but ourselves? By making assumptions and taking things personally, we only hurt ourselves.

Every person has a lens. Every opinion is biased, including the ones *you* hold. The question is, what created the perception leading to a particular bias? Does the bias benefit you or not? Is the bias warranted? Does your own bias prevent access of information that might benefit you? Is your bias based on fact?

When it comes to childbirth and parenting, when someone dismisses information as 'biased', what it actually means is the information does not fit with their *already held* biases. It is our insecurities that bring up defensiveness in the face of judgment, or perceived judgment, as the case may be.

If someone were to pass judgment on you for something you didn't do or something you felt confident about, do you think you'd feel defensive or hurt? Not likely. You would simply shrug off the comment or the person making it.

This work and the works listed as resources are very much **unbiased** as they are based on scientific and experiential knowledge. In fact, the most common selections currently passing for "balanced" or "unbiased" childbirth information are actually very biased and highly prejudicial, based on nothing more than a slick PR campaign.

Judgmental? Let's see: *judge/judgment/judgmental: to form an authoritative opinion by discerning or comparing; an opinion so formed; the capacity for judging; discernment.* By this definition, yes, it could be called judgmental as this information is very carefully weighed and considered. I will not own the term 'judgmental' in the way it is usually used, however.

One last human tendency that gets in the way of clear communication is making assumptions, especially from a 'right' or 'wrong', 'good' or 'bad' mind-set. This has created an enormous chasm between those of us trying to help women create better births and the women themselves.

Is 'better' a judgment word? Only if it is applied in the context of 'my birth was better than your birth'. Current birth management leaves us with **27 countries with fewer babies dying than the US.** (March of Dimes Perinatal Data Center, August 2002) This is worse than when I began teaching 10 years ago. Current birth management is leaving mothers feeling that they can't cope, with war stories instead of joyful birth stories. Current birth and parenting advice, in the noble attempt to not offend *anyone*, gives advice that helps *no one*. We can do better. That is how I use the term.

In any case, assuming one personal choice makes another one wrong distorts communication about the choices themselves.

- It is *assumed* that if a mother has a homebirth she hates doctors and hospitals.

  Truth: Homebirth mothers recognize that hospitals and doctors are necessary in special circumstances. If they were sick or injured in pregnancy, they would not hesitate to gratefully utilize technology.

- It is *assumed* that because natural birth advocates want parents to have truthful information about labor drugs they are against compassionate use of, or medically indicated pharmaceuticals.

  Truth: Not so...only unnecessary or inappropriate used, without full disclosure of risk.

These are personal examples. I have faced judgmental attitudes for my choices many times. No one can make me feel anything I do not choose to feel. The judgment I've encountered doesn't phase me because I am confident that I've made the best choices for myself and my family with the information I had at the time. I'm not concerned if anyone agrees with me or how *they* feel about what *I* do. At times I've attempted to explain my decisions, until I realized that the people making assumptions and judgments don't actually want to hear about solid decision making strategies if it conflicts with what they already believe to be true. They don't even hear, much less listen or consider.

As you work through this book and start making decisions that may be different from what our society considers the norm, you may hear comments with a lot of anger and hurt behind them, seemingly directed at you. Comments like, "Well I did [such and such] and my kids are just fine!" when you never implied that they weren't. You may never even had a thought in your head that the other person could have or should have done anything differently, but they are seeing *your* actions though *their* own lens and *making assumptions*. It doesn't have anything to do with your choices or why you made them.

In fact, if you tried to explain why you made a particular decision, they probably won't even hear you because *they aren't upset about you and your decision*...they have issues with their *own* decisions. They are stuck in an either/or mind-set.

If you think your decision is right, the assumption is you think their decision was wrong. It's best to just let it go. We are only responsible for our own heath and well-being.

It is true that those of use who have been trying to improve the safety and experience of birth for decades get *frustrated* when we hear horror story after preventable horror story.

We want so much better for women and babies, not because we're judgmental or think that every birth can (or should) be the same, but because we've seen so much sorrow that didn't have to happen!

If you were psychic and could foretell a train wreck about to happen, would you be frustrated that a person ignored your warning and was hurt?

If your adult self could go back and tell your child self what you know now so that her life could be better, would you? Would you be aggravated if she didn't listen?

Natural birth supporters aren't trying to scare you by telling you what you don't want to hear, we are trying to help you! What you don't know *can* hurt you! If you don't know your options, you don't have any. If you make decisions that net the expected, with all the unhappiness mothers now complain of, we are sad that you have to endure that...not judgmental. Closing one's eyes to the truth does not make it cease to exist...it only makes one powerless to deal with the reality.

Which brings us to 'objective'. Natural birth advocates are often passionate about natural birth. Passion does not preclude objectivity. If a person's personal opinion is based on emotion alone, then obviously they are not objective. However, if their passion arises from facts *'existing outside and independent of the mind"* and there is no distortion of the facts *'by personal feelings or prejudice'*, then the information is quite objective. How does one know the difference? Test the validity of the assertion. In this work, I have provided the resources to do just that in the notes. Yes, I'm passionate. I'm also objective.

So who am I and why would what I have to tell you matter?

I am you. I am a daughter, a wife, a mother. I grew up in the Midwest in the typical American family with 2.2 children. I was influenced by the same cultural ideas about pregnancy and birth that most people have.

The 'point two' child came into my family when I was 13. As a strong willed child prone to testing the data, I questioned everything my mother went through. I wanted to know 'why' to everything. I found it strangely disconcerting that there were no logical answers to my questions. Even the answers that were supposed to be logical didn't compute.

Why would a woman need to be cut (an episiotomy) to get a baby out? If nature were so incompetent as to make the birth passage inadequate to birth a baby, why weren't all mammals walking around with damaged vaginas? As it seemed to me, only human mothers were...due to the episiotomy! There were dozens of other illogical (to me) rituals in becoming a mother. Often the only 'reason' for them was because "That's what *they* do." (Ah! The ubiquitous *they*!)

My husband and I were faced with infertility when we decided to start our family. In researching reproduction, I began to learn that my instincts about birth were right. Not only was there no good reason behind much of the technology routine in modern birth, but much of it was actually proven harmful. I began a path toward midwifery, certain that with all of the information available...information that eventually enabled me to have a wonderful, safe birth without being cut, poked or drugged once we finally conceived...women would soon be looking for ways to have empowering births like mine.

> I COULDN'T FIGURE OUT WHY WOMEN WERE RUSHING OUT TO LEARN WHAT TO EXPECT INSTEAD OF LEARNING TO EXPECT BETTER.

That didn't happen. In fact, in the 80's and 90's a plethora of unproven technologies continued to be unleashed on women with no improvement in outcomes(1), many with serious questions of not only efficacy but safety. Women became more fearful than ever. The harder those of us in the know tried to impart vital knowledge, the faster women ran toward the burning barn. I couldn't figure out why women were rushing out to learn what to expect instead of learning to expect better. It took me years to figure out the reason. It had nothing to do with facts and everything to do with belief.

I set aside my midwifery aspirations to concentrate on what had, at first, been a steppingstone to midwifery...education. I focused my attention on writing and teaching. Still, the ones who 'got it' were few-and-far-between. I felt like I was spinning my wheels. Why couldn't I get through to these intelligent parents?

I couldn't get around their fear.

Whether consciously acknowledged or unconscious in nature, until the fear is dealt with, the belief holds firm. I educated myself on how to release false assumptions and applied critical thinking skills to our common cultural beliefs about birth. *Mother's Intention* and *Woman's Wisdom* sprang to life.

If used in pregnancy, birth and early parenthood, success—and by results this means the safest birth possible for you and the easiest transition into parenthood—is inevitable.

You will find that this material is based on evidence-based care...and that what you think you know just isn't so when it comes to maternity care in the US. I feel a duty to use my life to educate women on evidence-based care, which they *believe* is what they are getting. Women in America today are basing life-altering decisions on *belief* that they think is *fact*. Each subsequent decision is affected by that very first belief. Everything I share will be substantiated so that the reader can research the data. Not only do I encourage it, I expect it.

Sometimes wisdom comes from odd sources...I live by this little gem I found on a tube of lip balm years ago, "Examine everything you've been told. Reject what insults your soul."

Being Honest about Motherhood

Recently daytime talk(2) has featured shows on the difficulties mothers face today, from dealing with postpartum depression and the loss of 'self' to not wanting to be mothers at all.

Mothers are in crisis. They are having trouble coping. Many are disillusioned that no one told them how hard this job was.

Some are angry at the discovery that it's not a task that fits neatly between day jobs and isn't even a simple day job itself.

They feel unable to deal with the problems and challenges they are faced with, assuming they are somehow deficient.

> "EXAMINE EVERYTHING YOU'VE BEEN TOLD. REJECT WHAT INSULTS YOUR SOUL."

They wonder how other mothers do it, or they insist the mothers who say they love it are lying. Some may be faced with challenges they didn't sign up for. Even more have created problems where none would have existed but for the choices they made, yet our 'feel good' society is loathe to point that out for fear of seeming to 'mother bash'. How can anyone learn from their mistakes if everyone is too afraid point out that the mistakes exist?! The emperor is naked, people!

If you are one of the mothers feeling overwhelmed, you may feel it's unfair that your life seems out of control. Maybe it is. I don't want to minimize the magnitude of the job. It is enormous. It's the best job in the world, but that doesn't mean you'll love doing it 24/7. The fact remains that it is what it is and you need to find a way to manage it. You need to know what you are culpable for so that next time around you don't make the same mistakes. Most women will only get a couple of cracks at this motherhood thing.

This book won't tell you what to expect. What you can expect will change based on your own actions. Without action behind intent, there is no growth...no change. You get what you put into it, for better or for worse.

An open mind is essential for creating the birth you want. Letting go of resistance is imperative. Believe me when I say that there will be long held ideas that will be challenged. Give the new ideas a fair chance. Test their accuracy and validity.

For most parents-to-be, someone else is controlling your outcome. Parents are just rolling along with no plan, leaving the most important work with which they'll ever be entrusted to chance. These parents will live with the consequences of their choices for a lifetime, yet decisions are made without true informed consent or worse, under duress as their fear and love for their baby is played upon.

Are you holding yourself, or those making life-and-death decisions for you, to the same standards to which foster or adoptive parents are held? What's in "the best interest of the child." Or, are you doing what 'everyone else' does just because everyone else does?

How did we get here?

We didn't arrive by accident at this place where common sense is uncommon in obstetrical care. The progression is easy to dissect and examine.

Human behavior in obstetricians is the same as in the rest of us. Some of the traits we will explore in ourselves (and in these human beings who have bore the weight of our perceptions) are not pleasant to face.

It is necessary though, because nowhere else are they more damaging than in our experience as parents. For as a parent, you are not only accountable for your own life, but the life you have created, and, by extension, all the lives *that* life touches. Talk about a ripple effect!

Very pulled together people, people who excel in every other area of their lives, still will not ask themselves the questions that beg to be asked regarding parenthood. Mothers are drowning in guilt already, so it's become politically incorrect to talk about accountability. "Of course, it's a choice" we say of so much of parenting, and of course it is. But few are willing to say there might be *better* choices. This is unfair to

> IF FIFTY MILLION PEOPLE SAY A FOOLISH THING,
> IT IS STILL A FOOLISH THING.
> *(Anatole France 1844-1924)*

the mothers who are yet to come, for implying that all choices are equal when they simply are not cheats them out of the opportunity to make the better choice. It is a symptom of a destructive human trait...denial.

Parents are not immune to the tendency to make assumptions without testing their integrity or accuracy. Every choice made from an erroneous assumption is then flawed. In pregnancy and birth, the consequences can be fatal. Shutting out additional possibilities because of the 'rightness' of what you *believe* means you fail to see what *is*. Thinking that stems from this may seem logical, but the conclusions are wrong. Just because you want something to be true doesn't make it so.

Many obstetricians are stuck in this place. They'd rather be right than be safe. Show them the evidence that 'standard of care' is ineffective or harmful and they will dismiss it, or even manipulate the data to substantiate their position. Most of the time they aren't questioned. The media carried the 'news' that a study now confirmed that VBAC(3) is dangerous. They didn't say that it was the same study that ACOG(4) used to *support* VBAC just a few years ago, or that there are a multitude of better designed studies that also say VBAC is safer than repeat cesarean(5). It didn't take long...not even weeks...for this recommendation to become 'we need to support *elective* cesarean". Watch the numbers of surgical births...they are about to skyrocket. This is not a good thing. I hope that by the end of this book you will understand why.

Then the companion book, *Woman's Wisdom*, can help you avoid being a statistic.

I must state here that the human tendency to *assume* can color how the above information and that which follows is interpreted.

Therefore, I need to make clear from the outset that when I provide information on evidenced-based care and the dangers of 'obstetrical management', I am critical of a <u>broken system</u> that is statistically, scientifically and experientially <u>not working</u>.

I am not condemning the doctors within that system, nor do I have comment on particular institutions within that system.

There are shining stars trying to fix what's broken from the inside, and their work is difficult. If you are one of the fortunate that cannot reconcile your experience with what you are reading, you have probably found one of them. Reward them with a Certificate of Commendation from the Association of Nurse Advocates for Childbirth Solutions or nominate the institutions in which they work for Mother-Friendly Childbirth Initiative designation through CIMS, the Coalition for Improving Maternity Services. (See notes for further information)

Unfortunately, these special people are all too rare. Results don't lie. Again, unfortunately, I have to say that this book will benefit those that *think* they are in the ideal situation, but may *not* be.

Maybe they are, but I've seen far too many women who loved their doctors because they were 'nice', assuring them they would not do anything that wasn't medically necessary, only to end up with the same unacceptable results so many women face everyday. Lulled by a caregiver's reassurance that "of course pregnancy and birth are a natural process, but..." throughout pregnancy, they are blindsided in the last 6 weeks with one of those "buts". There are a multitude of reasons, it seems, to 'get that baby out of there'...baby is too small, baby is too big; premature labor threatens, mom is 'overdue'; too much amniotic fluid, too little fluid. These are all very real concerns...in an extraordinarily small percentage of pregnancies. Yet, an alarmingly high number of women are 'diagnosed' with these conditions. What's a parent to do?

I am encouraging healthy skepticism, not fostering distrust. Asking for evidence beyond "Because I say so" is reasonable adult behavior when adults must make important decisions. If results back up the words, your relationship improves...your trust grows.

An example of this is that there are doctors and nurses attending homebirth as well as midwives.

There are many within the current non-functioning system that have done their homework and will tell you, if you ask, that it is a viable option if you are healthy and have a skilled attendant.

Still, the 'official' opinion, and the one you will hear most often from doctors is that homebirth is not safe. What is that based on? Two 'studies' done by...doctors. They don't usually share that these 'studies' are virtually identical in their questionable methodology and stand in lonely opposition to every other **independent study** indicating homebirth is as safe (or safer) as hospital.

Also not mentioned is that the studies did not compare hospital to planned homebirth with midwives. In order to get the results they included abortions, stillbirths, infanticide and unplanned out-of-hospital births...i.e. taxicabs and elevators(6). Not quite a fair representation.

Lack of critical thinking isn't questioned by many within the profession or without. (Please notice I didn't say all. A good OB who practices evidence-based care with an open mind is worth her weight in gold...keep her!)

Another example is that gestational diabetes testing is routine for most women, devoid of symptoms or any risk factors what-so-ever. The American Diabetes Association does not advise this, and for good reason. It's not reproducible 70 out of 100 times! It's not accurate, it's harmful to women, yet it is the 'standard of care."(7 8)

Yet another example: I have a friend who broke her tailbone four days past her estimated due date. It hurt like crazy.

At the hospital, she was told all they could give her for the pain was a commonly available pain reliever because anything stronger would be bad for the baby. BUT...if she went into labor, (or if they just would let them induce her), she could have an epidural or Demerol. Excuse me? Why is it not OK to relieve the pain of a pathological condition that is by it's very nature painful, but it is OK for a normal, physiological process that can be quite comfortable without drugs? (more on that later) If she went into labor in 10-minutes she could have the drug, but not now? How does the difference of 10 minutes make it less dangerous? The same rational makes it <u>not</u> ok for a mother to have narcotics or a 'caine derivative in her system if *she* puts it there, but it is OK if the *anesthesiologist* does? (I am not advocating illicit drug use here...simply pointing out that epidurals, which an estimated 90% of our babies are born under the influence of nationally, are comprised of narcotics and 'caine drugs.)

Why are women undergoing painful obstetrical procedures often scolded for complaining, or told their pain is imaginary and that it's 'not so bad', but it's considered 'cruel' to encourage birthing without drugs?

Our faulty logic regarding pain, labor and women's capabilities has led to some truly convoluted thinking about what is 'normal' in the postpartum period. Our double standard concerning labor drugs vs. other applications of use has required that we distort what is considered 'normal' newborn behavior, with disastrous consequences to the mothers who based their decisions on misinformation without question.

Mothers may not want to consider that a simple uninformed decision had consequences for their child that might have been avoided, such as a continuous ear infection since birth, deathly food allergies or diabetes relating to artificial infant feeding (9). They may choose to believe that their child's neurological challenges couldn't possibly be due to the non-medically indicated, repeated ultrasound exposure (10), the epidural exposure (11) or a combination, despite the studies that suggest these technologies should be used sparingly. Our wondrous brains provide us this natural, protective mechanism to help us avoid agonizing over things we cannot change.

41

However, if we chose to resist the notion that choosing the behavior is choosing the consequences, mistakes are repeated and blame continues, improving nothing. I can only help those that expect more *of* themselves and *for* their children.

Have you made choices that might be setting you up for an unintended outcome? Is this a second child and you wonder if something you did, or didn't do, created a problem with your first child? Do you wonder if yours was an unnecessary cesarean, or if jaundice was a result of the labor drugs that your baby had to try to process with an immature liver? Angry that no one told you what you didn't dream you would need to ask? You shouldn't have to, but until overall outcomes improve, you do. It's a lot of work you shouldn't have to shoulder, but you do if you want to be safe. You have no choice at this time in history.

If you are angry about that, I feel the need to say very clearly, find a way to process that anger. I'm not here to judge, but to support and educate. I am here to tell it like it is, which means some people will be facing some painful epiphanies. However, guilt and shame will paralyze you. That's not it's purpose. It's an internal emotion meant to help us modulate our own behavior in a positive way. No one can 'make' you feel guilty if you do not choose to hook into that. If you feel good about your choices, knowing in your heart that your intent was well-meaning and you did the best you could, there is no purpose in feeling guilty. If you did make the best choice you could with the information you had, and later find out there was a better choice, you need to ask yourself, "Would I make the better choice next time?" If the answer is 'yes' the feeling of guilt has done what it was meant to do. If the answer is 'no' and rift with excuses or justifications, then it's *supposed* to nag you.

Either way, what is, is. All you can do is deal with what's before you. You can't change the past. You may be able to compensate or you may need professional help to let it work through your feelings, but holding on to it will eat at your soul.

If you are feeling over-whelmed, that's understandable. We should learn all of this in college, or better yet in high school, so we can enter this most important transition with calm confidence and joy. I'm trying to build that reality for my daughter. I hope you'll help me for the sake of your own daughters as well as yourselves.

After you've done the work in this book, you may wonder how anyone could make decisions you now see as clearly unfortunate. You've done the work, you've stepped through the looking glass, and it's painfully obvious that others haven't. You are free of the cascade of deficits that handicap those working from faulty assumptions and are confident in your ability to be the best parent you can be. It may feel lonely until they catch up.

Parenthood is the toughest job that you'll ever do. It's also the most rewarding. It begs us to stand alone sometimes, even when we are uncomfortable with it, because our children expect us to be the best we can be. Their lives are in our hands.

Journal Exploration:

What assumptions or beliefs regarding birth are you willing to challenge? What might be a problem not acknowledged or too painful to face? Is there something you fear about birth and labor? Are there concerns about new motherhood?

There is a high probability that what made this list are things over which you have at least some control, through your thoughts, choices or actions, even if that seems unlikely with your current thinking. Are you afraid of complications in birth? Most preventable complications, and many are preventable, are related to nutrition. Have you learned about how you need to eat to grow a healthy baby? Have you stopped smoking?

Some complications are seen almost exclusively in obstetrically managed births...have you interviewed midwives, made a birth preference list or do you need to find an ob that shares your birthing philosophy? If you avoid the non-medically indicated intervention, you avoid the complication. Do you know what would constitute a medical indication for specific interventions likely at your place of birth or with your current caregiver? Do you know what complications are common to certain interventions?

Knowing what you have control over allows you to be more accepting of what you don't.

How Important are Parents?

Many of the choices parents make on behalf of their baby with little or no conscious thought, from the childbearing year through the first 3 years, will set the stage for the life the child for as long as they draw breath.

There has been a five-fold increase in childhood diabetes in the last 10 years (12) that many logically attribute to low breastfeeding rates in the US. (13 14 15) Autism has increased by at least 400% in the last 10 to 15 years which some speculate may be due to vaccinations (16) and others to mothers who smoke or inappropriate birth technology. (17) Other autoimmune disorders, like MS, are also on the rise, with suspected origins in infancy or early childhood. Life threatening allergies are such a problem that schools have 'peanut free' zones. Is it coincidence that the first four ingredients in formula are four of the top ten allergens, including peanut oil?

Children with no attachment skills, empathy or sympathy are becoming so dangerous that my fourth grader had to have practice 'lock downs' with her tornado and fire drills. In her second grade class, if the timing was off it was impossible to even get into the classroom until the line of kids waiting for their a.m. Ritalin had been dosed and cleared away. I had home-schooled for a while and people asked me if I wasn't concerned about socialization...what socialization would that be? What she got from the kid who tried to stab her with a pencil? Or, the kid who pushed her face into the pavement on the first day? (18) Or maybe the 'socialization' she got that had her vomiting for days and spiking a temp. of 103 degrees? The child that shared that with her told her mother she didn't feel good as she was dropped off at school and her mother told her 'when you start puking, call me.'

We've lowered the bar on 'normal' so that we can feel good about what can, not should, be expected of our children. Mothers of gently, naturally born, attachment parented, breastfeed babies are often told "I could never take my kid everywhere! They would drive me nuts!" or "Wow! Your baby is so smart! Good genes!" or "How *lucky* you are that you 'get' to stay home." That last comment made *to* a mother who gave up a lucrative teaching position for a few years to stay home with her children, *by* a mother who then went on to talk about the liposuction on her butt and the new home she was having built, which she "had" to work to pay for!

Postpartum depression (PPD) got a lot of press after the Yates case, in which a mother murdered her five children due to postpartum psychosis. PPD got some much needed attention, but it wasn't long before it was deemed 'normal' as long as it didn't degrade into psychosis. Why? Because so many women experience it. Is what they experience due to birth? Or what has become of birth when all of the natural mechanisms in place for the perpetuation of the species are tampered with?

Finally, some researchers are looking into that and wondering if maybe what American women are experiencing isn't postpartum depression (PPD), but posttraumatic stress disorder (PTSD)(19). Listen to mothers of the typical American birth tell their 'war stories' as they show off their scars and it's an easy leap to make.

If the process of birth were the cause, it would stand to reason that other cultures would be experiencing the same rise. That doesn't seem to be the case. Plenty of mothers here and around the world aren't experiencing PPD or PTSD at the rates seen in obstetrically managed mothers in the US.

It would be ridiculous to insinuate that any one thing is responsible for all of societies ills, yet there is undoubtedly a cumulative effect on health and emotional well being when brain development is disrupted due to poor nutrition, smoking, drugs (including non-medically indicated labor drugs), lack of brain stimulation and/or lack of mother's milk. The majority of these things also disrupt the bonding process, which leads to other problems in the mother-baby dyad. Thus, mothers begin their new relationship in the red and wonder why they are having a rough time!

Mothers need to know what true 'normal' is and where 'average' lies so they know when to ask for help. They need to know what choices or actions can contribute to 'abnormal' so they can avoid them. Instead, growth charts for babies are printed by formula companies, with 'average' determined by children who have never had a drop of milk that their mother's body made specifically for them! Mothers who do feed their babies human milk are being told their children fall outside of the 'norm'! It doesn't seem to occur to many people to ponder the fact that cows milk is made for baby cows with four stomachs, weighing over 100 pounds at birth. Mothers are instructed not to give babies under 12 months cow's milk because of the allergenic properties, yet most formula is made from, you guessed it, cow's milk. If not cow's milk, soy, which is also on the list of top ten allergens.

The corruption of the natural processes meant to ensure the continuation of the species can only go so far. We are only glimpsing the ramifications of our actions. Women who have had, or are having, empowering experiences, who are making choices that bring themselves and their families peace and health, need to pass on their wisdom.

This is a book about how we all contribute to or diminish, the world we live in. It's about fact gathering and basing decisions on solid evidence instead of belief.

It's about judging success by results. How's the current system working?

- 25-30% of babies are cut out
- In a recent Harris Poll conducted by the Maternity Center Association, there were NO natural births in the study, despite the fact that 45% *said* they agreed with the statement that "giving birth is a natural process that should not be interfered with unless medically necessary".
- Women are so afraid of birth they are fueling these insane trends themselves.
- Women are forming support groups to 'get through' the weeks or months it is taking them to love their babies, declaring that bonding is a myth because they didn't experience it.
- Women are saying their breasts are bleeding due to normal usage in the physiological function for which they were designed, as all other mammals use them without incident.

Folks, this is NOT NORMAL or healthy.

Journal Exploration:

Take a serious look at excuses you might give yourself to justify failing to make meaningful changes to improve your birth outcome. Be honest about ways you might sabotage yourself. If your caregiver is leading you down the path of cascading intervention that leads to an unnecessary cesarean, will you make a stand? Why or why not? If you leave his office in tears, unsure, confused, angry or afraid, will you fire him? Why or why not? Have you quit smoking? Are you eating healthy? If not, what do you tell yourself to make that ok?

Is what you're doing working? If you say the thing you are most afraid of is a cesarean and your doctor insists that you will need one because your baby is breech, do you seek out a caregiver skilled in breech, knowing that a cesarean for breech is five times more dangerous for the mother with no improvement in outcome for the baby(20)? Do you try any of the known successful techniques for turning a breech to head down(21)? Why or why not?

If you desire a VBAC and your doctor will only allow it if you have an epidural and augmentation, do you gather the evidence against such dangerous protocol? Do you insist he follow evidence-based practice or let him know you plan to find a provider who will?

Are you happy, empowered, healthy? Do you feel confident, knowledgeable and safe? Be honest with yourself. Is every visit a confrontation or exercise in futility? Are you heard? Really heard.

Are your provider's actions and words saying the same thing?

"WHEN PEOPLE SHOW YOU WHO THEY ARE, BELIEVE THEM. THE FIRST TIME."
Maya Angelou

"Oh, we only use intervention when it's necessary" doesn't hold water when you are routinely given every non-medically indicated test in the book.

If coercion is used to manipulate you in pregnancy, why would you expect different at your birth? If intimidation seems second nature, pay attention. A good doctor never says, "Am I the only one that cares about this baby?" Good doctors react in a reasonable manner to reasonable requests. They appreciate a parent responsible enough to participate in their own good health. They see the wisdom in a good working relationship with actual informed consent. Find those doctors...or a good midwife. Not doing so means that you have agreed to the outcome, good or bad.

A picture paints a thousand words, so let's paint...

A woman comes to an independent childbirth class. She takes everything she is learning to her care provider, expecting to be able to talk about her concerns. Her provider refuses to look at the material from her class, with the comment that it's all garbage because the instructor 'didn't bother to get an education'. (I'm not sure if this means her knowledge isn't relevant because it didn't come with a nursing degree or what, but it certainly shows ignorance over what certification to become a autonomous childbirth educator entails.)

The mother keeps going, keeps pushing for care that is individualized to her. He continues to become more irate with each visit, with each question, until finally, he (fairly) tells her, "If you don't like the way I do things, find another doctor!"

For whatever reason, she doesn't.

Her biggest fear is of episiotomy and the affect it could have on her life. She shares this with her doctor, who tells her that he will only do it if he has to. He become irritated that she asks how often he finds it's necessary.

His actions become increasingly punitive, yet she keeps going back.

Her birth includes a huge episiotomy that extends into a 4th degree laceration (when the tear extends through the rectum...seen almost exclusively with an episiotomy). She is told that it's a good thing that episiotomy was done because her baby's shoulders were stuck and would have died without it.

The medical term is shoulder dystocia. It is a real condition, happening primarily to larger babies (and by larger I mean 11 or 12 lbs., not 9) in which the shoulder of the baby becomes wedged behind the mothers pubic bone. There are classic signs of shoulder dystocia that a care-provider looks for. What if none were present at this birth? What if video showed a perfectly normal 2nd stage. (This is why so many hospitals now ban video recording of the birth.)

While there are certain instances when an episiotomy might be helpful in rectifying shoulder dystocia, it is <u>not</u> what *resolves* the situation. Think of it like this...if you were trying to walk through a full screen door that is 4 ft. wide, while carrying a 6 ft. long board, parallel to the floor, would cutting the screen make it possible? No. You would have to turn the stick 90 degrees, break the stick or break the doorframe. The screen is pretty much irrelevant. However, what if there *was* no dystocia...the birth team was simply unaccustomed to physiological 2nd stage. If all they've ever seen are babies shooting out because mom is purple pushing with a big slice to her bottom, the relaxed pace of 'breathing the baby down' can be misinterpreted as the mom being 'too tired' or the baby being 'stuck'.

Say the mother wants to blame the doctor for everything gone wrong in her life since the birth by suing the doctor and she asks the childbirth educator to help her.

If the CBE subscribes to the philosophy of responsible decision-making I'm talking about here, how do you think she would respond to such a request? She would refuse, of course, and remind the mother that she chose the care-provider and the birth location with full knowledge of the probabilities. The outcome is her responsibility alone.

Alternatively, if you accept such treatment and find yourself saying, "It's the price you pay for a good doctor" kick yourself...and then find a new doctor. I've got news for you.

Good doctors charge paper money for office visits—they don't demand pieces of your broken soul or abused body.

You deserve better. Your baby deserves better. Husbands, your wives...the mother of your children...deserve the best. However, no one can change a situation like those above but you. Mind you, these are all real examples and sadly they aren't all that uncommon. The above examples happen so often because they can.

Good physicians know all this is true and try to provide safe and effective care. They have formed groups Physicians for Midwifery(22) and the peer pressure they face is incredible. They will be the first to tell you that good care does not mean bad treatment. That's why this book is so important...it helps you spot the good guys.

Notes on Chapter One

1   "Maternal mortality statistics have not improved since 1982.
The Safe Motherhood Quilt Project is an effort to bring attention to this fact and
find solution. www.rememberthemothters.org/inamay.html
World Health Organization, revised 1990 statistic (published in 1996) put the US
at 24 in maternal mortality, which had dropped from 21 in previous years. Efforts
to find a more current published report were unsuccessful.
US infant mortality rating (1998, March of Dimes) is 28th in the world.

2   September, 2002

3   Vaginal Birth After Cesarean

4   *"What Every Midwife Should Know About ACOG and VBAC: Critique of
ACOG Practice Bulletin*   *No. 5, July 1999. Vaginal Birth After Previous
Cesarean Section"* by Marsden Wagner, MD, MSPH   "ACOG is not a college
in the sense of an institution of higher learning, nor is it a scientific body. It is a
'professional organization' that in reality is one kind of trade union. Like every
trade union, ACOG has two goals: promote the interests of it's members, and
promote a better product (in this case, well-being of women). But if there is a
conflict between these two goals, the interests of the obstetricians come first."

5   The Assault on Normal Birth: The OB Disinformation Campaign, by
Henci Goer©2002 Midwifery Today, Issue 63, Autumn 2002.

6   "Out-of-hospital births pose a 2-5 times greater risk to a baby's life than
hospital births",1978 news release passed off as a 'scientific study' by
ACOG."Outcomes of Planned Home Births in Washington State:
1989-1996. Pang, J., Heffelginger, et al. August 2002 100 (2): 253-259
Basically, the same poor science dressed up, claiming the same
outcome.

Fifteen scientific studies that refute the above findings,
http://www.qis.net/~mfm/studies.htm.

Detailed account of the problems with the Journal of Obstetrics and
Gynecology report: *Obstetricians Use Dubious Method In Attempt to Discredit
Homebirth, Motives Questioned by Parents, Midwives, and Public Health Researchers,*
February 11, 2003 http://www.ican-online.org/news/headlines.htm

7   Understanding Diagnostic Tests in the Childbearing Year, Anne Frye,
Labrys Press

8   American Diabetes Association, www.diabetes.org

9   *Breas milk prevents Childhood Diabetes*, 1999, Dr. Gabe Mirkin
Breastfeeding and Allergies: Protection Now and for the Future, P. Christine
Smith
www.breastfeed.com

10   *Ultrasound Unsound?*   Beech & Robinson 1996, Association for
Improvments in the Maternity Services, London.

Ultrasound: More Harm Than Good? Midwifery Today, Issue #50, Summer 1999, Dr. Marsden Wagner, neonatologist, epidemiologist.

11 *The effects of Maternal Epidural Anesthesia on Neonatal Behavior During the First Month*, Sepkoski, Lester, Osthemimer, Brazelton, Dev. Med Child Neurol 1992 Dec: 34(12); 1072-80

12 http://outreach.rice.edu/~trsler/nurse/2002/obesity_diabetes_article.pdf

13 www.drmirkin.com/diabetes/D216.htm

14 E.J. Mayer et al. *"Reduced Risk of IDDM among breastfed children"* Diabetes 37 (1988): 1625-1632

15 www.midwiferytoday.com/articles/foodforthought.asp

16 www.909shot.com/Diseases/Autism.htm

17 www.no-smoking.org/july02/07-30-02-1.html
www.garynull.com/Documents/autism_99.htm

18 *Ghosts from the Nursery: Tracing the Roots of Violence*, Robin Karr and Meredith S. WileyAtlantic Monthly Press, New York, 1997

19 Birth 28:2 June 2001, *"Do Women Get Postraumatic Stress Disorder as a Result of Childbirth? A prospective study of incidence"*. Susan Ayers, PhD and Alan D. Pickering, PhD.

20 *Mode of Delivery for Breech Presentation*, a bibliography, www.childbirth.org/section/vagbreech.html

21 Hypnosis and Conversion of the Breech to the Vertex Presentation, Lewis E. Mehl, MD, PhD, Dept. of Psychiatry Univ. of Vermont College of Medicine, Burlington Arch. Fam. Med. 1994; 3:881-887

22 www.well.com/user/zini/pfm.html

BIRTH BELIEFS

It's easy to tell the women who've done the work from those that took the ride.

Those who've done the work are enjoying the path of parenting, whatever has befallen them along the way. They are informed and confident in their decisions. These mothers can't wait to tell you about their incredible labors, drug free, ecstatic, pain free, or at least manageable births. They are so blissful they seem almost evangelical in their zeal to share the joys of motherhood, even if Mother Nature tosses them a few challenges. Because they have more good days than bad, these challenges are met head on and probably soon forgotten. They forgive themselves when they mess up.

Those who took the ride feel ripped off, assuming the joyful mothers aren't for real, that such an ideal doesn't exist. Others are angry and bitter. They believe great births exist, but believe *they* can't have them, as illustrated by the following mother, reviewing Naomi Wolf's book, <u>Misconceptions: Truth, Lies and the Unexpected on the Journey to Motherhood</u>:

"...all the happy-earth-mama books about midwifery and doulas and all those candlelit bonding moments with a new squealing infant are put in their place---as happy fairytales that happen to a few women in America."

The irony is, it happens to so few women **because so few women make the choices that result in those births...**<u>not</u> because they aren't possible! The 'fairy tale' births should be the norm!

The women who *have* been 'lucky' enough (who might argue that luck was just a small part of their experience) are women with imperfect lives—nobody is perfect—but they educate themselves, they have a support system and they operate from a place of empowerment. Their convictions are strong because they are sure they are doing what works for themselves and their babies.

These happy mothers, because they want others to be able to enjoy the journey as much as they do, are often accused of trying to make other mothers 'guilty' for making different choices, when what they are trying to do is share the choices that brought them joy. Of course, in any population there *will* be a few judgmental people, but in my experience, most of the time, it's not the happy parent that is doing the judging, but the unhappy parent. The happy parent's only mistake is assuming that when women say they wish their lives could be like theirs, they really mean it. Knowing it <u>can</u> be, they give advice they thought was solicited, puzzled by the 'yeah, buts...' that follow.

Naomi Wolf, in *Misconceptions*, doubts the existence of these happy moms who face few challenges in their new role. (Note that I did not say 'no challenges'.) While her book is an excellent read with invaluable information, she draws some interesting conclusions that I didn't expect from such a smart woman.

Pages and pages are devoted to exposing the detriments of the current system and praising the possibilities if we were to adopt something closer to the midwifery model of care. She concedes that homebirth is as safe or safer than hospital and backs it up. She also concedes that VBAC is preferable to repeat cesarean. Being a mother who felt cheated by the system the first time around, she does make *somewhat* different choices with her second baby, still ending up with a cesarean. Her reasoning for not having the homebirth that she admits might have had a different outcome? Birth is so excruciating (another belief that pervades the book is that this *must* be so without the aid of drugs) that if she wants an epidural she can't have one at home. True. She can't. Why? Because it carries such risks that they can't be dealt with at home!

However, that's not the part that made me go 'huh?'. If a woman is laboring at home with a qualified midwife or competent doctor and there is a complication or she decides she just can't manage without an epidural, she's free to get up and go to the hospital for any assistance she may need. The odds are that at home neither she nor her baby will need medical assistance or experience the sort of pain that she felt in the hospital the first time (1). If she does, it's a short trip to most hospitals. However, I'd like to see a women in active labor at the hospital declare that she's feeling good and wants to go home to push out her baby!

At first glance, her reasoning seems logical, but it stems from a faulty belief, which makes it illogical. This is also an example of what I pointed out in the last chapter about smart women making bad choices. I admire Naomi Wolf immensely. She's written a scathing expose' on American obstetrical care that's cuttingly witty and strong on data. She *seems* to get it, at least on paper. Yet, she makes choices contrary to what she knows intellectually. She makes many faulty assumptions based on fear. She says the words, but her actions say something else entirely. It's the unconscious nature of the fear allowing so many women to coast through pregnancy without questioning much because, after all, they feel fine and *they* aren't scared. Some women will freely admit they are terrified, but many more fall into the 'see no evil' category.

Illustrating that Wolf really doesn't get it is that her book is heavy on blame and short on responsibility. At one point, she blames her hospital childbirth class and the books she read for not being truthful. She contends they misled her into making bad choices. She admits that independent childbirth classes do give more useful information, and that yes, there are books out there that actually do give solid strategic planning advice, just as there are caregivers available that have proven to have better outcomes. She doesn't go to those classes, or use the information in the books, or seek out the caregiver with the best outcomes.

She's angry that the classes <u>she chose</u> didn't tell her the 'truth'. Would she have wanted to hear the documented risks of epidurals? Of course not, that's why she didn't go to the other classes. It's a moot point anyway because her hospital class very probably *could not* have given her that information. Her hospital CBE probably was not free to share that the studies the friendly visiting anesthesiologist used to support non-medical use of medications was *conducted by anesthesiologists and funded by drug companies!*

Hm...no conflict of interest here. For a childbirth educator to even let on that she possesses such information is cause for termination. Why? Remember who signs her check? When you are low man on the totem pole it isn't wise to expose the great and powerful Oz. I'm not being cynical, I'm being brutally honest. I've been there, I know. I have also been fortunate enough to teach in a hospital where evidence and result-based success is valued, so I know those exist as well. However, they are a rarity. Even in those institutions, the teacher must teach what the parents want to learn or the seats will sit empty. Sadly, many parents take a class to hear the wonders of drugs, not the risks, and to become familiar with the hospital layout and protocols.

Most childbirth educators went into the profession to help women have safer, more comfortable births. It's very frustrating to be relegated to tour guide and drug pusher.

Ms. Wolf dismisses all of her admittedly better options for a variety of reasons...all based on her beliefs and fears about birth...yet somehow the fact that *she* deems other options not credible is somehow *their* fault. A childbirth educator that claims birth can be comfortable without drugs and doesn't use the 'p' word (pain) is "lying"?

Thousands of women are giving birth quickly and painlessly though Mongan Method HypnoBirthing®, thousands more are doing the same spontaneously. Some women even give birth orgasmically. Because she doesn't believe it can be anything other that what she experienced...and what her friends have experienced...she insists painless birth can't possibly be true. It never occurs to her that she and her friends have made the same choices and got the same outcomes.

Those that get the good births are the ones who don't allow fear to rule their thinking. Fear that 'something' will go wrong. Fear of how they might look to others. Fear that they'll make a wrong decision.

Those that don't 'get it' base their decisions on fear. They operate from a 'just in case' mentality, yet they have no firm idea of what the actual possibility of 'just in case' is. When I was pregnant and people learned I was having a planned homebirth with a midwife they would exclaim in horror "What if something happens?!" I'd ask, "Like what?" "What if the cord is wrapped around the neck and chokes the baby?" they would say, as if I was an idiot for not considering that.

Very rarely the cord will be very short or wrapped more than once, which makes it tight enough to restrict the oxygen exchange through the cord or impedes descent...then it needs to be cut and the baby born quickly. At that point though, the baby's head is already born so it's rarely a problem. In utero, babies don't breathe through their windpipe...they get oxygen through the umbilical cord. 30% of the time, there is a loop of cord around the baby's neck. It's a variation of normal, not a complication. There actually was with my baby. Midwives either un-loop it over the baby's head, loosen it so that the baby can be born through the loop or 'somersault' the baby through. No big deal.

Of course, it only sounds prudent to approach birth 'proactively'... except that the 'proactive' approach currently in use isn't working. Parents don't realize or won't admit that fear is actually the motivating force behind their decisions. Most of the time my request for specific 'what ifs' are met with either stunned silence because they can't come up with something, or the story of their own birth with some tragic complication. A large percentage of the time, said complication was iatrogenic (doctor caused) or nosocomial (hospital caused)...not common in natural (and what should be 'normal') birth. Fear of the unknown is at the bottom of it all...irrational fear not substantiated by fact.

Those that don't get it are the 'blamers'. They blame doctors for not giving them the perfect experience or the perfect child. It's someone else's fault when bad things happen. Someone always has to pay for their misfortune. These people drive the malpractice rates up and create the current environment in which defensive medicine thrives...creating the vicious cycle of overused and abused technology.

Fear rules these people. They insist pregnancy and birth are rift with calamity. This fear has permeated the caring professionals within the broken system. They aren't being mean...they are very afraid! According to the World Health Organization, at least half of all cesareans (at least 500,000 a year) are unnecessary and it all comes back to fear.

Fearful parents will torture themselves with guilt, second-guess themselves at every turn...and then make the same decisions again, and again. This reinforces their belief that they can't get a break because choosing the same actions results in the same consequences. They may spiral into severe PPD or even PTSD, all the while demanding to know 'why me?' Women who have done their homework, will sometimes be able to see 'why', but they will be hesitant to volunteer what they know, lest they be labeled 'judgmental' for pointing out that there were a multitude of choices that, by virtue of commonsense and evidence, might have netted a different outcome.

To break out of this vicious cycle, we have to challenge what we know that isn't really so about the current maternity care system in the US. How effective is it at improving the lives of mothers and babies? Not very as the statistics in the previous chapter pointed out. What perpetuates it? Are there better alternatives to the choices that 'everybody else' makes? Failing to investigate these questions means you can't possibly make educated choices. If you don't know this stuff you are operating without the necessary information and skills to create the results you want.

I hear examples of unintentionally created results so often I can finish a mother's story before she does.

I've been accused of being psychic 'cause I beat them to the punch-line. I'm not psychic, it's just that predictable.

A woman goes in for 'her' (because it's 'standard of care' it's just part of this right of passage deserving of a personal pronoun) gestational diabetes test. She's labeled gestationally diabetic and put on a low salt, low calorie, and yes low-sugar, restricted diet. (**Not** the commonsensical and healthy low sugar diet recommended by the American Diabetic Association that is similar to what midwives recommend) This leads to pre-eclampsia, which necessitates an emergency cesarean.

The shortcomings of this particular test were presented in the last chapter. (2) None-the-less, it is standard of care that often leads questionable treatment, which leads to unnecessary surgery.

Another woman, laboring quite nicely, is 'too comfortable'. Her caregiver is afraid that her labor has petered out since she looks too calm and relaxed. He suggests that they break her water to 'speed things up'.

She doesn't know that studies show no significant difference in length of labor(5) with amniotomy (breaking the water). She doesn't know that if a baby is high in the pelvis when water is artificially ruptured, there is a high likelihood that her baby will drop down malpositioned. The fancy term is "transverse arrest", which basically means the baby is stuck. This is a situation that was created, not encountered.

Amniotomy also accounts for the largest portion of cesareans for infection, failure to progress and cord prolapse (when the cord is washed down with the tide of water ahead of the baby...remember, the baby gets oxygen from the cord)(6). Ask ten women to tell you about their births and nearly all of them will contain the words "...and then they broke my water." Interesting terminology, instead of "...and then I let them break my water", considering this action requires someone's fingers having access to the mothers vagina.

"Birth" is blamed for these frightening situations. We don't have such high cesarean rates, or some of the worst mortality and morbidity rates, in the developed world because *birth* is dangerous, but because *obstetrically managed* birth is. Countries with better outcomes know better than to have surgical specialist dealing in pathology care for healthy women for a normal physiological process.

The idea of surgical specialists being the preferred caregiver for a normal, physiological process is analogous to a cardiovascular surgeon doing all routine exams on men over 50 or orthopedic surgeons for skinned knees!

Sure it sounds ridiculous, unless it were introduced the way obstetrics was, over 80 years, with powerful spin-doctors. (Ha!)

After all, a fall bad enough to break the skin could cause a broken bone. Sometimes falls in the elderly required specialist care because their bones are brittle, and the very young because their bones are still growing. If it's good for them, think how we can help everyone else!

Some people would resist, of course. Then word would get out that those seeing specialists got strong pharmacological pain relief!

A sprain hurts really bad, even if it's not a break...but without going to the specialist, one can't get the drugs...and gee, maybe there could be something worse wrong.

It might not even take 80 years for people to start imagining that there is no safe fall to handle at home. Band-aids would seem primitive. "You didn't take your kid to the doctor for that banged-up knee?! Don't you want the best for him? What if there is something wrong you can't see just by looking! You know, my nephew would have died if he hadn't been in the hospital after his skiing accident! He thought it was just a sprain, but good thing he went because he almost bled to death during the knee replacement!"

This is essentially how the normalcy of birth turned into a medical event.

Fear of birth, and fear of pain in birth, has created such panic that women prefer elective paraplegia to being an active participant in the most amazing event in their lives. They submit unquestioningly to rituals with no basis in reality. Statistically, they have a better chance of dying on the way to the hospital (20 in 100,000 for car accidents in women of childbearing age) than they do during a normal, natural birth (6 in 100,000) yet IVs aren't standard issue in cars. Of course, if they are one of the 1 in 3 or 4 women who will get a cesarean their odds of dying are highest of all, 35 in 100,000.

As for pain, there are plenty of women giving birth comfortably, even painlessly, so it is possible to do it without drugs and there are ways to learn how.

Where does the fear that allows this madness to continue come from? Is it misinformation or lack of information? Is it that we've given up making decisions for ourselves altogether?

Please bear in mind as you read examples of how choices in the childbearing year have gone awry, that I speak in generalities, though I use specific, real-life examples. I am using the most common stories I hear, so they may very well seem familiar. They are what has become 'the norm'. This may bring up issues from previous births that should be explored in a journal or a support group like ICAN (7).

No matter what choices you make, they are yours to make. If you want every intervention, useful, dangerous or just plain nonsensical, go for it. Just know what the consequences of your actions are so you can own them when the inevitable happens. If somehow you cheat the statistics, great, thank your lucky stars. At least you will have made your decisions consciously and with purposeful intent.

My primary goal is to help women have safer births that are unique, rewarding and dignified, if that's what they want. Somehow, women have gotten the idea that safety and emotionally satisfying are mutually exclusive in birth, which is patently false.

You don't need to give up your power and autonomy to have a safe birth. There are cause and effect relationships every step of the way to motherhood that influence the experience. Knowledge makes you the one in control, which is where you need to be. You are the one that will live with the consequences of your actions— or non-actions as the case may be. You sign the check, either directly or through a proxy in the form of your insurance provider. Your caregiver works for you. You have the right, and the responsibility, not to be a spectator. If your insurance company is owned by doctors, it still comes down to you and how hard you are willing to fight for the safety of your baby. No one said this tangled mess would be easy to unravel, but no one should invest what they can't afford to lose. In this case, the investment is your baby's life. Will you trust that to luck and bad information?

64

A healthy relationship must meet the needs of both people. This is a universal truth that applies to more than just your primary love relationship. It applies to your relationship with your care provider and later to the mother-baby relationship.

In the US we are not taught to take responsibility for ourselves or the condition of our relationships. We are not taught how to parent. We are not encouraged to question authority. We *assume* our care providers always have a good reason for doing what they do and that it's for our own good. We tend to do what our own parents did or what our friends do, *assuming* there is a good reason they do what they do.

This reminds me of a story I read once about a young woman making her first holiday ham. When her husband saw her cut the ends off the ham, he asked her why she did that. She pondered a moment and replied "I don't know. That's just how my mom always did it."

She called her mother to ask her what the purpose was in cutting off the ends of the ham. Her mother told her she wasn't really sure why...it was just how *her* mother did it.

So the mother called the grandmother and asked, "Why do you cut the ends off the ham? Does it make it juicier? Does it cook faster?"

"Not that I know of." replied the grandmother. "I always do it because the ham never fits in my pan!"

There was a time when an elite few held all information. In my mothers day, it wasn't an easy feat to compare and contrast the incoming data, what little of it there was. Today, books like *The Thinking Woman's Guide to Better Birth* and *Obstetrical Myths versus Research Realities*(8) should be on the bestsellers list. They aren't, not because they aren't useful, but they don't tell women what they want to hear. They only tell the truth.

My mother's generation should feel good about doing the best they could with what they had. They should not feel it's an indictment of their choices if their daughters know more and do better. "I didn't know" is not an excuse anymore.

We spend four to twelve years in college learning to do a job that may last 40 years if we're lucky. We will hold a position that, when we leave, will be filled by someone new in a matter of days.

We will work with people who, for the most part, know nothing of our hopes, dreams or fears even though we will spend more time with them than our own children.

Yet, I have parents from my classes complain that eight hours of childbirth preparation classes takes up too much of their time. Parents are parents for life. Mothers hold generations within them. Your children will never forget you and cannot replace you. Through them, you either make the world a little better...or a little more scary. It's my own personal opinion that three semesters of 'Parenting' ought to be a mandatory in every high school diploma or college degree.

Journal exploration:

Who will you allow to shape your future? What are their motivations? What are their biases? Their beliefs? How might their beliefs color what they experience as real or possible? Are their beliefs, or yours, based on fact? Personal experience? History? Are you open to the idea that perception is reality? Is it time that some concepts be modified or abandoned in order for you to create a better birth experience and smoother postpartum transition?

This is a crash course in responsible parenting. You must be willing to gather data every day staring right now. Make a commitment to your baby and yourself because there are no 'do-overs'. You get one chance to grow this baby the body it will inhabit for a lifetime. You may only get to experience birth once or twice in your life. Make those memories precious. In 50 years do you want to be swapping horror stories with your bridge club, or will you be misty eyed with joy as you pass empowerment on to your granddaughter?

Talk to women in nursing homes. Ask them which they remember better, the births of their children or the amounts of their bonuses? Do they recall their first promotion with the same sweet sadness as the first time their nursling gave them a milky smile?

Sure, there are women who thrive on the accolades of the competitive business world. More power to 'em! I'm all for women's empowerment in all forms. I believe in having it all, maybe just not all having it all at the same time.

However, if you are reading this book because you are pregnant, you volunteered for mom-duty...make every effort count. You won't get another chance to shape your baby's life in such a profound way.

People spend more time shopping for a car or home than they put into their births. They sacrifice years and thousands of dollars to go to college while they live on boxed macaroni and cheese, but balk at the investment of a couple of years of love and maybe some penny pinching during their children's most important developmental years.

Whether you've looked at mothers and thought "I hope it's that easy for me" or "Boy, is she lucky she can stay home." Or, even "What a brat that kid is!" know that coincidence and luck play a very small part. Ask the mothers who loved giving birth, and love being a mom why they do what they do. Ask mothers who like to be around their kids, and who's kids you like to be around what they did or didn't do and why. Then emulate their success.

Notes on Chapter Two

1   Mehl, L, Peterson, G., Shaw, N.S., Creavy, D. (1978) *"Outcomes of 1146 elective homebirths; a series of 1146 cases."* J Repro Med. Neonatal Outcomes: In the hospital, 3.7 times as many babies required resuscitation. Infection rates of newborns were 4 times higher in the hospital. There were 2.5 times as many cases of meconium aspiration pneumonia in the hospital group. There were 6 cases of neonatal lungwater syndrome in the hospital and none at home. There were 30 birth injuries (mostly due to forceps) in the hospital group, and non at home. The incidence of respiratory distress among newborns was 17 times greater in the hospital group than at home. The factors that make home birth more comfortable by maintaining the relaxation response will be covered in some detail in later chapters. For now, a couple of web sites that expand on reasons to choose homebirth (including safety) are:
http://www.gentlebirth.org/ronnie/homesafe.html
http://www.goodnewsnet.org

2   For more information see *Understanding Lab Work in the Childbearing Year*, Anne Frye

3   *Expecting Trouble*, Dr. Thomas Strong
    A Guide to Effective Care in Pregnancy, based on the Cochran Data Base, the most comprehensive collection of information on what works and what doesn't in medicine.

4   Terbutaline or not Terbutaline, Kim Wildner, Midwifery Today, Fall 2002

5   Fraser WD et al. Effects of early amniotomy on the risk of dystocia in nulliparous women.
    N Engl   J Med 1993;22;328(16):1145-1149.
    Seitchik J, Holden AE and Castillio M. Amniotomy and the use of oxytocin in labor in nulliparous women. *Am J Obstet Gynecol* 1985;153(8):848-854.
    Rosen, MG and Peisner DB. Effect of amniotic membrane rupture on length of labor. *Obstet Gynec ol* 1987;70(4):604-607.

6   Kariniemi V. Effects of amniotomy on fetal heart rate variability during labor. *Am J Obstet Gynecol* 1983;147(8):975-976.

    Levy H et al. Umbilical cord prolapse. *Obstet Gynecol* 1984;64(4):499-502.
    See *Obstetrical Myths versus Research Realities* by Henci Goer for abundant resources on this and other birth intervention.

7   International Cesarean Awareness Network, www.ican-online.org Phone: (310) 542-6400

    9   The Thinking Woman's Guide to Better Birth is also by Henci Goer and indispensable.

MOTHER GUILT

This book will not cheat you by telling you what you want to hear, sacrificing what you need to know. Too many books out there are telling you what to expect, but so few are telling you that you should expect more.

I believe it's time to be honest about some of our collective sacred cows. We have been politically correct about so many things for so long that we've lost sight of common sense. Many women come to their transition into motherhood confused and afraid instead of strong and excited to be a part of the Mystery. Many spend their lives feeling guilty for what they could not control, others, conversely, not taking the responsibility for what rests squarely on their shoulders.

Discussion of mothering has become as taboo as discussing religion or politics. Women have so many 'choices' now that to suggest one choice is better for babies than another is to risk offense. We tip-toe around certain things under the guise of 'being sensitive'.

What has happened is that in our attempt to be sensitive to mothers who can't make the choices they know are best for their babies, we have made all options seem equal when in reality they simply aren't.

The problem with this is two-fold. First-of-all, it doesn't shield the mother who is truly, unequivocally unable to give her child what she knows is best. What it <u>does</u> do is put women who *can* but *won't* in the same category, providing an excuse to take the path of least resistance instead of putting the best interest of the child first. The courts use the willingness of a custodial or adoptive parent to put 'the best interest of the child first' as a measure of good parenting. Examples abound of natural parents not being held to the same standard.

I know for a fact that there are women who've lost their breasts to cancer who are very envious and a more than a little angry with women who have perfectly functioning breasts that refuse to feed their baby the milk made specifically for him because they say they 'can't' when they really mean 'I don't want to'.

There are single mothers, with no support system, who cry every morning when they have to leave their child with an allomother(1), working two jobs and going to school with their only reward watching their child sleep in the moonlight with the hope that their hard work will eventually allow them to spend time with their child when he's awake. How do they feel when they hear a fellow working mother say she works because she couldn't stand to be with her whining, teething baby...a baby obviously in need of mothering. (I am not talking here of a mother who has just had enough for that day or that week and needs a break, as all mothers do, but of a 'mother' who dislikes the very act of mothering on-the-whole.)

How does the mother who lives on a restricted budget, who has put a lucrative career on hold to cherish the few precious years her little ones will be little, feel when a past co-worker comments on how 'lucky' she is to be able to stay home? How does the stay at home mother feel when the working mother explains that she "just couldn't afford to stay home", she *has* to work...then in the next breath talks about her new car and upcoming Caribbean cruise for two? Who considers how diminishing their willingness to mother well affects these mother's feelings?

Consider the woman who has eagerly anticipated her labor and birth as rite of passage but must have a cesarean due to cord prolapse or some other real medical indication. Grateful for the surgery that saved her child's life, or her own, she still grieves the loss of her dream. How might she feel when she hears about a woman who could have birthed naturally, but instead chose surgery for something as trivial as knowing the birth date in advance to plan around it. The surgery that is used with medical indication to save a life is the same surgery that carries a five times greater mortality (death) rate when it's done in the absence of a medical reason. How can anyone seriously say that to point this out is in any way, shape, or form a disservice to the woman did what she had to do to save her child?

To put these mothers all in the same category isn't *fair*. To suggest that fathers (or co-parents) are superfluous, or that it doesn't matter whether a mother or substitute mother raises their baby, or that the stay at home mother is 'lucky' is an insult.

Are there 'stay-at-home' mothers who don't actually *mother* at all? Of course. Are there very loving corporate mothers who are able to organize their time so that their baby never has an allomother? Naturally. Are there mothers who are the primary bread winners or who have functional insurance through work that the family needs, who go to extraordinary measures to ensure that even though the situation isn't their ideal, it has minimal impact on their children? Absolutely. Remember...no all or nothing thinking. There are always exceptions to the rule.

However, the way that this wide range of parental personal philosophy is dealt with is that it isn't. Certain topics are approached with prefaced with 'Of course it's a mother's choice, but...' or not considered at all. I don't sit on the fence and I don't see the value in avoiding the truth just because someone, somewhere might not what to hear it. Does that mean I have the right to judge anyone for making different choices than I?

I don't have the right because I don't have the power. And quite frankly, it makes absolutely no difference in my life if you, in Wooskerpoot or Topeka, choose to use what I'm about to share or not. I don't know what's best for your child, in your circumstance. I know what's probably best for *most* children in *most* circumstances. I know what's *possible* for most moms when they are determined to do their best. Only you know what is best for you...if you've made your decisions with the best of intent, or if guilt is an appropriate, self-imposed emotion.

> "NO ONE CAN MAKE YOU FEEL INFERIOR WITHOUT YOUR CONSENT."
> *Eleanor Roosevelt*

Yes, a self-imposed emotion. No one can make you feel guilty unless you agree to feel it. The purpose of guilt is that it guides us to aspire to "do the best we can with what we have, and when we know better we do better" (Maya Angelou). We must learn to distinguish true guilt as a message from our conscience from the useless punishment we heap on ourselves mistakenly labeled as guilt. Language often reveals the difference. Using the breastfeeding analogy again, an adoptive mother does not apologize for bottle-feeding her infant. She has no reason to and she knows it. (I know that someone will write to tell me that some adoptive mothers are able to breast feed. I am aware of that, but not all, and even those that do probably won't do so exclusively. Artificial baby milk originated out of orphaned baby situations so it's a valid analogy) A mother who made the choice not to breastfeed is likely to say "I really wanted to breastfeed, but..." Anytime "but" is in a sentence, everything that comes before is negated for what comes after it. Try it. Ok, now reverse it. Have you ever heard a breastfeeding mother ever say "I really wanted to formula feed, but..."?

At least a woman who says, "I know that the milk from my own body is the best for my baby that grew in my body. I still didn't want to breastfeed" is being honest. I may disagree with the intent behind the decision, but I respect that she'd have the bold ovaries to stand up to it. A mother that is defensive or makes excuses knows in her own heart that her intent is less than noble, and isn't even brave enough to take responsibility for it. She does a fine job of judging herself. Of course, often that is externalized so her perception will be that others are judging her, but that doesn't change that it really is a reflection of what she knows in her heart.

I can speak on this subject of mother-guilt with certainty because as a mother I have had nearly every single action I've taken on behalf of my child, from birthing at home to vegetarianism to my spiritual path, questioned and judged. Sometimes quite vocally and with great hostility. I feel no guilt for my choices, even when they are different from most of the people I know. I am confident that I had the information I needed to make the best choices for <u>my</u> child and hold dear my right to do so.

I can count on one hand the number of times that I have felt even a moment of regret when information came to light that might have altered a past course of action. In that moment, I had a couple of options. I could feel guilt and punish myself indefinitely, but make the same choices I've made in the past, or I could use the new information to make a different choice, forgiving myself for the past that I cannot change. I chose the latter.

Sometimes the truth is painful, but I can only speak the truth as I know it. I feel it is important to be impeccable with my word and use my life to a greater good. I share this information with compassion and the best intent. I have no control over how the facts are received or perceived.

I share it because of the many mothers who have regrets these days. Things they wish they knew then that they know now. It is those mothers I write for.

> "IT'S EASIER TO BE NICE THAN TO BE HONEST, BUT IT'S MORE IMPORTANT TO BE RESPECTED THAN TO BE LIKED."
> (Eli Wiesel)

Like the mother who smoked like a chimney, as did her husband, who got defensive during class when smoking was discussed. The parents who didn't want to hear about the effects of smoking on pregnancy, birth and babies. The parents who didn't appreciate people 'making them feel guilty' for their choice to smoke, insisting it's no one's business to judge their lifestyle.

The very same parents who lost their baby to SIDS, and upon researching 'why' as part of their healing, found that smoking parents(2) are much more likely to lose babies to SIDS (only one among many issues regarding smoking mothers). The parents who wanted to know 'Why didn't anyone tell us!" instead of "Why didn't I listen?" As a mother, defensiveness and avoidance of information that evokes feelings of guilt can be deadly.

The mom did choose to stop smoking eventually. She was a good mom...just a mom who paid a terrible price for not being able to look at a hard truth. Hindsight is always 20/20.

There are too many women living with the 'what ifs'. The stakes are too high to be worried about egos.

This book is not about 'you should'. It asks 'should you'? It gives you 'the rest of the story' and demands that you compare, contrast, and check in with your own heart. Granted, this carries a certain amount of courage, and it demands that we take back responsibility for our own choices. Our children deserve no less.

How does one know what is 'right'? The answer lies inside you, with your conscience and that 'wiggly' feeling in your stomach, as my daughter calls it. However, if following your intuition and your body's innate wisdom is a new concept, ask yourself these questions when you are faced with making a decision that will affect both yourself and your child.

1.) If someone else makes a different choice, how does that make you feel?

2.) Is this choice in the best interest of your baby? How do you know? How much do you know about the ramifications of both of (or all of) your options? What does common sense logic tell you? Intuition? Science?

3.) If there is a doubt about whether this decision is in the best interest of your child, what have you done to make a better choice more attainable?

4.) If you look into the future at the possible and probable consequences to you, your family and your baby for this choice, what do you see? Could you live with the worst case scenario with a clear conscience?

5.) What sacrifice is being asked of you? Do you make it for your child willingly? How does it compare for the sacrifice your baby is being asked to make? If your child were able to speak, what do you think he or she would choose? Why?

6.) In a perfect world, would this be your choice? If not, why? What can you do to <u>make</u> it perfect *enough* for this choice to happen?

7.) Is this choice irreversible?

8.) Is this a life decision? Does it contribute or contaminate your relationship with your baby? Does it contribute to or contaminate your baby's health? Do you like yourself for making it?

9.) Do you feel the need to make excuses or defend your choice?

10.) If you are aware that there is an option that is better and/or safer for your baby in the short or long term, why do you choose not to consider it? It is because you can't or because you won't?

11.) Does this act, above all, give expression to the words "I love you." Does it show your baby or child that you love him or her above all else?

12.) If your baby could speak, would you make this same decision? Would you want someone to make this decision for you if you were unable to communicate your wishes? If your life were recorded, would you do the same?

13.) Would your actions be any different toward an adult that you love if they were helpless and totally dependant on you? Does your baby deserve at least that much?

Choosing a Care Provider for Your Pregnancy and Birth

At the first sign of pregnancy, many women automatically make an appointment with their primary care physician or obstetrician. Some, aware that the birthing philosophy of their ob/gyn is different than their own, or who realize that adequate well-woman care does not necessarily translate into good maternity care, will seek out a different doctor for their pregnancy and birth.

Individual circumstance and personal preference play a large role in whether parents will look outside of their geographical area, or if the experiences of friends and family members influence their choice of provider.

In other cases, fear is a silent participant in the process of selection. Fathers-to-be rarely give a second thought to who will care for the love-of-their-life at her most vulnerable time. At this stage of the game, it's still in the realm of 'women's business' that they've never been involved in before. Before now, it's never been about who will be the first person to meet their child. A child who is still very much 'abstract' at this point.

Early pregnancy is a very emotional time. Even if the pregnancy has been planned for, or possibly orchestrated with intensive reproductive technology, there may be a moment or two of ambivalence...a feeling of "Oh no! What was I thinking?!" With unplanned pregnancies, there may be a sense of panic or fear. In any scenario, there is a sense of the world shifting with the emotional enormity of how life will change. Sometimes, it's a confusing, emotional feeling that begs for stability and familiarity to balance the excitement and the mysterious unknown.

The fierce protectiveness of mother-love hasn't usually kicked in. Mom doesn't necessarily feel any different physically just yet. Because she feels so 'normal', it may seem quite logical to make the call to someone who's been part of her 'normal' life. It may be the wise choice...or it may not.

This first choice as a parent may make the difference between life and death for you or your baby. Sound dramatic? It is. The sad part is that American mothers aren't even aware that they have choices to make, much less that their empowerment in making those choices could very well change the direction of the rest of their lives.

Knowledge is power. How well do you know your doctor? Do you know his cesarean rate? Do you know the infant mortality (death) rate for your state? For your county? For your hospital? Do you know what routine practices your doctor has as part of his standard protocol? Do you know if those practices are supported as safe and effective by scientific evidence? Does it sound overwhelming that one should even have to consider all this stuff?

Again, it is. However, it's very important. It's not as intimidating to gather this data as it sounds, for the most part. As a researcher and author, it took me a couple of hours to look up the information for my own region on the internet. If I were pregnant, I would have considered it a small investment in the safety of my child. Instead, it was a small investment in yours.

I simply started out with the big picture and narrowed the field. Using my home state for this illustration (3), I began at the national level so that I'd have the ability to compare my state's outcomes with other's. I already knew that international statistics from previous research(4) show that plenty of other countries have few mothers and babies die than the US and that at least 25% of the baby deaths in the US are preventable. The recommendations from The World Health Organization for improving outcomes include...choice of caregiver.

So first, I looked up US infant mortality rates with the Centers for Disease Control (CDC)(4). For vaginal birth it's 5.7 per 1,000 births for white babies. For African-American babies, the rate is 14.1 per 1,000.

Next, I went to state statistics (7) to determine state, then county mortality rates. The World Heath Organization recommends a 12-15% cesarean rate for optimum outcomes (the most live babies and mothers). Once the rates rise above that rate, the balance of this life-saving technique of last resort shifts so that more lives are lost than saved...hence at least a few preventable deaths. Statistics from countries with the best outcomes bear this out, as do statistics of midwifery communities where cesarean rates are kept low (8).

The graphic on the facing page shows which counties have the best (shaded gray-fewer than 6 deaths per 1,000 births) and worst (shaded black-9.9-22.2 deaths per 1,000 births) mortality rates for Michigan counties at the time of my research.

(The original graphic had five categories. I have only listed the highest and lowest rates for simplification. The non-shaded counties in this example fall somewhere between.)

Rate per 1,000 live births
Gray: Fewer than 6 deaths
Black: 9.8-22.2
Non-shaded:
Somewhere between those
State rate: 8.2

What might this information tell me? For one thing, I know the most dangerous places in the state to give birth (black) and the safest (gray), but there are a number of variables to consider.

Since we know that more African-American babies die than white, usually born to inner-city mothers with few resources and many challenges, we would expect to find that the counties with bigger cities including this population to have higher mortality rates. It's also important to recognize that counties that report the least deaths may be quite rural and have a large number of mothers delivering in neighboring counties, where the deaths might be reported. We also must consider that some counties have a high proportion of midwives, who have much better outcomes than obstetricians on the whole.

A county with active midwives may have a better rating than the hospitals within it. For some women trying to use this formula to determine the safety of birth in their area, there may even be out-of-the ordinary circumstances like a particular sort of pollution or other environmental factor that leads to higher infant mortality...but that would be unusual. Finally, some counties have many hospitals, others just one. In order to utilize the information you've gathered, there must be some small amount of familiarity with your own county resources and population. Once these things are considered, we are left with an educated guess that must be weighed along with the information gathered at the personal level.

For this I had to check into cesarean rates, which are an indicator of appropriate birth technology. If I were pregnant and had regular visits with my doctor, I could simply ask for his or her rate, but since I'm not I had to go searching. Because individual doctors and hospitals are not *required* to divulge mortality, morbidity (injury) or cesarean rates, patients may not get the answers they seek, but there are other sources, like the ones I used (9). Doctors and hospitals with low rates are very proud of that accomplishment, so if you can't get the data, you actually *are* getting some very important information.

In a large community, sorting this out may require help from organizations existing solely for the purpose of helping mothers make wise choices. Groups of other mothers, like Le LeLeche league (a breastfeeding support group) or ICAN (a cesarean prevention group) can be valuable resources (10). Friends and family are another. Just listen carefully to what they *really* say. If most of them have had the same doctor and they all rave about him, but most of them have had cesareans, episiotomies, postpartum depression that seems to boarder on post-traumatic stress disorder, sick babies, premature births or some other catastrophe or another, there's a problem. Birth just doesn't carry that much risk!

If it does with that particular doctor, there's something wrong with that picture. You've already read the mortality rate for vaginal birth and for car accidents for women of childbearing age. If a particular automotive company's cars were involved in far more than the statistical average of deaths, most people would refuse to buy cars from them...even if they came equipped with standard issue IV bags.

Dawn's (11) doctor was honest with her. When she asked what his cesarean rate was he replied "Oh, quite a few." But she liked him. "He sits by the bed with his hand on your belly." She explained. He also used inappropriate and dangerous technology routinely when all of the other doctors in his hospital had abandoned them for more evidence-based care. When she asked about this, he promised that even if he disagreed with her, it was her birth and he'd only use interventions if he had to. He 'had to' a lot.

One of these interventions was routine episiotomy (12). Her postpartum period was a nightmare, feeding the baby was hard because I was just in too much pain to get comfortable, and forget sex! The pain lasted for months. Her husband tried to be patient, but he couldn't understand that even sitting and walking hurt long after the cut healed. She justified the pain she suffered, defending her doctor by saying "Well, I guess that's the price you pay for a good doctor."

Good doctors charge standard currency for good care...not body integrity or first-born child. This doctor came highly recommended by friends who also found justifications for his actions instead of *questioning* his actions. His words reassured her all along the way, but his actions were always contrary to his words. He said he believed that pregnancy and birth were natural events, yet test after non-medically indicated test was ordered. He said he believed birth was safe, yet 'just-in-case' technology was employed, revealing his real fears.

Another example of how important it is to pay attention to non-verbal cues and intuition is Phoebe. Her doctor was very personable. She searched long and hard using many of the methods here. She and her husband were smart, savvy parents who weren't willing to settle for second best. Once they found the doctor they liked, subtle changes started to take place. Where they had been told that this doctor believed in minimal technology in the absence of medical indication, new tests were ordered at every visit.   Being an informed consumer, Phoebe did her homework.

Often she would find that a test was either not medically necessary or that it was useless...not accurate or developed for women with illnesses she did not have. She would bring in the information. Faced with evidence contrary to his practice, he'd get angry. Phoebe and Ted would leave feeling stressed, often Phoebe in tears and coerced into taking yet another test.

Still they went back. At each visit, they'd try to tell her she was sick. She did the research and knew she wasn't. She was very healthy, but they kept trying to label her 'high risk' even though she'd go back with information proving them wrong. Her doctor would get defensive, then concede that maybe she didn't have that particular condition, but the latest test showed she did have another one that would require further testing.   The entire pregnancy was wrought with frustration and far more work than any woman should have to do in pregnancy. These parents were not displeased with their experience. I could conceive of so much better and wanted more for them, but what matters is their perception, not mine. They had *their* best birth.

Had they listened to this doctor's actions instead of his words, and listened to that small voice inside that cried out after every visit, how much more might they have enjoyed their journey? Ironically, the reasoning behind seeking out this doctor and consenting to all of the testing was to get reassurance that everything was 'alright' so they'd feel safe.

If you want a comfortable, empowering, safe and joyous birth, but all of your friends have to tell are horror stories, pain, and sick babies, *don't do what they did!* Doing the same thing over-and-over but expecting a different outcome is the definition of insanity! Talk to women who rave about their births, who had alert babies that nursed with no problems, who talk about how wonderful it was, who had smooth postpartum transitions...then find out who their caregiver was!

In smaller towns, it may be easier to discern who the safest providers are. Say in one of our sample counties, there is only one hospital with three obstetricians. If said hospital has a nearly 30% cesarean rate we already know one thing...that at that hospital twice as many mothers will face a surgical birth than WHO recommends. Surgical births have a greater mortality rate than natural births. Knowing, as we do now, that such high cesarean rates means preventable deaths, we can see that there are many problems with choosing to give birth here.

Inadvertently, our map tells us something else. It illustrates the safety of birth and how irrational our fear of birth actually is.

Counties on the map listed as 9.8 to 22.2 baby deaths per one thousand births have higher infant death rates than Cuba, Kuwait, Hungary, Bulgaria, Russia and Romania. Simplifying then, in a county with one hospital delivering only one hundred or so babies a year, it would take about 10 years to compile the data on a per/1,000 basis. On the low end, (9.8/1,000) that would be only one or less baby deaths a year. That doesn't seem like much...unless it's your baby (as caregivers like to point out to justify inappropriate technology).

However, not all doctors practice the same. Many are working diligently to bring their practices in line with evidence-based care recommendations. What if one doctor in our example uses a non-invasive approach when possible, utilizing integrative therapies, and has brought her cesarean rate down to 12%. If this is your doctor, your work is done. Happy birth-day! When this doctor says "I may not agree with you, but we'll do it your way unless there is a medical indication for intervention." She means it. How do you know? Her numbers don't lie. Her actions back up her words.

If this is not your doctor, you still have gained a lot of insight into the other two doctors. If the above physician has a 12% cesarean rate and the hospital has only two other doctors but a nearly 30% cesarean rate, how high are the rates of the other doctors? So now, you have several options:

Do nothing, keep with your original choice and hope nothing bad happens. This basically means you are playing the odds. Don't wager more than you can afford to lose. If you had a million dollars, would you bet on 1 in 3 or 50/50 odds that you'd lose? Your child's life is more precious than a million dollars. As with any choice, ask yourself, is it in the best interest of the child? Am I making this choice because it's just easier to do nothing or out of fear? If so, that might be something to explore before the birth.

Stay with this doctor but research every recommendation, fighting for evidence-based care at every visit. Do-able, but exhausting. In a relationship of equals this is more likely to be a workable solution, but doctor-patient relationships are seldom equal. If the relationship is based on a power struggle, someone must lose. Usually the least powerful. Wouldn't a win/win, cooperative relationship be more desirable?

Change caregivers. Maybe more than once. Possibly extending out of a convenient geographical area. In a bigger city where a woman is probably a faceless chart this may not be difficult. In a small town, uncomfortable social moments may crop up from such a decision. When the subject is the life of a child vs. saving face, again, the question is, "What is in the best interest of the child?" We pay our caregivers a lot of money to work for us. It is reasonable to expect well-researched care. It is responsible parenting to seek it elsewhere if caregiver is unwilling to provide it. Good doctors have already taken the initiative to keep up on the scientific literature...reward them for their efforts and it's a win/win situation.

Another option is hiring a midwife. Ask the same questions of a midwife that you would of a physician attending your birth. Frequently you won't have to ask...midwives often provide their statistics at the initial visit without needing to be asked. If the midwife determines at that visit that for some reason you are a poor candidate for a homebirth, she may be able to refer you to a sympathetic doctor. Think about what it is you want at a birth.

Find a freestanding birth center. This is a birth center independent from and outside of a hospital. Some consider this a compromise for those that don't want to be at home, but don't want to be in the hospital either. Others choose freestanding birth centers on any of their own plentiful merits. They provide a homey atmosphere within the midwifery model of care, usually with physician backup.

There may come a time when all birth providers share important information voluntarily as providers, proud of their stats, do now. Or, other states may enact laws to protect the consumer, wherein the health department collects the data and provides it to mothers in a brochure so that mothers can make informed decisions as New York has.

No one would dispute that safety is first-and-foremost in choosing a pregnancy care provider, but there are other considerations.

One concern is financial. One questioned often asked at an initial visit with a midwife, or during a phone pre-interview is "Do you take insurance?" Insurance companies that aren't owned and operated by doctors are seeing a financial motive for covering homebirth and birth centers, albeit at a snails pace, as more women choose these options.

Parents need to look at the higher short-term cost of inappropriate technology as well as the long-term financial picture use of these technology paints. With a higher number of birth injuries and cesareans in what we think of as 'usual' care, parents may well be paying a co-pay on major abdominal surgery instead of a vaginal birth. Many midwives charge about what parents would end up paying out-of-pocket for their hospital birth insurance co-pay for a vaginal birth. For the uninsured or underinsured, the financial choice is easy...physician at an exorbitant price or midwife at a fraction of the cost. My baby's safety was worth what I'd spend on a vacation or save by not smoking...and then some. I know people whose children are starting school who are still paying on their births!

The other problem is of an emotional/relational nature.

Human nature dictates that if I say, "Michigan is a great place to live!" someone will take that to mean that that some place else isn't and reply, "What's wrong with Ohio?"

When we make a choice that might be different from what our peers are doing, it can seem to them as if we are questioning *their* choices, even though it has nothing to do with them.

When all of my choices were different from that of my mother, her response was to ask questions and often she'd say "If I had known that, I would have done a lot of things different." No guilt required on my part or hers. I was doing the best I could with what I had and so did she.

Some with friends or family who are unfamiliar with alternative options will opt to educate them by sharing what they learn along the way. Very often, objections are simply due to ignorance of why parents are making a particular choice or of the facts pertaining to that choice. I have seen families firmly opposed to homebirth become homebirth advocates once they were assured of it's safety. Often fathers and grandfathers become the biggest advocates, taking great pride in their wife's, or daughter's, empowerment.

In my lifetime I hope to see evidence-based care become the norm, midwives become better utilized and the US one of the top three safest countries in which to give birth. Unfortunately, if you are in your childbearing years now, that is not your reality. In fact, without your help, it won't be the reality of your children either. Here are some concrete things you can do to ensure safer care for you and your baby.

	Yes	No
1. Do you utilize prenatal testing only when medically indicated?	—	—
1. Are you supportive of dialog regarding my care?	—	—
2. Do you encourage evidence-based childbirth education?	—	—
3. Is your cesarean rate under 15%	—	—
4. Is your episiotomy rate under 10%	—	—
5. Is your induction rate under 10%	—	—
6. Is your VBAC rate at least 70%	—	—
7. Do you 'allow' pregnancy to go past 42 weeks if baby and I are healthy?	—	—
8. May I labor without a time limit if both my baby and I are tolerating labor well?	—	—
9. Do you allow vaginal birthing of babies deemed "large" via ultrasound?	—	—

	Yes	No
10. Do you discourage routine circumcision?	—	—
11. Do you support breastfeeding by not giving out formula samples?	—	—
12. Will you support requests that are not standard protocol as long as they are reasonable and not medically contraindicated?	—	—
13. Will you allow me to video tape my birth?	—	—
14. Can I be sure that you will be attending my birth?	—	—
15. If not, would the attending provider share your philosophies?	—	—

If your provider responded 'yes' to all 15 questions, you have found a responsible, safe and respectful caregiver. Your own best birth can be expected.

If your provider responded 'yes' to at least 10 of the above question, your caregiver might be willing to work with you, but a pathological view of birth may be unconsciously be under that willingness. Clear communication and a little more work on your part may be required for an optimal experience. Give them a month or two. If, after attempts at being a partner in your care, you are not being met halfway, find someone who is willing to meet you there.

If your provider responded 'yes' to 5 or less, 6 or 7 months is simply not enough time to bring this caregiver around. Remaining with this caregiver means there is a high probability you will be a statistic in the sad state of American maternity care. The chance that you will have a safe, dignified and empowering birth is next to nil.

Also, keep in mind that underreporting, not just of mortality and morbidity rates, but of certain procedures, is the norm in our health care system, as evidenced by a quick web search of the word 'underreporting'. Verify 'internal sources' with *independent* sources of information. There are often huge discrepancies between the two statistics.

Finally, remember to be sure words and actions say the same thing.

Notes for Chapter Three

1   Allomother is a term used in *Mother Nature: A History of Mothers, Infants, and Natural Selection* by
     Sarah Blaffer Hrdy, Pantheon Books, 1999 in reference to mother substitutes.
2   *Smoking and SIDS*, www.motherisk.org/updates/Spring2002.php3
3   The research for this book began in early 2002, through 2003
4   March of Dimes Perinatal Data Center, Aug. 2002 shows that the US has fallen from 21st place it held in previous years to 28th. Cuba, Spain, Portugal and Ireland now have better outcomes than the US.
     World Health Organization, www.who.org
5   Centers for Disease Control,
     www.cdc.gov/nchs/fastats/pdf/nvsr50_15tb34.pdf
6   The socio-economic reasons for this discrepancy are beyond the scope of this work. However, the differences are relevant for the purposes putting the statistic in your own geographical are to use.
7   www.michigan.gov/documents/InfantMortalityFEb00_10492_7.pdf
8   www.thefarm.org.charities/mid.html
9   Michigan Hospital Report, www.mha.org/mhr6/
10   Le Leche Legue International, www.lalecheleague.org/
11   Not a real name. All mothers are composites.
12   A cut between the vagina and anus (or into the leg) to enlarge the birth canal. Almost never required.

PART TWO
MOTIVATION

OUR ACTIONS ARE BASED ON WHAT WE THINK WE KNOW ABOUT BIRTH. NOW THAT YOU HAVE AN IDEA OF WHAT MAKES BIRTH SAFER, DO YOU KNOW HOW TO MAKE IT HAPPEN FOR YOU? DO YOU KNOW HOW TO BE MORE COMFORTABLE? ARE YOU READY TO EXPLORE YOUR OPTIONS? PART TWO BUILDS MOMENTUM IN YOUR NEWFOUND MOTIVATION.

(PRO) CREATION

How can America be one of the most technologically advanced countries on earth and be one of the least safe places to give birth? One reason may be simple American hubris that we are known for throughout the world. I think it's learned in medical school. In trying to discuss traditional birth wisdom of Caribbean doctors and nurse-midwives with one young med student, she scoffed, "Yeah, those 'medical degrees' are a big joke at school".

Another reason may be that our technological capability has surpassed our ethics or common sense. In any case, how is it that American parents can be under the assumption that they are safe due to the technology, when all of the evidence says otherwise? The technology has the *potential* to save lives. It seems to make sense that better technology means better outcomes. Now that you are aware that the outcomes are proof that the system *doesn't* make sense, let's look at what's broke so we can fix it.

Accountability is paramount to the solution. Everyone who shapes the current system of maternity care, from the doctors to the consumer, needs to be accountable for their part in the reality we have.

This is not about blame. Blame is part of the problem. Blame and accountability are not the same. Blame releases us from accountability because it puts responsibility for outcomes 'out there'. We didn't break it, so we don't have to fix it. "I'm only doing what the women demand" is blame. "My doctor didn't tell me" is blame. "I'm only doing my job" is blame.

However, we are all responsible for how a situation affects us personally. Without acknowledging that our choices matter, we won't make better choices.

This means good, bad, fair or unfair, every choice you make as a parent affects the outcome of your birth. Likewise for caregivers. There are no inconsequential actions. That may not be the way you want it to be, but it *is*, none-the-less. It is an inescapable fact-of-life. If you've never considered it before, it's essential that it is understood now because now you are making choices for two.

Let it be understood that I am talking about normal, healthy women here. I am not suggesting that an illness or injury is within your control—though there are a number of situations in which it might have been.

What I am saying is right here, right now, you are constructing your own reality with the choices you make...or don't make. By the end of this chapter you will understand what you control, and what you only control your *reaction* to. If you are thinking to yourself right now that there is <u>no way</u> your feelings of fear, your lack of confidence or some pregnancy 'condition' you've been diagnosed with is under your control, keep reading. You will be surprised to learn how much really is. I promise.

However, you have to consider there may be a grain of truth to what you are about to learn or you'll be giving your power away. Don't victimize yourself by accepting the illusion that someone else is running the show. No one can control your life unless you allow it.

If you really want a healthy pregnancy and joyful birth, and you truly understand that you are the one in control, then you must examine what you have or haven't done so far to create the outcome you want.

How do you know where your current choices will lead if you are newly pregnant for the first time? Do you have the same attitudes and hold the same opinions as your friends? Most of us do. What were their outcomes? I'm not talking about a healthy baby. That should be the expectation of most parents. Nature is very efficient at the survival game. There are very few things that *actually* go wrong in pregnancy. There are many things that *could*...but not that many that actually *do*. That is one of those things that people assume about pregnancy and birth...that they are crisis in waiting. As you will see, it's not true.

Past behavior is the best indicator of future outcomes. So, their choices have resulted in a healthy baby, that's the good news. What did it cost them? Not in dollar amounts, though that is a disgrace. Midwives deliver the same results or better for far less. What did it cost them *personally*. Did they have postpartum depression? Did they have trouble bonding or nursing? Is the baby healthy or been plagued with ear infections, digestive problems, behavioral problems? Does the mother have an episiotomy scar that is affecting daily living? Did she have to try to mother a newborn and heal from major abdominal surgery at the same time? Did she 'almost die' having her baby? Did she need to be 'rescued'? These are all awfully high price tags for something that is a woman's birthright.

Does that mean bad things never happen? No. It means that they happen so often in modern obstetrical care that we are now beginning to consider them 'normal'. They happen infrequently in the midwifery model, but the woman still gets the baby 'prize' and so much more out of their mothering experience. How fair is that? I'd be mad at hell if I had to pay for something that was already mine!

Self-assess where your motherhood journey begins by answering these questions :

What is important to me regarding my pregnancy and birth?
What do I want to avoid during my pregnancy and birth?
What have I done to ensure one or avoid the other?
What can I do to make the preferred outcome possible?
Can I accept that I may have to examine some of my choices or gather more information?

Am I trusting unwisely? Am I missing important 'red flags'?
Am I communicating my needs clearly to my care-provider and partner?
Have I deceived myself because I wanted to justify inconsistency in my providers words and actions ?
What choices have I made that resulted in something I didn't want?
Have I chosen the right caregiver and birth location for my wants and needs?
Did I fail to act on an intuition that led to an undesirable result?
Am I standing up for my parental rights and asking for what I need?
Am I treating myself with dignity & respect? Am I requiring it of others?
What actions can I take right now to move in a more positive direction?
Are there behaviors that I can adopt to improve my birth outcome?
Are there behaviors, detrimental to my birth if continued, that should be examined?
Am I realistic in my pregnancy, birth and parenting expectations?
Am I realistic in my expectations of my capabilities and those of my provider?

Obstetricians can ask themselves the same questions to understand why they are the most sued profession. There are no accidents. By taking some responsibility for it instead of blaming lawyers and patients, they can address the real issues and become part of the solution.

It's hard to accept the idea that we are responsible for the outcomes of our actions, I know. We live in a time when it's easier to be right than be responsible. Not accepting responsibility means we can't heal...can't grow. This reality must be internalized if it means stopping here to journal and digest. It means entertaining new ideas about victimization.

Anita was a smart, strong woman. She took an independent childbirth class and read books about making her experience better. She decided she didn't want to make a big fuss about the all the prenatal testing...it was easier just to do what her doctor said. She knew she could choose a midwife, said she wanted to, but her husband wouldn't 'allow' it. Besides, she was healthy and took great care of herself. The tests wouldn't show anything bad.

Her triple screen test indicated that her baby had a chromosomal abnormality. The recommendation was to do further testing. She read up on further testing, only to discover there was a unacceptably high chance, to her, of her losing the baby due to the test. The next test was also no more reliable than the first, although she did agree to an extra ultrasound, which confirmed the diagnoses. There was nothing to be done about the problem. She was advised to abort.

She couldn't bring herself to do that. She was under an incredible amount of stress, was constantly being told that now she was high risk and would need a cesarean, though a cesarean would not change the outcome for either her or the child. She got genetic counseling. She took classes on caring for a special needs child. She was fearful about whether or not she could love enough and how all of this would affect the rest of her life.

Her baby boy was born completely healthy. Of course, that's all that matters, right? Wrong. I doubt *she* would consider the pointless assault on her emotional and psychological health, or the toll this took on her life, her work or her family insignificant.

You can believe that what's wrong with the system has nothing to do with you. That woman was not the first who went through this with this particular doctor and she wasn't the last. She asked questions, but she didn't act on the answers. She sacrificed so much of what should have been the happiest time of her life. Were there long term repercussions with bonding? Did the stress hormones produced by her body negatively affect her baby's brain development as scientists postulate? What would be the point in knowing for sure? What's done is done. Unless other parents would be spared her torment, why go there? Would your decisions be affected if you knew for sure her child *had* suffered the consequence of her actions? Would you think it couldn't happen to you? She knew the reputation of this doctor and that's exactly what she thought.

Parents can keep feeling as if they are mistreated and powerless and they *will be* mistreated and powerless. They can shut their eyes to books full of scientific studies about our current birth technology and the evidence of misuse contaminating the process of birth. They can insist that anyone who would question the status quo is just wrong.

What if they aren't? **If** the 'normal' choices are right, and the 'weird' choices are wrong, why are the ones making the 'wrong' choices having the faster, more comfortable births and sometimes even a blissful experience of motherhood?

You can be angry that it seems unfair that so few women have 'fairy tale' births, or you can become Cinderella . You have to be willing to be flexible in your position, humble enough to admit maybe there are other possibilities or that you might be robbing yourself of the potential to improve your situation.

> YOU CAN BE ANGRY THAT IT SEEMS UNFAIR THAT SO FEW WOMEN HAVE 'FAIRY TALE' BIRTHS, OR YOU CAN BECOME CINDERELLA.

You can keep doing what you are doing, what all of your cesarean friends have done, if you want a surgical birth...preparing to deal with all of the difficulties that it entails. OR you can decide that there might be an alternative for you. The Universe may reward you for your initiative.

Let others blame the system, the books they read or the bodies they have been led to believe are deficient or defective. Let them blame everyone else and God for their pain, disappointment and suffering. You be the one to truly change your life. Stand up and take what's yours. Do it for your baby. Stop looking in the wrong place for answers only you have.

Realize that every decision you make from this point on has consequences you own. Also realize you had this power before today, as well. As you consider that past choices led to present results, you may have to adjust personal perceptions. It's important that you remember 'responsibility' is not the same as 'fault'. Allow yourself the space to acknowledge how your actions affect your present circumstance, then *release the negativity that affects your life.*

Journal Exploration:

If you have felt like an outsider to your own pregnancy up until now, take some time to relive the situation behind the emotion so that you can re-evaluate accountability.

Thinking back through your pregnancy to date, or to past pregnancies, list 5 times when you felt mistreated, ignored, not dealt with fairly and compassionately, made to feel incompetent or defective. Detail the situation until the emotion associated with the interaction is clear. Leave enough space under each entry to go back in a moment.

Now go back to the spaces under each entry, identifying how your action or inaction contributed to the result that made you feel victimized. Were there warning signs? Intuition? Be really honest with yourself. It's hard work, but you will use this information to your advantage when you begin to take control over your rite-of-passage...birth.

What should become clear is that looking outside of yourself for why you may feel the way you do is nonproductive. Thoughts, choices and behaviors become yours to change. You have the ability to purposefully change the birth experience you create. Resolve to analyze the events of your pregnancy as they relate to the choices you make.

Doing so reframes how you interact with your partner, your caregiver and other mothers. "Why me?" becomes "Why not?" You will begin to wonder, "How can I change this situation or my reaction to it? How might it be different? What are my options and do I have all of the information I need to explore each one?" If you don't know your options, you don't have any.

If you've been programming yourself for what you don't want, it should become clear that you can also program success. Success is what *you* want it to be. It isn't about what anybody else thinks or what is 'right' or 'wrong'. How you feel when all is said and done reflects if the choice was right *for you*. Do you feel confident, strong, certain that your choices fit your situation? That the choice was right for you? Since these things can't be answered until it's too late to make changes, the only way to know is to weigh the evidence that's available to you. That's the purpose of this book.

It's certainly easier to place blame than to be accountable. Our culture supports the victim mentality. That's why malpractice rates are so high and frivolous lawsuits are out of control. By not accepting responsibility for how we are affected by our own actions, we don't have to expect more of ourselves.

It would be easy to believe that we are victims of the broken obstetrical system because of the obstetricians, but that's not entirely true. The specialty of obstetrics developed because sometimes we need them. We must accept that often, inappropriate technology is used because we ask for it.

Doctors must take responsibility for allowing parents to dictate inappropriate care, for sure. However, the hypocrisy of saying that the epidural rate is only so high because women demand it, yet meeting reasonable requests with snide remarks like, 'where did you go to medical school?' has to stop. Would an internal surgeon open you up and look around just because you demanded exploratory surgery? The system is partially shaped by the women in it, partly by caregivers. At least two other forces are also a factor... economics and fear.

Inappropriate technology used in the name of defensive medicine exists because parents sue doctors. Not just doctors with bad judgment or malicious intent, but good ones too. All doctors (and parents!) are being punished in this complex situation.

It may seem that the world is unfair or unjust, that you were only doing what you were told; that just because something *should* be so it *is*. I'm sorry to say it is not likely to be so if you don't put action toward it. The odds are against it right now, which means you must actively work toward the outcome of a healthy, whole child and an unwounded body and soul for yourself at the end of your journey.

If you don't want to hear that, you aren't alone. Listen to people talk about what's wrong in their lives for the next week. You'll hear it everywhere. Ask your sisters and friends about their births. They may have a gorgeous, healthy baby...but what unnecessary sacrifices were they asked to make? Did they sacrifice their dignity? Integrity? Their sex life? Their marriage? Further childbearing capability? Their child's potential? What justifications do they use to make it okay? Is blame involved, including blaming of themselves? Many women internalize blame, and I'm afraid there are many ways that this is encouraged in the current system. It deflects blame that could cost someone cold, hard cash. Accountability is essential, blame is not acceptable.

FAR TOO MANY WOMEN ARE BEING REQUIRED TO SACRIFICE FAR TOO MUCH FAR TOO OFTEN.

Sacrifice is a part of motherhood so we accept it without question. Certain sacrifices *are* a mother's lot in life. Sleep deprivation. A change in body structure resulting from growing an entire human being within your body and birthing it into the world. However, far too many women are being required to sacrifice far too much far too often. It's up to you to determine how much unwarranted sacrifice you are willing to heap on top of what is already inherent in motherhood. To bear more than your fair share, assuming the role of victim by your own free will, starts you out on your new path with a deficit that makes the job so much harder.

It is our very nature to blame others for our problems. You'll see it in your toddler eventually and it's painfully obvious as we look about our world right now.

It's self-preservation to try to escape accountability, to justify and rationalize. It's not right, but it is natural. We have a hard time being objective when we are emotionally involved. Our ability to determine solutions is hindered by our lack of objectivity in those instances. It's imperative to adopt new ways of thinking. Nothing is more emotional than motherhood.

Once able to change a victim mindset, though, the possibilities are endless. You decide only you can change what you don't want in your birth. You stop hoping for magical solutions and start dealing with the issues at hand.

You can't solve a problem with blame. You can't just coast along because the truth hurts. Doing nothing *is* doing something. If you are feeling frightened, confused, overwhelmed, unsure or downright powerless about how your pregnancy is progressing, how your birth will end up or what to expect from your new life with baby, you need to accept that only you can change it.

- You choose the food that builds your baby.
- You control the stress hormones that reach your baby.
- You control the books you choose, if any
- You control the images of birth you accept
- You choose what kind of childbirth class you take, if any
- You choose your care provider.
- You choose how you will allow your caregiver to treat you.
- You choose what tests you will allow.
- You determine the level of understanding you have of your care.
- You choose your birth location.
- You choose to believe the facts of safe birth or the illusions of danger.
- You choose to smoke, or not.
- You choose to take drugs, or not
- You choose to drink alcohol, or not.
- You choose natural birth, or not

Can you add to this list? I realize that if blaming has been one way of interacting in the world until now, it's a tough habit to break, but it can be done. People improve their lives everyday by doing it. I've done it. I didn't make the rule, but I will attest to it's truth. There's no way around it if you want the best experience of motherhood possible.

Remember, blame and responsibility are not the same. Mistaking the two will cost valuable time. Recklessly disregarding consequences of actions, or intentionally inflicting harm, warrants blame. Responsibility means being accountable for actions that were under your control. Intent makes the difference.

Guilt is often the end-result of blame-worthy behavior. Guilt is a message from our inner self that says we knew our intent was less than honorable. It is meant to help us navigate difficult situations so that even if we make mistakes, we learn from them and don't repeat them.

As seen in previous chapters, there is a need to be willing to look closely at feelings of guilt because, unfortunately, misplaced guilt is common. Neither real guilt nor misplaced guilt is meant to be carried around as punishment. True guilt guides. Once we recognize it, we decide to do better next time, we let it go and we move on. Misplaced guilt simply has no purpose.

This should be liberating news. If you really don't have control over something, you can release feelings of guilt that were not yours to carry. If you made a bad choice knowing there was a better one, you can allow the guilt to guide you in the future to make the better choice, and release the guilt that's done it's job.

The only thing we are assured of is the here and now. From this point on your expectation can improve because you are no longer an observer in your own process.

You can't change the past, you can only choose your reaction to it and learn from it. Letting regret or misplaced guilt taint future decisions only hurts you. It's far better to be pro-active in making sound decisions you know you'll feel strong about, no matter what the outcome.

> "THOSE WHO DO NOT LEARN FROM THE PAST ARE DESTINED TO REPEAT IT."
> *Winston Churchill*

Has your doctor belittled or berated you for asking intelligent questions? Have you avoided asking questions because you feared he would? Were you coerced into dropping a great childbirth class because your doctor played a power trip? Threatening to discontinue care with you if you kept going? Has he censured you in some other way? The bad news is, only you have the power to change the situation. The good news is, you have the power.

Briefly, I'd like to introduce just how thoughts and feelings affect your birth. I realize the idea is very abstract and far off for some readers. I didn't understand it for a long time.

The mind affects the body in very concrete, biological ways. The body your child calls 'home'.

Are you a blusher? Then a *thought* causes blood to rush to your face. Do you get an upset stomach from stress? Then your *thoughts* cause your body to make more stomach acid.

In pregnancy, one way that this can detrimentally affect your experience is a phenomenon known as 'white coat hypertension' (1), which is elevated blood pressure that only shows up in the doctors office. Considering women are now expected to take tests through the entire pregnancy, it shouldn't be surprising that blood pressure would be higher when they go in to "see how they did".

Anxiety induced elevated blood pressure occurring only in the office is not usually a serious problem. High blood pressure all of the time can be. If the only time a woman has her blood pressure taken is at her prenatal visit, and it's high at every visit, the interpretation of that could be that the blood pressure is elevated all of the time, when it's not. It's diagnosed and treated, when in actuality, treating a non-problem can *create* problems. (2)

It's more important to understand the mind/body connection in pregnancy and birth than any other time. It can make the difference between painless, drug-free birthing and suffering.

Your choices now literally program your experience later. Please do the work you need to do to get the result you want. Getting a handle on any negative 'self talk' now will make parenting easier and more enjoyable later.

Journal exploration:

What negative tapes do you have about birth? List the top ten and choose to stop sabotaging yourself now. For each negative comment, think of a positive affirmation using positive language. Focus on what you want, rather than what you don't. For example:

Negative tape: I don't even want to think about the pain in labor!
Affirmation: My body is perfectly designed to give birth.

Negative tape: I can't do this!
Affirmation: I have all the resources I need to give birth gently.

Negative tape: I can't ask my doctor that! He'll think I don't trust him!
Affirmation: It's good parenting to be assertive in seeking the best care for my baby.

Mongan Method HypnoBirthing® taped affirmations are available through practitioners teaching *HypnoBirthing®* classes as well from the *HypnoBirthing®* Institute. Affirmations can also be found in the book, *Birthing from Within®* and the *Better Birth Decks* sold wherever *Mother's Intention* is sold or through the order form at the back of this book.

Taking your newfound insights into the world may require practice. It's easy to get overly excited about empowerment, to start <u>demanding</u> better treatment. There may be a time of transition as questioning, once a rarity, becomes commonplace.

Consider that 'what comes around goes around". How you approach your caregiver means a lot. It's all right to give people the benefit of the doubt. Do you want to be a partner in your care? Mutual respect is the foundation.

What is your communication style? What is your partner's? What is your care provider's?

Professional and personable:
This is the "dream" caregiver. Doctor, Midwife or CNM, this care provider is the perfect fit. They seem to like everyone. They are open to new ideas and treat everyone as valuable. Even if they disagree with you, they'll tell you they disagree, respecting that this is your birth and your life. If there is a medical reason for something, they will explain everything to your satisfaction. The important thing here is *they back it up*. Others may say it, but words and deeds contradict each other. Not here. This is someone who will go the extra mile to look up new information so they can give you a fresh perspective, even changing their thoughts on something if the evidence supports it. They actually respect a parent who does their homework.

Hopefully, this book will help parents to *be* these types.

Prickly:
Nothing is ever right. These people take it personally. Defensive and easily offended, a simple question sets them off. He'll use manipulative tactics to get you to comply. He doesn't expect you to question him and will personally attack if you do, often with "If you want to kill your baby..." sort of maneuvers. As clients, these people don't ask questions, they make accusations.

Jeeves:
Arrogance drips off these people! They have to look at your chart to remember your name and may argue if you tell them they have the *wrong* chart. They hate being wrong. They don't get angry about questions though, because they deftly avoid them, not really taking you seriously. You may not realize your questions have not been answered until you're on the way home. If you persist, the response is likely to be "Where did *you* go to medical school?" (Though these are the people who also say they only use unnecessary technology because the patient demands it!) When both parents and caregiver exhibit these characteristics, it's almost comical...neither knows the other is even in the room.

Bubbles:
Always cheerful, not very deep. They check the mirror on the way into the office. They seem distracted because they have their mind on something else...usually having nothing to do with you. When presented with a birth plan they'll say "Sure, sure, anything you want". Don't expect it though...he hasn't even actually looked at it and won't 'find time' before your birth. In mothers, these would be the ones for whom the realization that *there's a baby in there* doesn't hit until the baby is in their arms. These mothers often have difficult births because they don't prepare at all...they just assume someone else always takes care of stuff. Fear takes over in the end when reality sets in.

Control freaks:
Dominating and insufferable, they know *everything* better than you, including how you should think and feel. They tell you, too. These doctors will 'fire' you as a patient if so much as look at an unauthorized book or set foot in a class of which they don't control the content. Loss of control over you is not tolerated. Women who are perfectionists of this sort may have difficult births if they can't lighten up. Motherhood is all about adaptability and if that realization isn't made, these mothers are miserable.

High Drama:
Nothing is ever simple. A stitch in your side requires a battery of tests. Requesting any deviation of the usual routine is likely to be met with "I don't like to deliver dead babies!" There is a catastrophe around every corner and she is the only thing keeping you safe. Don't expect evidence-based care from her...she doesn't look at scientific evidence, but acts on adrenaline and fear from her every day experience. Parents that fall into this category wear their caregivers out.

Victim:
Nothing is their fault. Routine technology harmful? They only do it because they have to! The lawyers are out to get them, the

patients are out to get them, *you* make them do it! Everyone's out to get them anyway, what difference would competency make? They won't bother to look at new information because as far as they are concerned, they're damned if they do and damned if they don't. Sometimes quiet and won't look you in the eye. Like the donkey character in Winnie the Pooh, mothers in this group may have an 'Eeyore' attitude...going along with everything, asking no questions, thinking everything bad in life always happens to them and there is nothing they can do to change it. Doctors like these patients...as long as everything goes as planned. If the parent inadvertently gains knowledge about evidence-based care, there will be trouble for the doctor. Parents in the group are the 'why me-s' and blamers...they are the ones who most often sue.

Analysts:
Maybe boring, but a safe bet in a caregiver. They are scientists at heart. They love knowledge, whatever the source. Every day is a learning experience. They love it when you bring them new information that can be substantiated and incorporate it into their practice. These types are also dream clients when the caregiver is practicing evidence-based care. They look up what you tell them to verify it themselves, but each time they get confirmation, they trust more, the relationship strengthened. These clients rarely sue because they feel that everyone played fair and know that sometimes, bad things still happen, though the odds are in their favor with knowledge. Doctors not practicing evidence-based care hate these patients because it makes them work too hard.

We all have all of these traits and many more besides. In balance, they make up a positive interaction. Out of balance, they can affect your decisions in ways you might not want.

Choosing to remain in an unhealthy relationship with a caregiver is as harmful as remaining in an unhealthy relationship with anyone else...maybe more so. Make no mistake, even choosing not to act in a bad situation is a choice. Each choice leads to the one-and-only birth-day of your child. Be consciously aware of what you are creating.

> EACH (PREGNANCY) CHOICE LEADS TO THE ONE-AND-ONLY BIRTH DAY OF YOUR CHILD.

It's human nature to resist change. Our ancestor's survival used to be contingent on the known and familiar. Our brains work the same way now. As you move into awareness you may be uncomfortable at times. Other people may react to you differently. It will feel more 'right' with practice.

By being willing to embrace, or at least explore, new thought, you will be amazed at how much you enjoy your pregnancy, and eventually, your birth. After that, new motherhood. Being judgmental or dismissive just because ideas are new or unusual will deprive you of nature's gifts to new mothers.

Being willing doesn't mean abandoning good sense. It doesn't mean accepting uncritically. Quite the opposite.

Chloe's story:

Chloe was a strong young woman. She and her husband read everything they could about birth early in their pregnancy. In their second trimester, they decided to see a midwife.

In their community, the medical establishment refused to provide back up to qualified midwives. This put the couple in the undesirable position of continuing prenatal care with their doctor without informing him of their homebirth plans in order to be able to transfer to the hospital in the event of an emergency. The midwife would have preferred a better arrangement as well, but it was better than the alternative of no emergency plan at all, so she went along with the decision.

One day, Chloe appeared at her midwife's door, days before her next scheduled prenatal/midwifery appointment, miserable and scared. During a routine doctor's visit, she had been told she was in premature labor. This diagnosis was made on the basis of a (useless, routine) vaginal examine that her doctor told her showed dilation of two-three cm (not necessarily unusual at 36 weeks), as well as an electronic-fetal monitor strip (also proven to be useless without medical indication) that showed she was having contractions (which she didn't feel—had never felt). From that visit (where she was told all sorts of horrifying stories of the effects of pre-maturity) she was sent to the hospital. There she was given IV terbutaline to stop premature labor (which has been proven ineffective) and then sent home with an oral medication, Brethine (which the Physician's Desk Reference says not to use in pregnancy). After only a few days on the drug, this mother, who had taken excellent care of herself and been healthy up until that last visit, began to feel very ill. Her heart raced, her baby moved non-stop as it's heart rate did the same. Nausea kept her from eating and drinking. She couldn't sleep.

Her midwife sadly informed her that once drugs were introduced, this became a medical event. Midwives deal with normal pregnancy and birth, which this no longer was. The midwife offered to accompany Chloe to the hospital for the birth, but could not help her at home while she was on the medication. Besides, Chloe had not reached 37 weeks...the earliest midwives will allow homebirth.

At that point, Chloe confessed to having reduced the dosage of the drug of her own volition. She asked if the midwife would attend her at home if there was time to clear the drug from her system and if she could make it past the 37 week mark. Her midwife conferred with her partner and agreed, if those conditions were met, and there were no complications resulting from the treatment, they could do it at home. All of this was contingent on whether the mother really was in premature labor. After checking

111

Chloe's cervix and finding it high and closed, the midwife determined that Chloe had *never been* in premature labor.

Chloe called her midwife a few days later. She was 'spilling protein' in her urine, her blood pressure was up and swelling had worsened. All of the symptoms of pre-eclampsia, which is very dangerous. Also signs of a compromised liver (one of the risks of terbutaline, according to the Physician's Desk Reference).

Chloe had reached 37 weeks, but she would still have to birth in the hospital.

At the hospital, the doctor was rude, rough and disrespectful. He didn't ask Chloe or her husband how they might like to proceed or offer any options, which they knew were available from their reading.

He told them what he would do, then abruptly left, leaving orders with the nurse.

Chloe asked her midwife if she could help her use imagery to bring her blood pressure down long enough to go to a different hospital. She knew that allowing the interventions this doctor was intent on using would, in all likelihood, result in a cesarean. After discussion with the understanding that a cesarean might still be an option as sick as she now was, it was agreed to at least try.

Relaxation brought her blood pressure down to normal levels. Chloe got dressed and was ready to sign out AMA (against medical advice) when her doctor returned. He was furious. He yelled at her. He accused her of trying to kill her baby. He detailed all of the tragedies that would befall her if she walked out the door. He not only made her sign the AMA form, but he made her *write out and sign a letter* he dictated, stating that she knew she was killing her baby by making this choice. This brave mother stayed relaxed throughout his entire tirade and walk out.

She went to a different hospital. She explained what had happened, all the while, remaining calm and keeping her blood pressure down.

Once settled into the new hospital, Chloe did have medication to lower her blood pressure, and she did have low dose pitocin to get labor started. It took a long time to get labor going...she was only 37 weeks and had never really been in premature labor...but eventually her own body took over. She had to work hard to stay relaxed as her condition made it impossible to move to a more comfortable position and she needed to be hooked up to two IVs for true medical indications.

But she did it. She had her own best birth. It didn't turn out as she planned, but she knew that she made the best choices for her baby and avoided what would have been an unnecessary surgery.

Notes on Chapter Four

1   *"White coat hypertension during pregnancy leads to unnecessary Cesarean deliveries"*
    Journal of the America Medical Association 1999; 282;147.
    By: Thomas Pickering, MD, DPhil, FRCP, Director of Integrative and Behavioral Cardiology Program of the Cardiovascular Institute at Mount Sinai School of Medicine, New York.
2   *The Tentative Pregnancy*, Barbara Katz-Rothman

HUMAN NATURE

In previous chapters, we've looked at the safety of birth in America. We've examined the role fear plays in our decision making process, as parents and professionals alike. We've seen how skillfully our subconscious beliefs manipulate our actions. We now clearly recognize how belief affects perception, which <u>is</u> reality.

It's a lot to absorb. You may be noticing you view the world a little differently now that you've done the work in the first chapters.

You may have changed some behaviors. You may have revised some long held beliefs and are wondering why others do what *they* do. You may be thinking differently, but have not put the new knowledge to work, and can't figure out *why*.

Why do parents support a system that in large measure treats them poorly and puts their children at risk? Why do doctors perpetuate a system that continues to generate more lawsuits than any other profession? Why do publishers publish useless information and why do producers make frightening birth programs? Why do midwives keep trying to improve a system that doesn't seem to want to improve when the effort might land them in jail? Why do lawyers prosecute the midwives when every shred of credible scientific evidence supports midwifery for healthy mothers and babies?

All of us play a part in the system we now have to deal with. The blame cannot be placed with just one group. The responsibility must be met by all, and all must hold the others accountable for their portion of the problem if we are ever to find a solution. We must step up to the plate for our mothers and babies.

We all do what we do for the same reason. On some level there is a perceived reward for our behavior. Sometimes it's obvious, sometimes not.

Our behavior creates our outcomes. Success is measured by results. Is what we are doing, and have been doing making birth safer? Is what we're doing helping produce happy, healthy, well adjusted children? Is what we're doing helping doctors care for high-risk patients and midwives care for healthy mothers? If our results are indicative, no, what we're doing certainly isn't working!

Mothers are so afraid of a natural, gloriously designed process that they are choosing to not feel a thing, detaching emotionally and physically from the most rewarding effort they'll ever make in their lives.

Doctors are being sued so often they are choosing not to practice obstetrics.

American mothers are so dissatisfied with the institution of motherhood it's been relegated to a two hour a day 'life style choice'.

More mothers and babies die in the US than 27 other countries.

American babies and children suffer a whole host of disorders and problems not seen anywhere else.

It doesn't *look* like it's working—so why do we keep doing the same things over-and-over again? Why are we not learning from our mistakes? Why do our collective behaviors create results benefiting no one? Denial is certainly part of the problem.

Here is an example of this in action. A popular morning news program recently ran a series about "Having a Baby Today" in April of 2003. In one portion of this series, several *opinions* were expressed by the physician interviewed. These opinions were based on faulty core assumptions and contradicted by the scientific literature. When I told a friend that I was going to write to the show and point out these inaccuracies, I was asked, "If what she said wasn't factual, how could she say it?" I asked my friend, "Did you question her advice?" The response was "No." The show didn't verify the facts, why would the viewers?

If you saw it, did you question the advice? Probably not. Most wouldn't. After all, she's a doctor, on the show to help us make safe decisions, right?

One assertion is a nifty little sound bite, "Pizzas are home delivered, not babies" but the explaination that homebirth isn't safe, is patently (and demonstrably, as you'll see throughout this work) false. Another opinion, that elective cesareans save pelvic floor function, is also not supported according to US researchers reporting in Obstetrics and Gynecology (2002;100:226-229), which states that women who have never experienced childbirth are just as likely as those who have given birth to develop urinary incontinence, a finding that casts doubts on the theory that vaginal deliveries increase the risk of incontinence. What does cause pelvic floor damage is *episiotomy*, still routine for many doctors.

This sort of thing happens all over the nation every day. Blindly accepting opinion as fact keeps the erroneous beliefs in play. Few have been willing to admit the existing dysfunction. Yet, make no mistake...no matter how logical or rational you pride yourself on being, if you aren't part of the solution, you are part of the problem.

- That means if, as a parent, you are seeing a provider that's not practicing evidence-based care, you are part of the problem.
- That means if you are a doctor not supporting midwifery, you are part of the problem.

- That means if you are a lawyer supporting frivolous lawsuits, you are part of the problem.
- That means if you are consenting, or conducting, non-medically indicated, routine testing and intervention, you are part of the problem.
- That means if you are watching crisis oriented birthing programs, you are part of the problem.
- That means if you are producing fear based programming, you are part of the problem.

We know that in pregnancy, diet and exercise are two of the most important factors in outcome. What are you growing your baby on? Are you growing your baby on whole, fresh foods, or junk?

We know that smoking is responsible for numerous, potentially fatal, pregnancy complications and childhood illnesses. Have you stopped? Have you eliminated as much second-hand smoke from your home and work environments as possible?

We know stress is at least partially responsible for several pregnancy complications. What are you doing to create a peaceful environment for you and your baby?

We know the five standards of safe childbearing are:

- Good nutrition
- Skillful Midwifery
- Natural Childbirth
- Homebirth
- Breastfeeding

What kind of commitment have you made to your baby's safety based on this knowledge? Are your choices based on scientific evidence or obstetric myths?

To create your own best birth, you need to stop behaving in ways that interfere with what you want, and begin behaving in ways that bring the positive results you desire.

You may believe on the surface that what you are doing is working for you. Ask yourself, are you fearful and anxious? If you think you're not, allow yourself a little honesty about what drives your decisions. A 'just in case' philosophy is built on fear. Testing for conditions that you are not at risk for, and have no symptoms of, is fear-based. Prenatal visits that focus on things that *might* go wrong instead of what *is right* are fear-based.

> TO CREATE YOUR OWN BEST BIRTH, YOU NEED TO STOP BEHAVING IN WAYS THAT INTERFERE WITH WHAT YOU WANT, AND BEGIN BEHAVING IN WAYS THAT BRING THE POSITIVE RESULTS YOU DESIRE.

Prenatal visits that leave you crying or with a wiggly feeling in your belly mean your intuition is screaming at you!

Logically, we know this isn't what we want, but we feel powerless to change. Parents do what they do out of love, first-and-foremost, and safety. But if that is true, as we know it is, why make decisions that are proven unsafe? It seems illogical.

We come back to fear and belief. They *believe* that they are making the safest choices, yet fear is the root of their choice.

This may not be a conscious fear. Though many will come to a childbirth class fully willing to admit that they are (consciously) terrified, I believe in most mothers the fear is subconsciously lurking. Only about one quarter of the mothers giving birth annually even come to classes. There are a number of reasons for this, but if you ask a first-time mother who has the means, transportation and support why she didn't attend, she'd probably tell you she doesn't see a reason. Either she believes what will be, will be, because she has no control anyway, or she will say that she just expects everything to be fine because pregnancy and birth are normal and she is healthy. She might insist that isn't the least bit afraid...yet she makes choices that contradicts this because they are based in a 'just in case' mentality. Now, someone who says they trust in birth and have no fear as they plan an unassisted birth, I believe. Their words and actions match. Healthy mothers who get mad at anyone who suggests that fear is part of their process, all the while seeing a surgeon for a natural function are the ones I'm speaking of.

It's all right to admit to being afraid. We all fear the unknown. To what matter degree we allow it to impact decisions is what's important. It's whether we let the fear rule our choices, or illuminate the darkness so that the fear doesn't surface later to cause problems.

Those that start out consciously acknowledging fear at least can deal with preemptively. Denial of fear only means that it will lie in wait until some little thing sets it free. The current system provides ample opportunity for this to become a problem, even if it has been kept at bay for most of the pregnancy. The last few weeks of pregnancy, and labor itself, are when the majority of women will face their unconscious fears, because that is when inappropriate birth technology is abused the most. By that time, how many women are willing, or able, to question their 'low tech if you want me to be' caregiver who suddenly seems to have a personality transplant? The confidence the parents thought they had disappears in an instant. The 'just in case' (fear-based) philosophy they convinced themselves had nothing to do with fear is 'proved' necessary. They haven't prepared themselves on how to maneuver this kind of scenario...it wasn't going to happen to them. Since it did happen, they convince themselves *they* are part of that small percentage of people for whom the technology is beneficial.

The way that this 'of course pregnancy is a natural thing, but anything can go wrong at any moment' set up plays out, has been likened to the 'frog in a pot' analogy. (Yes, animal rights activists, it is horrible...I am not advocating, only repeating.)

If you toss a frog in a pot of boiling water, he'll jump out. If you put him in a pot of room temperature water and very gradually turn up the heat, he doesn't even notice the water getting warm until it's too late to jump.

An independent childbirth educator has seen a lot of frogs. She is probably able to see 'the big picture'. She may have had contact with hundreds of women in your community and may be able to tell you if the local induction rate your OB insists is 'low' is actually 60 or 70% instead of the 10% the World Health Organization suggests. She believes in the normalcy of birth.

Parental birth belief has been explored, but how is it a reward? If we act in ways that support our beliefs, no matter how erroneous they may be, we get what we expect. Having expectations met, even if they are negative consequences, is for some people, better than the unknown. Being fearful does not seem to be a reward, except that fearing what we 'know' seems less scary than the unknown.

Our erroneous beliefs about pregnancy and birth are not the only beliefs in play. Beliefs about authority, about self-esteem and even spiritual beliefs have some affect on how we birth. Do you believe that birth is a natural, biological process? Do you believe current birth technology makes birth safer? Safer than what? Do you know what made (or makes) birth dangerous? Do you believe birth must be painful? Excruciatingly so or manageably? Do you believe if some women have painless birth maybe many, even most, can? Do you believe that the US is one of the safest places in the world to give birth? Does your religion tell you women must suffer to bring forth life? Investigate your beliefs. See if they hold up to the facts. Don't just seek out information that bolsters what you already believe...see if other views have merit. Some of these we've already discussed in previous chapters, but did you verify them for yourself? Did you dismiss them or simply accept them with no proof? Beliefs are tenacious. If you want to change your experience, you must test your ideas constantly as they reassert themselves in the face of factual information. If they don't hold up to fact, discard them.

What about pain and birth? What would it take to convince you painless, or at least comfortable birth, is possible without drugs? "Suffering" is a judgment of a perception that you can choose to accept or reject.

An entire chapter is devoted to helping you work on your idea of the perception of pain so we won't dwell on that here. Just ask yourself, "Does fear of pain contribute to the choices I am making regarding pregnancy and birth?" The reward there would be freedom from pain, of course, but what if intolerably painful birth is *created or encountered*, not inherent in the experience?

One reward of abdicating responsibility for that which we are solely responsible for is that it allows us to place blame elsewhere if something goes wrong. This one is a tough one to accept, but the sky rocketing malpractice rate attests to it's validity.

Why would we choose to play the victim? Because we can.

Finally, one of our biggest fears is of being excluded. Most people will do almost anything to 'fit in'. Doing what everyone else does, even if we have reservations, seems to be part of our wiring. Social psychologist Stanley Milgram conducted controversial 'obedience experiments' at Yale University in 1961, expecting to show that American subjects would not follow orders that seemed to hurt another person. These experiments showed that indeed good people would do things under orders that they wouldn't do on their own. It seems we humans have sort of a 'pack' mentality. Sports frenzy resulting in riots is an extreme example of this gone awry. Unfortunately, when it comes to making safety decisions for precious babies, we can't afford to be blind followers.

Doctors and Nurses

Everyday, more doctors and nurses question where inappropriate technology has lead us. Organizations like Physicians for Midwifery and the Association of Nurse Advocates for Childbirth Solutions exist because of these courageous souls. (1)

Obviously, they are the minority or conditions would be improving, so what motivates the vast majority of those within the current system? Where are common sense and critical thinking skills?

Just as with parents, it comes back to fear and faulty beliefs. They spend a great deal of time learning about pathology and very little about normal, natural birth. They then see what they expect to see.

They create the reality they perceive to *be* reality. The medical model sees birth as a disaster waiting to happen, so it's based on fear. Facts that might contradict that belief are dismissed...unless the doctor or nurse is a scientist or non-conformist at heart.

Doctors and nurses are under even more pressure to conform than parents. Questioning procedure and protocol can be very expensive for them. 'Peer pressure' is taken to a whole new level. The ranks are so tight that even if a doctor is just flat out bad, his peers will clean up his messes before they will expose him. Even if ACOG's recommendations lack all common sense, they follow them. The reward is that they in turn are supported if they make a mistake. However, there is a difference in making an honest mistake, and true malpractice. If there was less tolerance for bad care within the ranks, parents might not be forced to take legal action as their only perceived recourse.

Fear for doctors and nurses includes this fear of litigation, in addition to a fear of birth and of being ostracized. There are financial rewards in sticking together. There are also financial rewards for routine use of technology.

For a long time I wanted to minimize financial incentive for maintaining the status quo when it means mothers and babies are put at risk. Conversations with doctors themselves who insist that money and power are at the root of the abysmal conditions we now face have convinced me that it is a reward that motivates at least a few.

Doctors (and at least one certified nurse-midwife I've talked to), have explained to me how the money and fear of litigation create a sort of circular logic that allows patients (and lawyers) to practice medicine.

They insist that they only do the things they do because the women *demand* it. If they didn't do what the women wanted, then the women would go elsewhere (taking their purses with them). By not doing something that someone else <u>would</u> do, they stand to lose a great deal (of money and acceptance both) if they follow the science instead of 'standard of care'. Standard of care means, basically, what everyone else is doing.

What I wonder is, why is it that birth is the only place we see this? Okay, we see it with antibiotic use also, which has led us to a place where antibiotic resistant organisms run rampant. But mainly, we see it in very limited situations.

If I went to a doctor and demanded Vicodin for common stress headaches, I'm guessing I'd be hard pressed to find a doctor who would buy into that.

What if I went in and demanded an appendectomy because I have an irrational fear of the pain and possible death of a ruptured appendix? Would I be able to find a doctor who would take it out 'just in case'?

My guess is that doctors would explain the actual incidence of ruptured appendixes, would only do appendectomies if clinical signs and symptoms were present, and maybe even educate the general public about their misconceptions. Hm...novel concept.

Most in the helping professions went into it to help. They believe they are helping. To think otherwise would be painful, so denial is useful in avoiding emotional pain. That makes total sense. Change is painful sometimes. Avoiding pain is a reward.

Another reward is one that I didn't think of until it was pointed out to me by someone in helping profession...being able to rush in and save the day is appealing to many. Maybe not consciously, but heroism addiction is easy to plug into. What a feeling of power to think that an event could not happen safely without out them. Certainly, we all like to feel needed. It's easy to see how seductive this reward might be.

What it boils down to though, is they do it because they can.

As for ACOG, what is their motivation for making recommendations that fly in the face of common sense and decency, not to mention science? It's not for the sake of mothers and babies, that's for sure.

Lawyers
Now, I know lawyers who have justice as their only professional motivation, but let's face it, they are few and far between in the age of the frivolous lawsuit. If this link in the chain refused to sue doctors for being human, doctors would not have to practice defensive medicine.

I've tried to think of another reward lawyers might have for their part in the mess we're in, but all I come up with is money and power.

Media
The media reflects society's core beliefs. What sells is the bottom line and what sells is drama, disaster, blood, death and rescue. The media portrays birth the way it does because you are watching it and they are making money.

In conclusion, while our maternity care system doesn't 'work' in that it produces the best outcomes or deliver affordable care, it does reward each participant in some way, shape or form, recognizable or not.

Are you on the path of least resistance? What if we all did one thing different?

- What if television and movies started portraying birth as joyful, easy and even funny without relying on the pain card?

- What if good doctors, practicing evidence-based care, refused to support the sub-standard practice of their peers?

- What if lawyers refused to try cases in which the doctor did nothing intentionally wrong?

- What if parents demanded respect and became informed consumers?

- What if we come back to common sense?

- What if...

Journal exploration:

List 3 behaviors that intellectually you know are not beneficial to your baby or yourself, but you continue to do anyway. Determine why it's detrimental to an optimal birth outcome, then identify what unconscious payoffs may be fueling the behavior.

My generation...

Aside from our motivating factors, we must examine some of our 'tendencies' as well.

We are said to be the 'me' generation...the 'now' generation. We've heard ourselves referred to as a 'feel good' society. We want it, we

> "IN OUR EVERY DELIBERATION, WE MUST CONSIDER THE IMPACT OF OUR DECISIONS ON THE NEXT SEVEN GENERATIONS."
> *From: the Great Law of the Iroquois Confederacy*

want it *when* we want it, and we don't feel we need to work to get it.

We don't tend to look past our own noses, let alone seven generations ahead.

Pain relief now as opposed to special education classes or Ritalin for a child 7 years from now seems to be a no-brainer. Feeling good <u>now</u> is a powerful motivator (and may well be how the baby got in there in the first place!). Consequences affecting ourselves, or our children, down the road seem remote possibilities...abstract and not very compelling...if faced with inevitable suffering right now. Is suffering inevitable in birth? Only if you want to believe it into being.

So, what are the real reasons stopping you from creating the best birth possible for you? Is there a social pay-off in being able to share the same war story as your friends? Is it to avoid emotional pain of rejection, or unreasonable fear of the expectation of unbearable physical pain?

Remember, if you fail to identify your motivators, if *you* fail to recognize them, others can manipulate you *with* them. It happens everyday. Women have been coerced into non-medically indicated interventions with their unconscious motivators with such tactics as being asked, "Am I the *only* one who cares about this baby?" or "Do you really want to kill this baby and put yourself at risk?"

Parents can be on the giving end of manipulative tactics as well. The word 'malpractice' comes to mind.

Nurses (and some female doctors...the highest rates of cesareans being nurses, doctors, and doctor's wives) who either didn't labor at all or labored with drugs have been known to tell women who don't want drugs, "Oh, come on! Done be a martyr!", even when the mother is quite comfortable and coping well.

Free yourself from the tools of manipulation by knowing your own system of motivation. If you are knowledgeable, if you know you are making a decision from a place of confidence, these power plays will have no effect on you.

One last thing that must be mentioned is that parents would not knowingly consent to worthless and expensive testing or birth technology, much less potentially harmful intervention. Yet, the premise of this work thus far is that consent is given millions of times everyday, and that current obstetrical management is harmful and unnecessary.

Motivating factors aside, would fear override good judgment if parents had all the facts?

Do they have 'balanced' information or is their fear and lack of unbiased pregnancy and childbirth information played upon?

Know what is normal for you and this won't happen. I had a client who had a caregiver that tried to manipulate her by saying accusingly, "Your hemoglobin has dropped to <u>12</u>!" as if it's a catastrophe. If you know that 12 is within normal limits late in pregnancy or what your hemoglobin has been at for the last few weeks, this tactic won't work on you.

Women have been coerced into a cesarean because "your baby's heart rate had dropped to 120...he's in distress and we need to get him out of there". 120 is within normal limits.

Mainstream childbirth information is held and dispersed, for the most part, by a self-perpetuating system. There is other information out there, but YOU MUST SEEK IT OUT.

It doesn't take mountains of scientific literature to break this cycle, though it is plentiful for those who want to avail themselves of it. A few questions can do the job. Start with an attitude of "Show me the evidence!"

In pregnancy or birth, when an intervention or test is suggested (2), ask:

- What does this test for, specifically?
- Where can I find further information on this condition?
- What personal risk factors indicate I may have/develop this condition/problem?
- What signs or symptoms indicate I may have this problem? Please supply me with normal parameters so that I may see where I am in regard to 'normal'.
- How accurate is this test? What is the rate of false positives? How reproducible is it?
- What are the possible risks of this test? (Beware of a 'none' response!)
- Could this test lead to others? What are they?
  (repeat all above questions for each subsequent test before consent)

- If this problem/condition is detected, can it be fixed? How?
- What is the incidence of spontaneous improvement of this condition?
- What is the success rate of intervention for this condition?
- Is this condition/problem considered a variable by some practitioners, or is it always considered a complication?
- How might someone who sees it as a variable proceed?
- What if we do nothing?

Some common examples might be routine ultrasound to rule out ectopic pregnancy.

Ectopic pregnancy is on the rise, and it is the 2nd leading cause of pregnancy related death. Sounds scary enough to a mother, right?

Well, the death rate for ectopic pregnancy is roughly the same as death from an auto accident for women aged 15 to 35....definitely something to be aware of, but probably not something you think about each time you hop in the car to go get a quart of milk.

There are certain identifiable risk factors that can lead to ectopic pregnancy. Routinely testing a high-risk population is probably prudent use of technology.

Ultrasound is undoubtedly effective in detecting this condition. Is it safe? There is some evidence that suggests we should use it sparingly because there are possible risks. Is there an alternative? How about telling women what early signs and symptoms are and making sure they know the importance in contacting their caregiver, reserving testing for high-risk women?

Premature labor is a complication dreaded by both caregiver and by parent alike. Parents, faced with the threat of pregnancy loss, are understandably desperate to save the life of their child.

Caring practitioners obviously don't want to see the parent endure the painful process of loss either, but in a litigious society such as our own, we must also recognize the imperative to give the appearance that every attempt has been made to avoid such loss, even if the futility of such an attempt is well known by the medical professional.

Modern medicine has tried very hard to reduce the number of premature deliveries, but sadly, very few of the current standard practices are able to stop a true premature birth. The incidence of premature delivery, before 37 weeks gestation, has *increased* by 11% since 1990. (4)

Does this increase suggest that mothers are becoming less healthy, despite numerous campaigns to improve the heath of mothers and babies? While that may seem to be the case at first glance, it may not actually be so. There are other causes to prematurity that are often ignored, including preventable prematurity due to increasing numbers of vaginal infections and the high number of unnecessary cesareans in the US (5) as well as a high number of cases of premature labor being diagnosed and treated where it does not exist as and a high number of inductions. The result is prematurity because the ultrasound was wrong on dates or baby's size...a common occurrence.

Consider, the mother who is expecting twins, who is told throughout her pregnancy that twins always come early. She takes excellent care of herself and goes past her doctors predicted six-week early delivery date. She goes past 34 weeks. Then she makes it to 36 weeks.

Her doctor tells her that she needs to be induced because 'the babies aren't growing'. Two babies nearly 7 pounds each are forced from the womb (not bad for early twins that 'weren't growing'...had she remained pregnant she might have had 8 lb. babies, laying waste to the claim that 'twins are always small'), and their birth will be listed as premature, strengthening the argument that 'everyone knows twins come early'.

Certain obstetrical 'complications' tend to fall into and out of favor. Premature labor is currently 'in vogue'. Of course it *does* really exist in a small number of pregnancies. Per 1,000 babies, 97.3 are actually born too early. However, alarmingly, many women are being diagnosed and 'treated' with drugs and protocol that aren't even effective for the true condition of prematurity, much less where it does not exist.

Remember Chloe's story? Not all similar situations end up with healthy babies and empowered mothers.

Most often the faulty diagnosis of premature labor examined here is made via unnecessary routine vaginal exams and superfluous electronic fetal monitoring devices in the doctor's office. Mom is not told that neither provides useful information. (6 7) Never mind that they definition of pre-term labor includes contractions that get longer, strong and closer together while opening the cervix. Is it reasonable to assume that this kind of progression could be determined by one routine internal digital exam and EFM per month, even per week? Not really...much closer observation would be required. Nevertheless, Mom is so alarmed at the possibility of losing her baby that she often isn't thinking critically. She's willing to do anything to save her baby. She also probably doesn't know that even if she is dilated a couple of centimeters, it can be completely normal.

So, the mom's cervix is sewn up (cerclage) or given terbutaline and put on bed rest. She's so grateful that her doctor 'caught' this, of course, yet there is more she doesn't know. She doesn't know that in study after study, terbutaline doesn't do a thing to stop true premature labor. She also doesn't know that this drug isn't approved by the FDA for pregnancy, labor, delivery or lactation, or that the FDA warns that it should not be used to stop or slow contractions because "serious adverse reactions may occur after administration of terbutaline sulfate to women in labor." (8 9 10 11 12 13) The pregnancy continues (because it would have anyway) but there is no way to prove that it wouldn't have, so the assumption is that the only reason it did was because of the efforts of the doctor.

Because the betamimetic agent definitely cross the placenta, baby experiences the same thing that mom is, including heart rate accelerations. (14) If the mom is unable to eat from the nausea, the combination of not being able to keep anything down, the effect on her already taxed liver, and the high blood pressure, she will quite likely develop complications that were completely preventable. Up to this point, very similar to Chloe.

Now mother and baby need to be 'saved'. Mom will be induced. If she really *had* been experiencing premature labor this would be easy, since she was on her way already, right? Except that in this case, she wasn't *in* premature labor. The induction doesn't work on this hard, high, closed cervix.

Since many inductions start with a prostaglandin ripening agent, rupture of the membranes and pitocin or misoprosol (an ulcer drug and chemical abortion agent, again, not only *not* approved by the FDA for this use[*], but known to cause a number of complications) the mom is on a clock. If she doesn't deliver in 24 hours or less), she will be sectioned. Of course, because her water has been broken and fingers have been inside her constantly since she arrived, there is a high probability that she will get a hospital acquired infection and the cesarean may be warranted. Although, again preventable and caused, not encountered. This woman will

---

[*] While Cytotec still does not have FDA approval for non-medically indicated use, during the writing of this book, approval was granted for medically indicated induction of labor. It was not proven safe. It was simply approved because it was already being used. The labeling that warns "Cytotec may cause the uterus to rupture during pregnancy if it is used to bring on labor" and "uterine rupture may lead to severe bleeding, hospitalization, surgery, infertility, or death" remains.
http://www.mothering.com/11-0-0/html/11-2-0/11-2-cytotec107.shtml

get an unnecessary cesarean and be eternally grateful that her doctor 'saved' her, completely unaware that all of it was avoidable.

Remember that premature labor *is* an actual medical condition. So how does a mother know if she really has it and does need medical assistance or if something else is going on? How is real premature labor diagnosed? What causes it?

How can a mother reduce her chances of going into labor too soon, and if it does happen to her, what are the *effective* treatments? What treatments, (besides terbutaline) have been shown to be *ineffective*, and what are their risks?

Twenty-five percent of preterm, low birth weight cases occur without any known risk factors. Prediction of this sector is nearly impossible. When it occurs, blame must not be placed at the feet of the practitioner who is treading a very fine line between prudent use of technology that could save a life, and inappropriate use of technology in the name of 'defensive medicine' that could cost lives.

Prevention is the best medicine when it comes to lowering the rate of prematurity. Nearly 75% of premature labor could be avoided if mothers took more responsibility for improving their health by quitting smoking, not using alcohol, eating better and preventing urinary tract infections. Sometimes this is not made very clear, as caregivers face being labeled 'judgmental' for trying to encourage mothers to stop smoking or for pointing out that negative behavior choices could have life-long ramifications. Unfortunately, those that cave into 'political correctness' around the issues may then be sued when a baby is premature because honesty and sparing the parents the emotional and financial hardships (conservatively projected at $500,000 for the life of the child) of raising a baby born prematurely might have made a mother 'feel guilty', which could have lost them a client.

Mothers need to be properly nourished for placental health. Mothers have complete control over what they put in their bodies (though admittedly not always what will <u>remain</u> in their bodies, at which point mom needs to remember to control what she can, accept what she can't). A baby who is not getting the essential requirements for optimal growth and well-being is more likely to be born prematurely.

In the same vein, smoking damages the placenta in a number of ways. Because 50% of what should be oxygen going to the placenta and baby is carbon monoxide, cyanide, arsenic, nicotine and countless other toxins, the placenta might grow over more of the surface of the uterus seeking oxygen, or, it might fail to grow large enough to meet the needs of the baby because it *isn't* getting enough oxygen. Small dead areas called "infarcs" are more common in smokers. Areas that cannot deliver nutrients and oxygen to the baby...which is why smokers' babies are smaller than normal babies and prematurity is more common in smokers.

Nutrition is also vitally important for the health of mom. Dr. Tom Brewer has done extensive work on the effect of nutrition and pre-eclampsia/toxemia.

Infections are another cause of pre-mature labor. Routine vaginal exams in pregnancy serve no purpose. It has been theorized that excessive use of this pointless ritual contributes to premature labor and premature rupture of the membranes by introducing germs to the cervix on the examiners glove. Even sterile technique isn't truly sterile. In any case, a pelvic exam without medical indication tells the caregiver nothing. A woman can be dilated to 2 centimeters at 34 weeks and still be pregnant past her 'due date'. Likewise, a woman can be 'high, firm and closed' and have a three-hour labor at 41 weeks.

Dehydration often causes premature contractions. Mothers must take in at least ten 8-ounce glasses of water a day, not including other liquids in the equation. In hot weather she needs more.

Insufficient water intake is also a factor in bladder infections in pregnancy, which can cause pre-term labor.

Multiples are often expected to be premature in the medical model, but is that expectation a given? No. Midwives attending well-nourished mothers of multiples often not only have moms who reach their 'due date', but go 'over due' to deliver healthy babies of normal weight. With twins, it may very well be the expectation of the caregiver (thus, the management of the pregnancy) that is the biggest factor in early delivery of twins, excluding the rare medical abnormality.

Avoidance of all non-medically indicated prenatal testing reduces the chance of being misdiagnosed or over-diagnosed, a subject which Henci Goer has extensively explored and documented in *Obstetric Myths verses Research Realities*.

Establishing communication with your caregiver about the medical applicability, risks and benefits to any-and-all interventions, not just in pregnancy but through the birth, is vitally important. Any doctor who is practicing evidence based care will welcome this exchange and be pleased that you would like to take more responsibility in your care. A doctor who becomes angry that you would like more information, defensive that you would require evidence of efficacy or condescending toward your efforts to be knowledgeable is waving a big ol' red flag.

What's a parent to do if, by some fluke of nature or circumstance, premature labor *has* become their reality?

Interventions that have been shown to be of questionable or no value:
- Home uterine activity monitoring
- Bed rest
- Repeated vaginal exams
- Ultrasound assessment of cervical length

Interventions that have been shown to be of questionable or no value **and** which may pose significant risk:

- Terbutaline
- Magnesium Sulphate (although this *has* been shown to arrest uterine contractions in women who are <u>not</u> actually in preterm labor...exactly the situation this article was written about...but with serious side effects)
- Cervical cerclage

Interventions that may help but not without significant risk:

- Prostaglandin inhibitors
- Ritodrine

Interventions that seem to help without significant risk and warrant further investigation:

- Calcium supplementation
- Progestogens
- Antimicrobial agents (antibiotics)

Interventions with insufficient data to warrant regular use:

- Diazoxide
- Oxytocin antagonists

Significantly effective with no risk:

- Hypnosis (18)

What is the very best way to avoid being treated for a condition that doesn't exist? See a midwife or holistic general practitioner in pregnancy instead of surgical specialist like an obstetrician. If an underlying medical condition dictates that you must see an expert in pathology (illness), such as an OB/GYN, initiate dialog early about appropriate birth technology specific to your situation. Learn about what you can do to be healthier and how you can best assist your caregiver in your treatment.

Don't be afraid to get second opinions or change caregivers if yours is not treating you respectfully and helping you to learn about your condition. People treat us as we allow. If you don't speak up now, you create your own experience.

Let's look at just one labor intervention as another illustration:

The policy of fasting in labor and an IV are two interventions that go hand in hand. The rationale given is that anything could go wrong at any minute, requiring surgery. If that were to happen they need to be able to 'have a vein open'. Also, if surgery becomes necessary, the stomach should be empty because one complication of general anesthesia is that it can cause vomiting.

This all sounds reasonable to the parents, after all, it is for their safety. Is it?

An IV is a good idea if the mother is vomiting constantly, unable to keep food and fluids down. Obviously, if a woman is <u>planning</u> surgery, an IV is required.

An EMT can find a vein to place an IV in a car crash victim who has been bleeding out into a ditch for fifteen minutes or more. Why can't highly trained nurses attending a pregnant woman find a vein in an emergency in which medical personnel have been no more than a few steps away?

Pregnancy complications rarely happen, but when they do, there are usually indications that something is going wrong long before.

Any time the skin is pierced, as in with an IV, there is risk of infection. In the hospital, that means super germs that can be fatal. IV fluids can dilute the mother's own birth-regulating hormones and comfort hormones, which means artificial ones are more likely to be required. (Many women, upon requesting their birth records, have discovered easy access to a vein allowed these artificial substances to be administered without their consent.)
If a mother is allowed to eat and drink as she desires in labor, dehydration is rarely a problem, providing she is not vomiting

everything she takes in. Most mothers are not allowed food due to the unlikely event she should require surgery. Note the circular logic of the simple act of placing an IV into a laboring woman *increasing her chances of needing surgery.*

It is true if general anesthesia is **incorrectly administered** it can cause vomiting that could theoretically be inhaled into the lungs. However, general anesthesia is rarely used since the advent of the epidural, even in emergency situations. If general anesthesia is used, and if it is administered incorrectly and if a mother aspirates the contents of the stomach...the acidic contents of an empty stomach are actually more damaging to the lungs than easily digestible food.

Asking questions and testing the validity of the answers with good old fashioned critical thinking skills can reveal the underlying unsound nature of most routine intervention.

Notes on Chapter Five

1   Physicians for Midwifery, www.well.com/user/zuni/pfm.html
Association of Nurse Advocates for Childbirth Solutions, www.anacs.org
Maternity Center Association, www.maternitywise.org
Citizens for Midwifery, www.cfmidwifery.org
Physician's Committee for Responsible Medicine, www.pcrm.org
Coalition for Improving Maternity Services, (CIMS) www.motherfriendly.org
Association for Improvements in Maternity Services, (AIMS) www.aims.org.uk

2   I have seen these questions adapted in many places since they were first
authored by Penny Simkin at least a dozen years ago. Anything done by her
is fabulous. http://www.pennysimkin.com/

3   Many resources on the questionable safety of ultrasound may be found at:
http://www.midwiferytoday.com/articles/default.asp?a=1&r=1&e=1&q=ultrasou
nd
http://www.gentlebirth.org/archives/preScreen.html

4   National Vital Statistics Reports, National Center for Health Statistics,
April 17, 2001

5   The World Health Organization postulates that a 10%-15% cesarean rate
optimizes lives saved...meaning that at the current rate of 25-30% about half
of the cesareans are at best unnecessary, and at worst, start claiming lives
the cesarean is meant to save as an emergency procedure.

6   Lenihan JP. Relationship of antepartum pelvic examinations to premature
rupture of the membranes. Obstet Gynecol 1984;63 (1):33-37

7   McDuffie RS et al. Effect of routine weekly cervical examinations at term
on premature rupture of the membranes; a randomized conrolled trial.
Obtset Gynecol 1992;79(2);219-222.

8   D.M. Main, E.K Main. "Management of Preterm Labor and Delivery"
Obstetrics: Normal and Problem Pregnancies. S.G. Grabbe, J.R. Hiebyl, J.L.
Simpson, editors. New York: Churchill Livingstone, 1986, p. 689

9   M.J.N.C. Deirse. "Bet-Mimetic Drugs in the Prophylaxis of Preterm
Labour: Extent and Rationale of Their Use. British Journal of Obsterics and
Gynecology. 91 (1984) 431

10   G.A. Macones, M. Berlin, J.A. Berlin, "Efficacy of Oral Beta-Agonist
Maintenance Therapy in Preterm Labor: A Meta-Analysis. Obstetrics and
Bynecology. 85(2001)313

11   K.D. Wenstrom, C.P. Wener, D. Merrill, J Neibyl. "A Placebo-Controlled,
Randomized Trial of the Terbutaline Pump for Prevention of Preterm
Delivery." American Journal of Perinatology. 14(1977)87

12   D.A. Guinn, A.R. Goepfert, J Own, K.D. Wentrom, J.C. Hauth.
"Terbutaline Pump Maintenance Therapy for Prevention of Preterm
Delivery: A Double-Blind Trial." American Journal of Obstetrics and
Gynecology. 179(1998)874

13   American College of Obstetricians and Gynecologists. "Preterm Labor"
ACOG Technical Bulletin.

14   A Guide to Effective Care in Pregnancy & Childbirth, Second Edition,
      Murray Enkin, Marc J.N.C. Keirse, Mary Renfrew, and James Neilson.
      1995, p.,166
15   Obstetric Care Providers' Knowledge and Practice Behaviors Concerning
      Peridontal Health and Preterm Low Birth Weight.
16   A Guide to Effective Care..., p.161-171
17   Multi-centered controlled trial of cervical cerclage in women at moderate
risk of preterm delivery, Lazar P, Gueguen S, Dreyfus J, et al: British Journal of
Obstetrics and Gynaecology 91(8): 1984
18   Medical Hypnosis in Preterm Labor, A randomized Clinical Trial. Dr.
      Donald C. Brown, Dr. Mary Murphy, June 1996

Mother Nature

Fairy tale births **do** exist! (I'll keep repeating that until you believe me!)

Creating a wonderful birth requires a combination of good decision-making, decent circumstances and a little bit of luck, in that order.

If you want a great birth, the odds are overwhelmingly in your favor to have it...if you seriously set out to have it. Nature has designed it that way. The way to keep it that way is to keep it close to the original design, which has worked as long as humans have been overpopulating the earth.

We know this design works because the healthy mothers who follow the plan are the ones of which other mothers are so envious. In fact, envy, one of those lenses that colors what we see, prompts the unhappy mothers into believing that the happy mothers are lying or, at the very least, just lucky.

Not so.

Keep in mind that while we have the blueprint for happy healthy mothers and babies, there will be a few, a very few, who do everything outlined and still be unhappy...just as there are a few, a very few, who will do everything antithetical to a fairy tale birth and still be quite happy with no unfortunate results.

Remember this book is not about 'right' or 'not right'. If you were induced and had an epidural with no negative consequences to your baby or yourself, fine. Not all women who have medicated births will have jaundiced babies, difficulty breastfeeding or challenging postpartum recovery resulting from the cascade of interventions that *usually* follow. There are mothers who intended to have homebirths that later were not happy with their choices and so condemn all homebirth. I don't believe in "all or nothing".

The elements of a great birth are what we scientifically know will result in the best possible birth *most* of the time. The conclusions are based on years of statistical analysis and matched populations. You are not a statistic. The best I can do is to tell you what joyful mothers do and and have done. If you make the same choices you will probably get the same results. If you make the same choices that unhappy mothers get, you will probably get the same results. That is just common sense.

By now, you should be able to see that options you didn't think pertained to you are really quite possible for you.

Remember the five elements (1) of the safest, gentlest births, resulting in healthy babies and happy moms:

- Good nutrition
- Skillful Midwifery
- Natural Childbirth
- Homebirth
- Breastfeeding

Good nutrition:

I have heard women complain about the nutritional ideals put forth by other books. Food to grow healthy babies on is not what we are used to eating. The foods are not what our palates are conditioned to prefer.

That doesn't change the fact that we grow our babies with every single substance we put into our bodies. These babies will have those bodies for the rest of their lives. You will care for those bodies for the next 18 years. Trust me, mothering is hard enough without starting a child's life encumbered by asthma or prematurity.

What does good nutrition encompass? Simplified, it means eating well. If you used to eat white bread, eat whole wheat while you are pregnant. If you've never eaten organic, make some of your produce organic. If you used to drink soda, drink water.

If you normally eat a lot of empty calories, ask yourself if what you are about to put in your mouth contributes to your baby's heath or is a detriment to it.

If you would be inclined to drink juice, eat the fruit. If you can't stand vegetables, drink vegetable juice. If you like pasteurized cheese products, choose real cheese instead. If you don't like milk, drink calcium enriched soy or eat yogurt.

There are several things to remember about diet that are more important than others.

Proteins are the building blocks of your baby. Not only is it important to ingest more protein (80-100 grams a day) to build your baby, but it's important in avoiding pre-eclampsia as well, according to practitioners who follow Dr. Tom Brewer's guidelines for healthy pregnancy. This recommendation for increased protein consumption in pregnancy is not to be confused with the new study that implicated over-production of a protein *made* by the human body in pre-eclampisa. It is NOT the same sort of protein that the body needs to build a baby and should not be confused as such.

Adequate water, calcium and salt intake are also important. In order to create 50% more blood, the body needs more fluid. Incidentally, more fluid means that there will be dilution of the components of the blood, which is why hemoglobin levels appear to fall. A contracted blood volume, for example from dehydration, would mean that substances are elevated in the blood stream, which is why premature labor can result from dehydration.

In any case, I visited one hospital where all of the babies in the nursery were delivered via cesarean surgeries due to pre-eclampsia. I was shocked, because in the previous months as a midwife's apprentice, pre-eclampsia was never ever seen once.

Pre-eclampsia is a very serious disorder in pregnancy. The medical establishment still maintains that they don't know what causes it and that it cannot be prevented. I've read theories that it has to do with everything from multiple partners to heredity, and the latest, that the body makes too much of a certain protein.

Dr. Tom Brewer's (2) extensive research on the topic suggests that protein, calcium and adequate salt intake are critical in avoiding illness.

Midwives using his information almost never see pre-eclampsia unless there is some underlying liver compromise. Gail and Tom Brewer have a web site (see notes) and several books on the subject of the importance of nutrition in pregnancy.

Babies need to grow on actual food, not prenatal vitamins. While vitamins can pick up some of the slack of an otherwise lacking food program, it's really best to eat the foods, which have the necessary extra calories needed to sustain a healthy pregnancy.

Prenatal vitamins cause some women more grief than they're worth if they contain ferrous sulfinate, which most prescribed prenatal vitamins do. Women report nausea and constipation. Nausea can lead to problems like low blood sugar, which perpetuates the cycle of nausea and vomiting. Constipation can lead to hemorrhoids, at the very least. This is because the body does not absorb ferrous sulfinate very well. Because only about

30% of what is ingested is absorbed they are manufactured with <u>more</u> than the minimum daily requirement for pregnant women.

There are products available with the more easily absorbed ferrous gluconate. Still, food sources are best. Iron is important in pregnancy because you are helping your baby build a storehouse of available iron until he or she produces his or her own, long after birth. Also, iron is important in the production of hemoglobin, which helps your red blood cells carry oxygen to your baby.

Sugar is a *huge* problem in our culture. In the public-at-large, sugar consumption (not only in the form obvious sugar, but in the form of foods so processed that they break down quickly into sugar) is responsible for high type-2 diabetes rates and obesity. In pregnancy, sugar and insulin work differently, creating problems just as serious.

While babies are <u>built</u> on protein, they <u>grow</u> on glucose...sugar. In order to produce healthy, plump babies, our bodies produce less insulin so more sugar is available to the growing baby. Of course, this design maximized growth when early humans ate whole foods. Now, it works against us.

Less insulin in the system means more circulating sugar. The concept of gestational diabetes is predicated on this natural phenomenon.

Currently, scientists are researching the theory that foods with a high glyemic index are the cause of many health problems, such as obesity and heart disease, within the general population. It would stand to reason that the solution to insulin/sugar problems in pregnancy would be to avoid foods with a high glycemic index in the first place.

Another danger is if all that sugar makes babies 'macrosomatic'...big. This is where the medical establishment's fear of 'big babies' comes from. Some big babies may result in 'shoulder dystocia', meaning the baby gets stuck, though one has to wonder just what the natural incidence is and what is due to mismanagement since midwives regularly help mothers birth babies in the 8 to 10 pound range or bigger with no problem.

If mom has been ingesting large quantities of sugar, baby may also have hypoglycemic episodes after the birth, when the sugar supply is cut off. Sugar water was given to babies after birth to avoid this very thing. If a mother has not been a sugar hound or isn't a true diabetic, and the baby is allowed to nurse to his hearts content after the birth, sugar water isn't necessary. Not only that, but it can set up breastfeeding challenges resulting in horrible pain for the mother and early weaning.

When I speak of big babies here, I mean over 10 lb...not 8 or 9 lb. as medically minded care providers assert is 'too big'. Cesarean sections for CPD (head/pelvis disproportion) are common for babies predicted (via ultrasound) to be too big to birth.

Over the years, many women in my own classes and those of my colleagues have consented to a cesarean because they were told their babies were **huge** (8 or 9 lb.) only to have a 6 lb. peanut-baby surgically removed. Ultrasound is not a good predictor of baby's weight, it's only accurate to within 2 lb. either way...for a total of a 4 lb. range. Neither does it 'change' your due date. How many times does your conception date change?

Eight or nine pound babies are healthy and most mothers, barring a pelvic abnormality, can birth this size baby just fine. Bigger babies are actually usually easier to birth than smaller because positional complications are not seen as often.

What people don't often think about is that nature has an interest in seeing that as many offspring as possible survive birth. We don't make babies too big to birth without some sort of outside variable. If a 4'10" mother makes a baby with a 6'6" father, her baby *might* be too big to fit through her pelvis.

If a mother grows her baby on a truckload of sugar, her baby might be too big to fit through her pelvis. If a mother was malnourished as a child and her bones did not develop properly, or her pelvis was damaged in some sort of accident, her baby might not fit. Most of the time, however, our wise bodies grow babies just the right size to be born through the body in which they were made and grown.

Not seemingly related to nutrition, but absolutely related to healthy babies and birth, is smoking. Now is the time to take charge of this monkey on your back if you are a smoking mother. Smoking robs the body of B vitamins, vitamin C and others essential to healthy pregnancy.

Skillful midwifery:

Skillful midwifery can mean certified professional midwives, certified nurse midwives or traditional birth attendants. It may also mean a doctor working within the midwifery model of care.

The midwifery model sees birth as a healthy, normal social event instead of a medical disaster waiting to happen. The care reflects that mind set.

Pregnancies are monitored with minimal invasiveness. Baseline readings are taken to establish 'normal' for a given woman. At a minimum, blood pressure, urine, fundal height, fetal heart tones and sometimes hemoglobin are assessed. The emotional and social needs of the mother are evaluated, with referral to support networks where indicated. Each visit will usually last at least an hour.

The mother is also counseled in the importance of good nutrition, with assistance in formulating a program that works with the mother's own preferences. If something is askew, the midwife refers to a physician to investigate further...where doctors are willing to work with the midwives. Midwives prefer to offer collaborative models where continuity of care can be established. Unfortunately, in some areas, their efforts are not reciprocated by other professionals.

To see how a fear-based paradigm differs from a evidence-based, safety-focused, mother-centered paradigm, consider the following:

Say a midwife has a client who comes early in pregnancy. The midwife refuses to take her unless she stops smoking and gets a back up physician.

At subsequent visits, the client first a.) says she forgot to set up an appointment with her doctor for blood work b.) says she missed an appointment with her doctor because she forgot and c.) says the doctor won't take her because she's planning a homebirth with a midwife.

Throughout, the mother's baselines (blood pressure, fetal growth & movement, urine dipstick readings, fetal heart tones, etc.) are all within normal limits.

Since the mothers last birth was within the last couple of years, with the same partner, the midwife agrees that if she gets her records and blood work from last time, at least they'll have a starting reference point.

Every time the mother leaves, the midwife gets a 'wiggly feeling'...yet she tries to ignore it because clinical signs all say everything is normal.

By the 20-week appointment, after several more maternal lies, omissions and discovery that the mother has not quite smoking, the midwife can no longer ignore her intuition. She dismisses the client with a registered letter, explaining that without trust and responsible action on the part of the mother, birth at home is not a safe option. The choices made by the mother are putting her at risk for certain complications that make the hospital the only safe option. The midwife gives the names of three caregivers chosen from the phone book...her only recourse because all of the doctors have refused to meet with her to discuss providing continuity of care for her clients.

Months later, the midwife runs into the woman who tells her that the birth ended up requiring emergency assistance due to placental abruption and hemorrhage...the exact complications the midwife didn't feel could be handled safely at home.

In a sane system concerned with the safety of mother and baby, this midwife would be congratulated recognizing her limits, referring to an appropriate professional and probably saving a mother's life or that of her baby.

In a self-serving, doctor centered system, the doctors are angry that they have to deal with a...gasp!...sick person. Petty and retaliatory measures are sure to follow. These could include everything from behavior bordering on restraint-of-trade, to making it impossible for the midwife and her family to receive medical care in their own community. There are even many cases of criminal charges leading to jail for midwives with better outcomes than the doctors that instigated the charges!

Midwives are trained to care for 'normal', recognizing abnormal. They are trained in emergency procedures in the event of time-sensitive complications.

Where the doctors and midwives work together, in the rare event of a medical emergency at a freestanding birth center or home, the 'decision to incision' time for a cesarean is about the same as it would be for a woman actually in the hospital, where she may have to wait for her surgeon to get to *her*.

Homebirth

Homebirth is safer not only due to the temptation in the hospital to inappropriately use the technology at hand, but for biological reasons.

The mother is immune to all of the germs in her own home. The most foreign thing there would be the care provider that came to assist her. Because the mother has immunity to everything in her environment, so does her baby. Hospital acquired infections cause a large number of the thousands of deaths due to medical mistakes. Why would we want to expose healthy mothers and fragile newborns to these 'super bugs' intentionally?

Next, the mammalian 'birthing brain' functions best in one's own 'nest'. Mothers are less likely to produce adrenaline, the fight or flight hormone, if the sights, smells and sounds around her are familiar. Adrenaline is counterproductive to oxytocin, the mother's own naturally produced birthing hormone.

Because mom is more relaxed, births tend to be shorter and more comfortable at home. Mom can eat and drink to keep her strength up, can move around at will and can utilize water to her advantage.

At least part of the reason that Mongan Method HypnoBirthing® helps women in the hospital achieve shorter, safer, more comfortable birth is because the self-hypnosis intentionally sets up a sort of 'cocoon' for mom. A environment perceived to be safe is one of the four requirements of eliciting the 'relaxation response'.

The 'relaxation response' is the term Dr. Herbert Benson gave the opposite of the 'fight or flight' response in his Harvard studies on the effects of stress on the body. His findings are applicable to simplifying the birthing process (3).

Studies have shown that births where the relaxation response is engaged...homebirths and births using self-hypnosis or similar techniques most notably, are as safe as, or safer than hospital birth, with fewer birth related injuries to both mother and child. (4 5)

Natural Birth

Avoiding unnecessary interventions is perhaps the most important element to a safe birth. The technology was created to help sick or injured pregnant women. It is helpful to those women. Applied indiscriminately and routinely to all birthing women, it creates most of the problems we see in birth today.

Many interventions may seem trivial in-and-of-themselves, but they lead down a dangerous path that results in disruption to the essential hormonal balance and natural physiological systems needed for comfortable, safe birth. In the absence of the medical indication for which they were developed, birth interventions are at best worthless, at worst, harmful.

None of what modern women view as "normal" birth...IV, medications, laying flat on the back, monitors, catheters, episiotomies/stitches, babies whisked off to warming tables, a room full of doctors and nurses...has anything to do with what *should be* normal birth the way Nature intended.

Truly normal birth...natural birth...is gentle, loving and peaceful. It is an intimate event between the mother, father and new being their love created. The organs and hormones that made the baby are the very same ones involved in getting the baby out. In fact, natural birth often sounds and looks very much like love-making. The same things that would disrupt a sexual encounter disrupt the birthing process.

Nature provides us with many mechanisms to be comfortable in birth. I've even seen orgasmic birth. I believe it is not birth itself that creates pain, but the fear/tension/pain cycle. Sometimes, our bodies use pain to communicate a need. On occasion, some abnormality causes pain. Pain itself does not have to be inherent in birth.

I bring this up before the chapter on pain because we now have a 90% national epidural rate. Virtually all women birthing in the hospital have some drug, even if it isn't an epidural.

All drugs tamper with the delicate balance nature provided, by a number of different mechanisms. All drugs affect the baby in a negative way, some by prolonging labor, some by restricting oxygen, some by hindering the reflexes meant to assist baby's transition from the womb to the room. Maybe short term, maybe long term, maybe obviously or subtly, but they all affect the baby.

Pain relievers, 'caine derivatives and narcotics disrupt the feedback loop for the mothers birthing hormones. These reach the baby and are hard for the baby's immature liver to process. They make babies sleepy, sometimes for weeks, and complicate the nursing process.

Pitocin fools the mother's body into thinking it doesn't have to make it's own oxytocin, which can lead to hemorrhage. As a synthetic oxytocin, it blocks endorphins which increases pain. Contractions stimulated by pitocin are abnormally long and strong, which increases stress on the baby. Severe postpartum depression (6) has been linked to both pitocin use and a decrease in the mothers own production of oxytocin.

Natural labor and birthing result in dramatic brain chemistry changes in both mother and baby. Bonding is not just a function of proximity, though that is important. Bonding includes a complex interchange of chemical messengers (7) that actually *change the brain structure of mother and baby to create a symbiotic partnership for survival.*

There are medical reasons to use both pitocin and epidurals on occasion, but women are choosing both thinking there is no risk to either...often because that is what they are told. Months later they wonder why they feel strangely disconnected from their children. The erroneous assumption has been made that bonding is a myth. It is absolutely a reality! It's just been sabotaged in the majority of mothers in America.

If birth didn't work, if Nature made a mistake, if birth were so dangerous, could we have survived in such huge numbers?

Hospitals and doctors, the currently assumed factors in safe birth, didn't even enter the picture until about 80 years ago! In fact, when birth was first moved to hospitals (for the sake of caregiver's convenience, not for safety as is often presumed) maternal mortality (death) rates *increased*. (8) Dr. Semmelweis recognized that this high rate of 'childbed fever' was due to the practice of doctors moving from cadavers to birthing mothers without washing their hands, but it would be another 50 years before his 'radical' ideas would be met with anything but derision by his peers. Some things never change.

Far more significant in the reduction of maternal and infant death are the contributing factors of improved sanitation, anti-biotics, birth control, better nutrition and disease managment.

Natural birth is important, not just one choice between two equals. There are reasons to educate yourself about the benefits to you and your baby. They are life long.

Breastfeeding

Babies aren't actually 'done' when mom's 'belly button timer' pops. Human babies are born before they are really ready to be out here on their own. They are born more helpless than other mammals because they have to be. Human babies are born earlier than other primates so that their relatively large heads, containing bigger brains, fit well through their mother's upright pelvis.

All mammals, animals with mammary glands, give birth to live babies that need to be close to their mothers until they no longer need the milk made just for them, specifically...at least two years, but much longer where nutritious food is scarce. Human babies brains grow at an astonishing rate in the first two years of life. Mother's milk gives their brains the building blocks to grow bigger brains with more neurological connections. Yes, that means higher IQ, but there is another brain size connection as well.

Researchers have studied children with ADHD who have smaller brains. (9) They thought that it might have been caused by the medications prescribed to control the disorder. There is now data that suggests that is not the case.

ADHD is a mild form of autism, which has increased by 250-500% in recent years. (10) While ultrasound exposure, medications in birth and vaccines have all been implicated in this rise, undoubtedly, lack of mother's milk is a huge contributing factor.

I have been asked in classes "If a mother isn't going to breastfeed, what is the closest thing to breast milk?" There is nothing like breast milk. That is not a judgment of mothers who don't feed their babies the milk made especially for them...it is a fact.

There are proteins in mother's milk that build your baby's brain. These proteins cannot be duplicated in a lab.

There are *living components* to mother's milk that help babies ward off illness until their own immune system develops that cannot be duplicated.

The composition of a mother's milk will change from feeding to feeding, *based on her own infants needs*.

The physical ailments that have increased dramatically with the advent of bottle-feeding are commonly discussed. One writer (writing anonymously, for she said she feared the 'nipple-nazis'...though what she feared—being forced to lactate at boob-point?) in a popular pregnancy magazine questioned just *how much* better breastfeeding was. The numbers on the differences childhood illnesses wasn't enough proof for her, it seems. In any case, she decided to focus on the bonding issue and declared that if bottle-feeding really was inferior to mother-feeding, we would have legions of angry, maladjusted kids, which she just wasn't seeing.

I read this incredulous as news reports of school shootings, kids killing their parents, mothers killing their children, hazing incidents, etc. followed on the news. I don't know where *she* lives, but if she just were to listen to the music of today's teens, she'd hear they are telling us how angry and maladjusted their world is! *Youth of a Nation*, by POD, *It Doesn't Even Matter*, by Linkin Park, and *I'm Hating All of This*, by Nickelback, to a name a few songs.

When the symbiotic mother-baby relationship is engaged, hormones are released each time, prolactin and oxytocin, that make babies sleep better and make mothers feel a rush of intense love. That is if the mother isn't in excruciating pain from cracked and bleeding nipples. Mothers are being told that pain in breastfeeding is normal, just as they are being led to believe pain in labor is. IT IS NOT "NORMAL" FOR YOUR BREASTS TO HURT WHILE USING THEM FOR THE FUNCTION FOR WHICH THEY WERE DESIGNED! If it hurts, there is something wrong. If it is allowed to continue, it will be a miserable experience leading to probable early weaning. There may be an adjustment period, with unfamiliar and sometimes uncomfortable sensations, while mother and baby learn, but it should not be allowed to degrade into an excruciating ordeal.

Think about it...Do men need to 'prepare' their penises to ensure successful intercourse? Do they need to roughen them up with a washcloth or apply special cream? Do they need to limit their interactions to five minutes at a time until they are 'used ' to this new function? After all, there is friction and until he learns how to do this he could get blisters or something. Now, there are a hundred different things that *could* make sex painful, but if something hurts, he's probably not going to just continue until his penis cracks and bleeds. He's going to figure out what's wrong. What if he was told that pain in the beginning is normal, so he just keeps doing what he's doing, thinking it will go away on it's own?

Feeding a baby does require coordination of partners who are both new to the relationship. It is essential that the things that are known to interfere with the relationship be avoided. It is imperative that help be sought out early if there are problems. Mother-feeding your baby is supposed to be enjoyable!

In any case, breastfeeding hormones are meant to reinforce the desire for mother to want to be around her baby, and for baby to prefer mom. This intense love is *biological*. When the birthing hormones are undisturbed and the nursing hormones are engaged, the result is the type of 'mother bear love' that keeps mammals from harming their offspring, makes them fiercely protective so others may not harm their offspring and triggers behaviors that make mothers *want to mother*. This foundation is very important, because when the babies reach the age of independence testing at around two, they aren't always very lovable!

The benefits of mother's milk are so numerous that entire books have been written. I suggest *Bestfeeding*, by Arms and Renfew, *Birthing Mother's Companion,* and *So That's What They're For!*
For now, I just want to take a common sense look at some misconceptions regarding mother's milk and formula.

The two are often represented as 'equal' choices to mothers. This is partly because no one wants to make a mother feel guilty if she *can't* nurse. However, many women "can't" because they get bad information and no support. Sometimes what they really mean is not that they *can't* but they *won't*.

Formula companies foster this idea of 'not making mothers feel guilty' because they make a lot of money if mothers think formula is just as good as human mother's milk for human babies.

The one ingredient in the first four that isn't an allergen is sugar. Childhood obesity and diabetes have reached epidemic proportions. There is no doubt that lack of exercise and junk food contribute, but we have to acknowledge that we start the trend in infancy when we confine babies to car seats, when they aren't even in the car, and assault their poor little systems with the equivalent of baby junk food.

Formula was made for babies whose mothers had died with no available wet nurse (other lactating mother who could feed the child). Orphans and infants whose mothers have had their breasts removed due to cancer, or the very (very) small fraction of women who actually have defects of the breasts that do not allow them to nurse, need an artificial mother's milk substitute to survive.

Formula does accomplish that. Babies *will* survive on it. Children will also 'survive' on nothing but ice-cream and chocolate syrup. That doesn't mean they'll be *healthy*! (Though my own child would love to challenge that assertion!)

Is it a woman's choice to bottle-feed? Of course. No one can force you to stay pregnant if you don't want to and no one can force you to use your breasts against your will. Your body, your choice. "Is it in the best interest of the child to bottle feed?" is the question. Further, is it in the best interest of the mother or the planet?

That's what all the work you've been doing in this book comes down to. It's time to get honest about this stuff, not to make mothers "feel" anything particular, for they can choose to feel what they want to feel. It's about the babies. It's about coming clean and getting real for the sake of the <u>babies</u>. As grown ups, mothers have choices, babies don't. It's up to us to make sure women have the information they need to make the best choices they can for their babies. Because we haven't been getting the truth for such a long time, the truth is going to be hard to take at first. I have faith in mothers, though. I know that once mothers can face the truth, they will do the best they can.

It isn't fair to them to enable denial and foster blame. Allowing parents to reclaim the mantle of responsibility allows them to take back their power. The art of effective parenting is on the verge of being lost as parents give their power away to 'authorities' in books. The only authority on your child is YOU. By making choices consistent with the five standards, you will be confident enough to make your own best choices as a parent.

Will parents find information on making their own best choices in the 'usual' places? Do hospital classes and pop-culture birthing book selections give you what you need to put together the elements of a great birth?

Nope.

Those sources tell you what you want to hear because it sells. They don't tell you what you need to know because they figure, as Jack Nicholson's character in A Few Good Men so eloquently states, "You can't handle the truth!" They reason it's for your own self-preservation that they can't be straight with you. It might hurt your feelings if the facts don't mesh with your beliefs. I believe parents are fed up with the results that sort of thinking leads to. I don't think it gives parents the credit they deserve for trying to do the best they can for their babies. I believe that parents who have made the effort to get this far in this book want to do the work that will get them better results than what everyone else is getting.

Those classes and those books will give you information that may seem 'balanced' in that they present all options as equal. They are lying to you, because all options aren't equal, but as long as they give the *appearance* of balance people will keep coming.

Independent classes are your best chance for real information. The books in the appendix are full of actually *useful* information.

I mentioned independent classes before. What are 'independent' classes? Most people assume that Lamaze® is the only choice they have, but there are many, many choices to choose from.

Lamaze® is a reasonable choice if it is taught according to the guidelines set forth by Lamaze® International. They support the five standards for safe childbearing according to their policy statements, including homebirth.

The organization acknowledges that childbirth education is integral to a safe, empowering birth and that leads to more confident parenting. Non-medically indicated interventions are discouraged.

The classes do assume that birth is painful, which was not Dr. Lamaze's original vision for his techniques, but other than that, the official recommendations are right in line with everything you have read here so far.

However, the official stance and what parents encounter in their hospital Lamaze® classes are often *very* different. Lamaze® instructors are usually nurses working in hospitals. They can't discuss homebirth or midwifery. They must give out formula samples if that's the agreement the hospital sets up with the formula company. They may not be able to fully disclose the dangers of certain interventions if doctors in their hospital use those interventions routinely. Rarely does the instructor have the freedom to teach the Lamaze® International mission for better birth. Very often the instructor does not believe in those tenets herself. Classes are between 4 and 6 weeks.

Parents report that Lamaze® is not helpful to them. Results bear that out. Lamaze® is the class parents usually take and we have a 90% national epidural rate.

The reason for this is that the classes no longer contain all of the elements that allowed mothers early on to have painless births. The technique has been reduced down to 'breathing'.

Lamaze® classes are subsidized by formula/drug companies (which are usually one and the same), so they are the least expensive.

Mongan Method HypnoBirthing® (11) does have all of the elements for shorter, more comfortable labor and birthing. Mickey Mongan, the originator, tries to assure that the program is not adulterated or diluted. HypnoBirthing® is a 5 week course that mainly focuses on the relaxation techniques. Complications are not discussed because most women will not encounter them, so 'why go there?' The philosophy is that our bodies know how to give birth and very often our minds just muck it up, so why complicate the process with a bunch of stuff you don't need? Keeping it simple is the plan.

Of all of the 'methods' today, this one is the most exciting in that the mothers are reporting 'fairy tale births'. Their testimonials can be found on the official website.

Beware that you are getting the original Mongan Method HypnoBirthing®. Due to the success these mothers are having, many hospitals and others are *saying* they are teaching this when they are not. This is what happened to Lamaze,® reducing what parents get to something nearly worthless. It's the original that is helping women birth gently, not the rip offs.

The class fee includes a book and two cassette tapes. These may also be ordered through the official web site.

Prices vary greatly. Practitioners who started out as childbirth educators and learned hypnosis tend to be on the low end of the scale, practitioners who started out as hypno-therapists tend to be on the high end of the scale, and those who are HypnoBirthing® practitioners only tend to be somewhere in the middle. Contact the HypnoBirthing® Institute for their preferred list of practitioners in your area.

The Association of Labor Assistants and Childbirth Educators (ALACE) is a non-profit organization that certifies childbirth educators. In my opinion, these classes are the most balanced as far as providing factual information of all options. Deep relaxation techniques are taught. Parents learn about avoiding unnecessary interventions, being informed consumers, and in some cases there is a class on complications.

ALACE (12) instructors have a great deal of freedom in what they may teach. They may be certified by other organizations besides ALACE. The classes may range from weekend 'get-away while you can still be alone' seminars, to up to 12 weeks, depending on the amount covered. Classes may be anything from just birthing information to pregnancy, birth and parenting.

For parents or mothers-to-be who are "information gatherers", this is going to be the class that gives you the most for your money. Prices vary. The textbook for this class, The Complete Book of Pregnancy and Childbirth by Shelia Kitzinger, can be found in bookstores and libraries. There are also *lots* of handouts provided with the syllabus for the class, which instructors may use at their discretion.

Fees are variable because there are so many variables in what might be offered.

The International Childbirth Education Association (ICEA) is another organization that provides professional certification programs. Like ALACE, it is an umbrella for so much more. Contact ICEA (13) for more information.

Bradley® Husband-Coached Childbirth (14) classes boast a high percentage (about 80%) of natural birth success. The classes can run 8-12 weeks and are somewhat high-end in pricing for the most part.

Birthing from Within Childbirth Preparation (15) classes are an innovative approach to childbirth education. Mentor (teacher) certification is relatively new (1999) so it may be hard to find a class near you. Information on pricing and class structure was not available on the website, but the book is readily available at better bookstores. It is an *awesome* resource for pregnant mothers!

As you can see from the few listed here, parents can find a childbirth class to meet any need. Restricting yourself to what 'everyone else does' will only get you what everyone else got. The numbers say that's a very sad limitation to place on yourself.

She's so lucky!

Does 'luck' play a part in what you can expect in birth? Does prayer? Synchronicity? I don't know how much any of these things might affect birth outcome.

What I do know is that in birth there is a very strong 'cause and effect' relationship between the choices mothers make, or allow to be made for them.

Birth is very predictable most of the time. Babies come out. How mothers feel about it, how fathers react, how caregivers *inter*act...all of these are variables under your control. There are just so few variables that are unknown. It is undeniable that on occasion the unpredictable occurs. Still, it is rare. Certainly, it doesn't happen as often as parents have been led to believe.

Nasty 'surprises' are only happening with such frequency in medically managed birth as it stands because it is set up that way. When more people start making choices from a place of knowledge instead of from a place of fear, this reality will be amazingly clear.

Notes on Chapter Six

1   As suggested by WHO and detailed in *Five Standards for Safe Childbearing*, Stewert
2   www.blueribbonbaby.org/
3   *The Relaxation Response* and *Beyond the Relaxation Response*, both by Dr. Herbert Benson who conducted the studies at Harvard in the 70s.
4   Schauble PG, Werner WEF, Rai SH, Martin A. *Childbirth preparation through hypnosis: the hynpnoreflexogenous protocol.* Am J Clin Hypnosis 1998; 40:273-83.
5   Harmon TM, Hynan MT, Tyre TE. *Improved obstetric outcomes using hypnotic analgesia and skill mastery combined with childbirth education.* J Consult Clin Psychol 1990; 58:525-30.
6   http://jama.ama-assn.org/issues/v287n6/ffull/jct10021.html
    www.naples.net/~nfn03605/dheapost.htm
7   The Scientification of Love, by Dr. Michael Odent
8   Historical information on this transition can be found at:
    www.goodnewsnet.org and
    http://www.cdc.gov/od/oc/media/pressrel/r2k0306c.htm
9   http://www.autism.com/ari/editorials/autismincrease.html
10 http://www.drgreene.com/21_1016.html
11 www.hypnobirthing.com
12 www.alace.org
13 www.icea.org
14 www.bradleybirth.com
15 www.birthingfromwithin.com

PART THREE
INTERNALIZATION

YOU'LL SEE BETTER BIRTH WHEN YOU BELIEVE IT. PART THREE EXPANDS ON THE CONCEPTS OF COMFORTABLE BIRTH AS A REAL POSSIBILITY IN THE RITE OF PASSAGE THAT IS BIRTH.

BIRTH RITE

Birth should be the most instinctual thing a woman does in her life. It is designed to be safe and effective at perpetuating the species. Certain built in mechanisms work at the instinctual and biological levels to ensure we will put our offspring above all else.

This book is for women who want that back in their lives. It is not intended to force anyone to birth a particular way. If you are happy with the status quo, that's wonderful. Sad, but fine. If you are happy with every decision you made with your last child, this book is not for you.

I put the work into this book to help women who are dissatisfied with their options...who are looking ahead at their probable outcome with disappointment, and already dread their expected experience.

I wrote it for women who instinctively know something isn't right about birth today, but didn't have a clue what's been so wrong about it.

It's for women who want their undisturbed birthing hormones to bond them so deeply with their baby that they don't *want* to be apart from them. It's for women who want quick, comfortable labors without fearing they are sacrificing their baby's health or their own safety. It's for women who refuse to believe that it's 'normal' for nipples to crack and bleed from using their breasts in the way nature intended. It's for women who want to spare themselves, their babies, and their families the pain and suffering they see around them. It's for women who know this mothering gig is hard enough without manufactured obstacles to overcome.
It's also for those women who are past childbearing, who did the best they could with what they had, and may feel cheated with what they got, who want better for their sisters, friends and

daughters. If you are one of those women, this book provides you with the emotional tools to help yourself and those you love.

The five standards known to result in safe childbearing are referred to repeatedly, as is the concept of evidence-based care. These are <u>ideals</u> resulting in safer mothers and healthier babies. By knowing what produces optimal outcomes, you can strive for your own best outcome possible in your individual circumstance. If we want mothers and babies, thus society, to reach the highest potential, we need to strip away the illusions that hold us down.

In order to assess what *your* personal best is, you must be completely honest with *yourself*. This is not a test. No one has to be privy to any of the work you do in your journal, so even the painful or ugly truths we don't like to admit to can be explored. It's time to ask yourself if the filter you view your world through is causing you to dismiss options as out of reach, when the reality may be that they are as available to you as anyone else.

So often options are invisible to us even when they are within arms reach. We trap ourselves with our own limited thinking. The universe is so much more generous with us than we our to ourselves!

By being honest about what doesn't create a safe, dignified and empowering birth (which would be all of what passes as acceptable in our culture today), we can identify and implement what *does*.

Taking ownership of what you can control allows you to surrender to what you can't. By acknowledging your role in the creation of your birth, you can improve your outcome. Refusing to acknowledge your role makes you resistant to change...it makes you a tragic statistic.

If you are a healthy woman and you still haven't become a partner in your care after reading this far, there <u>must</u> be factors you are not acknowledging that drive your behavior, such as unconscious fear. If you are still consenting to routine prenatal technologies, if you haven't interviewed a midwife, if you haven't made an effort to learn about normal pregnancy and birth by reading any of the suggested reading in the appendix, you are setting yourself up for a negative experience. It's a simple statistical fact. Why? Is there something you're not facing?

You have to be honest with yourself if you really want a shorter, more comfortable labor with fewer complications than the national average. If you really want better health, a higher IQ and emotional stability for your baby, you need to make the choices we know contribute to those outcomes. These are not the same choices that are considered the 'norm' in our society right now. I can't identify what choices are right for you. You must do the work. You must come up with your plan for your best birth.

Maybe there are no midwives in your area. Your choices will be different than a mother in Oregon where midwives are plentiful. You may have to look outside your geographical area for a birth center. Maybe you have no transportation, so you have to work with what you have locally, whether it's acceptable or not. You still have options. You just have to be more creative in finding them!

My point here is we always have choices—some easy, some not. It's up to us to decide what's important to us and make decisions that support what matters. We can't do that until we are honest with ourselves about what we want, and that we have the power to get it.

In order to do this, you must examine and challenge every belief and position you hold. When we discuss the facts of what makes babies safe, healthy and well adjusted, you must be willing to honestly assess your beliefs, patterns and positions against the truth. When it comes to pregnancy, birth and parenting, you can't afford the luxury of denial. Your baby's life depends on you taking responsibility for that which you are responsible.

As humans, we have a self-protective 'perceptual defense'. It protects us from those things our inner self deems too hard to cope with or things we don't want to face.

This is a wonderful gift of our wise self when it protects us from trauma. However, it is active in our everyday lives, too. It could be keeping you from seeing things you simply do not *want* to be true.

It may be causing you to dismiss your mother's intuition on a daily basis, keeping you from seeing warning signs in your caregiver's behavior or allowing you to light up another smoke.

Your subconscious mind, the seat of your mother's intuition, knows if you are not making the best choices for yourself and your baby, even if your consciousness is blocking the messages. This is where guilt and defensiveness originate. If you are blocking out the very information proven to result in what you *say* you want, you are living a fantasy to think you will actually get it.

If that is an upsetting idea, then consider the issues that need to be considered. Acknowledge these blind spots so that they can be changed. You don't have time to 'wait and see' if change will happen spontaneously to everyone around you. You need to make the necessary changes to get what you want.

Your expectations shape your outcome. We see what we want to see, sometimes with contradictory evidence staring us right in the face.

Remember the safe standards for childbearing? These have been determined, and are backed by, over 30 years of science. In the appendix you will find entire books with the compilation of science. Solid evidence is staring you in the face. Has your behavior changed? Has the evidence caused you to explore your options more fully? If not, you are still only seeing what you want to see. You are resisting the truth.

Years ago two Harvard researchers won a Nobel prize for their experiment on two groups of kittens fitted with special goggles. One group was raised able to see only horizontal lines. The other group was raised seeing only vertical lines. Once grown, it was discovered the group raised in the horizontal environment didn't recognize vertical lines in a maze, and those raised in the vertical world couldn't see horizontal lines. When the brains of these animals were examined, the researches found that there were no neural connections between the neurons responsible for recognizing vertical and horizontal lines in the respective groups. The kittens raised to believe the world is vertical simply could not see any other possibility. Likewise, those raised in a horizontal 'world' could not conceive of a vertical world, not because of their psychology, but because of their physical neurology.

While this study has implications reaching into the reality of how we birth and parent our babies and how their brains develop, I use it here to point out that they did not see what was clearly before them because they *had no experience of a different reality.* They didn't see what they didn't expect to see.

People come to childbirth classes with dread over what they will see. Women expect to see needles and cutting, men fear they will react in an 'unmanly' way to 'all that blood'. Their conception of 'birth' includes machines, a room full of masked strangers, being confined to bed in a hospital gown open down the back, drugs, wires and tubes. Even if it's dreaded (for some wisdom deep down inside understands that this all screams 'danger') it is expected. Parents simply expect nothing else and so have a hard time picturing anything else when I try to explain that birth...normal, natural, healthy birth, which about 85-90% *should be*...includes NONE of these things. Because they have not been brought up to envision strong women, birthing comfortably in the nest they have create at home, with candles, their own tub, their own food, freedom of movement with those they love around them as 'normal', the picture is a difficult one for them to form. In fact, even after trying to 'draw' this brain picture for them, some people will say 'Well sure, but who wants all that mess in their house? At the hospital they clean up all the blood!" Natural birth is very neat and usually quite clean. More than two cups of blood is a hemorrhage, which is not usual. Babies are born in a tide of clean, sterile water. If healthy tissue isn't cut, it's really not all that messy, just wet. But they shake their heads, unable to see safe birth as wonderful birth *because they've been conditioned to see safe and wonderful in direct opposition.*

Those of us who have seen, with our own eyes, what the evidence confirms...safe, comfortable, empowering, gentle birth...want you to see it too! Fortunately, you don't have to grow new neural connections. You just have to *decide to see it.*

Have you surrounded yourself with images, stories and pictures of empowered pregnancy and blissful birth? What are you conditioning your mind—and by extension your body—to accept? Expect? Are you relying on tests that in healthy women are inaccurate or useless at the expense of your intuition, your body wisdom? Your wise body knew how to create a human being from two single cells. Every day it builds these cells, organs, tissues. Amazingly, it will know when the work is done and the baby should be born, and even more amazingly, it will then know to produce the perfect food that only you can make for your baby. All of this happens without a conscious thought from you. All of it happens whether you have the tests or don't. It is happening for women with midwives, and women alone in the rainforest. Why should you be so fearful that the ubiquitous 'something' might go wrong when billions and billions of times, over thousands and thousands of years, the process worked just as it's supposed to? Yes, sometimes things happen that might have been prevented, but the scales have tipped so that now more problems are created than encountered. Vigilance and monitoring are in proportion to the risk and are appropriate...seeing things that seldom exist in healthy populations is paranoia.

Changing our point of reference again illustrates this point. A multitude of things CAN go wrong with any system in the body, but seldom actually DO. Take the heart/circulatory system for example. Heart disease is the leading cause of death in the US. 873 per 100,000 die of heart disease (CDC). (Remember, natural birth is between 6 and 14 per 100,000 in the US, depending on the population.) Some have arteries on the verge of clogging. Some have heart defects they are unaware of. Some have damage they don't know about. Something could go wrong at any minute and immediately available surgery can undoubtedly save lives.

Using the logic of obstetrics, all health clubs should be in hospital and all fitness trainers should be cardiac surgeons. Any independent health club with 'lay' trainers would be 'practicing medicine without a license', subject to prosecution. It's for your own good.

In fact, in order to know if a problem is developing, close monitoring and 'management' is required. We will need to place straps on the muscles to measure the intensity of the workout. Of course, it will be restrictive, but we need to know how hard the muscles are working to know if the heart can take it. We'll need to monitor heart rate, blood pressure, fluid output. We'll need to give an IV because with sweat excreted, you could dehydrate, and of course, we simply can't take the risk of letting you drink anything lest you need emergency surgery

Maybe all activity that increases heart rate should be monitored. How about sex? Again, blood pressure, heart rate, IV, speed and adequacy of penile erectile performance. Bright lights and strangers assessing a man every 15 minutes or so might be a bit distracting, but medically speaking, his heart is a time bomb. We don't want men's hearts to get to the point of stress. I'm sure they would be relieved to know that if they can't get it up or keep it up, or if it looks like his body is working too hard, we can always surgically remove the sperm so the his failure doesn't damage his reproductive system. There was a booklet out years ago called "Natural Love" by Janet Isaacs Ashford that detailed such a scenario to illustrate the parallels to birthing

For, as ridiculous as the above sounds, it does make very clear how current birth management disrupts the process. All of the same hormones involved in sex, as well as the same organs, are involved in birth. What would make intercourse difficult or impossible? The same things disrupt the balance of birth and make it dangerous.

It's not too late to maximize your positive potential if you are honest without yourself about what needs fixing before this baby comes. It means removing the filters that convince you that the current system is just peachy, when in reality it has you on the fast track to an unnecessary surgery. It means recognizing landmines beneath your feet in the form of inappropriately applied technology, as well as the emotional drain of a fear-based paradigm.

Maybe the truth you need to face is about yourself, or maybe your partner, caregiver or hospital. You are cheating yourself and your baby if you aren't willing to do the work.

It is easier to see other people's mistakes than our own. None-the-less, it's denial allowing this birth machine to keep on damaging women's lives. We all must be willing to consider our place in what we have and own it. Being willing and able to identify and acknowledge negative attitudes, ideas or behaviors is essential in order to change them. The hard part is that on some level, the level denying what you don't want to hear which operates under a perceptual defense mechanism, you perceive these attitudes to be 'normal' responses. You may even see them as positive.

How do you know for sure which each is? Judge by results and ask yourself if the *facts* support the *belief.*

Acknowledgment is only lip service if there's no commitment to change. If you *want* better, you must *do* better. If you are stuck in a 'yeah, but...' rut, you have to get yourself unstuck. There are a lot of things in life you can put off until later, but better birth isn't one of them. Your baby is growing closer to being in your arms every single day. If you don't face your shadows before he or she is ready to make an entrance, you won't get a chance later. You can't 'take back' a birth and you don't get a dress rehearsal. You are preparing for the real deal. The brain chemistry alterations inherent in natural birth are for keeps and they can't be made to happen at any other time. The health benefits of feeding your baby it's birth right of mother's milk are lifelong.

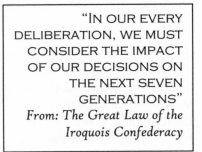

"IN OUR EVERY DELIBERATION, WE MUST CONSIDER THE IMPACT OF OUR DECISIONS ON THE NEXT SEVEN GENERATIONS"
From: The Great Law of the Iroquois Confederacy

The cumulative effect of choices you make from this moment through the next several years shape the kind of person your child will be. There is **no** job more important.

"Yeah, but..." clearly reveals you are not accepting this bottom-line truth. It indicates you are making excuses for not holding yourself to the highest standard. You are putting up with less than what you and your baby deserve.

This sort of honesty with yourself can be hard. It doesn't allow for political correctness. It draws a line in the sand that says "be the best you can be—or don't—but at least be honest with yourself."

People want reinforcement and validation for what they already think, right or wrong. They intentionally seek out the people, information and support for conclusions already reached, regardless of if those conclusions rest on a factual foundation. They want to hear what makes them feel good about choices they've made, good or bad. We all have this propensity. Mother's have been blamed for everything from bedwetting children to ax murdering adults, so the tendency is to tenaciously defend any choices mothers make to over compensate for decades of unfairness. This is not helping to create a better reality. The truth lies in the middle. Mothers are not to blame for everything wrong in the world...but they have the power to make so much right.

In writing this book, one agency declined representation because they felt the "market might be resistant to the message". Sadly, I know there will be some women who will be resistant. We have legions of mothers walking wounded. The truth comes too late for them and that's painful. I wish there was a way to help those hurting moms while helping you moms-to-be. I do hope someone will step up to service that need.

There will be women who simply will choose to ignore all of this good advice. That's fine, too. Keep telling yourself you can't have a better birth and you'll be right. You make yourself right by your actions. If you'd rather make decisions based on beliefs with no basis in fact, than be empowered, safe and comfortable at your birth, it is your choice to make.

This book is for the women who drink up the empowerment it provides like clear water in a desert. This is for women who want change, who want better, who know they deserve better and their babies deserve better. It's for parents who fully accept that they must do the work that makes it so.

Are you willing to work hard on your beliefs and behaviors? Are you willing to get past the security of the status quo? Are you willing to demand more of yourself? Are you willing to face that what's now considered 'normal' isn't normal at all...isn't even acceptable? It is so far from normal that true normal seems to be 'the unknown'. That's very scary.

Normal and natural aren't as hard to access as some would have you believe, though. Mothers with strong intuition have bravely maintained the natural that should be 'normal' on the outskirts. That is how we even have the data to compare what we have with what we've lost...or nearly lost. Follow the examples of these mothers and change for the better will happen—one mother-baby at a time. Birth is a defining moment in a woman's life.

It can be very threatening to acknowledge the problem. I'm fully aware that change is never easy and that as mothers reclaim ownership over their part of the problem there will be resistance from everyone that prefers things just the way they are. There are people with quite a financial stake in the current system, from pharmaceutical/formula companies to obstetricians as well as those too afraid to face their own fears.

"The hand that rocks the cradle rules the world" may be cliché, but it is reality. When mothers take back birth, when more and more mothers begin to tell their joyful stories, transformation is inevitable. When mothers realize what they've been missing, they will be a force to reckon with.

My wish for women is comfortable, safe birth. My wish for babies is health and stability. My wish for dads is a bonded, happy family. My wish for doctors is freedom from fear of litigation. My wish for midwives the freedom to practice their passion.

I know everyone isn't ready, willing and able to break through the system that keeps us in a self-destruct mode, but some people are more than ready. This is for those who know there are no accidents, accepting ownership for the experience they are creating for themselves. It's for the parents willing to commit to be genuinely honest with themselves.

Be willing to ask yourself the hard questions and face your own truth with no lies, no excuses...no telling yourself what you *want* to be, instead of what *is*.

Admit to yourself if—

--you are allowing other people to make your birthing decisions
--you are not requiring the best of yourself for your baby
--you are scared of birth
--you feel powerless in your pregnancy
--you are self-destructive in ways that could affect your baby
--you are just maintaining, day by day, with no positive expectations for your baby's birth
--you are breaking promises to yourself or your partner
--you are breaking promises to your baby
--you feel you don't deserve a wonderful birth

Half of the solution is defining the problem. Once you have the courage to admit fear and belief may be in the way of seeing the truth about the most common aspects of obstetrically managed birth you will be unable to accept the myths leading to the sadness and despair so prevalent in mothers and children today.

These circumstances did not occur by accident and they won't change by accident.

We need to stop making excuses for the inexcusable. You must accept responsibility for your own little corner of the world and create something better for yourself if you want better instead of 'good enough'.

Admitting being scared or confused is not weakness. It is the first step to empowerment. Being real allows us to stop making excuses and start making changes. If you really want better for your baby, you can't be only partially honest with yourself. You have to go all the way. You'll be a better mother for it because you'll be a better person. You have to want it for yourself...it's not about me, or anyone else *making* you want better. It's about you knowing you <u>deserve</u> better.

Give yourself permission to have issues that need attention. Distorted beliefs, thoughts or feelings about birth mean you are human, not bad. Our culture has heaped a whole lot of nonsense on mothers...baggage that we have to deal with. Allow yourself to take it one step at a time. Be gentle with yourself.

You are who you are because of your life experiences. You have incorporated these experiences into personal characteristics that may or may not be helping you when it comes to your own best birth planning, right down to how you interact with your birthing team.

Accepting that some of these experiences are different than how they may have appeared through our personal filter is imperative to lasting change. Allow this distortion to be revealed by educating yourself on what is really natural and normal in birth. Know what is actually possible through better decision-making. You will stand a much greater chance of having the 'fairy tale birth' other women only dream about.

INTENTIONS AND EXPECTATIONS

It's not what we *say* that matters, it's what we *do*. It is not our *intentions* that do good works, but our *actions*.

This chapter points out that intent without action means nothing in pregnancy and birth. Very often today, a 'successful' birth is judged by whether a mother has a live healthy baby in her arms. Of course, we all agree. What seems to have been lost is that it is what we should *expect*, since the overwhelming majority of time, that is the way nature works. It has become the hallmark of a 'good birth' intentionally...because it is justification for all of the sacrifices mothers are needlessly required to make. Iatrogenic and nosocomial complications are considered acceptable because, of course, all that matters is a healthy mother and baby. This idea makes the parent feel ungrateful for expecting more, even though the mother's life that will never, ever really 'be the same'.

I know of no other area of medicine (or any other profession) where someone is thanked for <u>creating</u> a problem...even if they *can* fix it.

What if...

You went to the doctor complaining of chest pain...not bad pain, but bothersome. To rule out a heart problem, the caregiver listens to your heart. He scowls, then excuses himself to make a phone call. He comes back in and tells you that you need to be admitted to the hospital for a test that requires the use of a drug. The drug has a low risk of serious complications, which is why you must be in the hospital, but he feels confident in taking that risk.

You go, and within minutes of having the drug administered, you have a heart attack. You are rushed into emergency open-heart surgery. Complications arise, but they are dealt with. You nearly bleed to death, but with blood replacement you recover.

The repair doesn't go well, which may mean you will need further surgery later...maybe even a heart transplant. You definitely will need to change your previously active lifestyle.

Later, you discover the call your care provider placed wasn't to a specialist, but an HMO lawyer who advised him not to let you walk out the door, *just in case* the routine examination missed a serious problem. You also learn that there were less dangerous ways to determine if there could be a minor problem.

It turns out, you really did have a minor case of heartburn. All you have been through was avoidable, but "As long as everyone's ok now...that's all that matters"...right?

A comment like that, to a mother who has suffered <u>unnecessarily</u>, when she would have-or could have-had the result of a live, healthy baby without such sacrifice, disregards her feelings of loss.

Parents *should* be expecting <u>more</u>!

When women discuss their upcoming births, they say, "I'm going to *try* to have a natural birth, but..." The statement is rift with subconscious communicators.

To say one will 'try', instead of calmly stating that they will be having a natural birth, implies a.) there is no belief that it can or will be accomplished and b.) the effort factor can be very low because there is no commitment. The "but" at the end of the statement further tells us to negate everything that came before it. So, forget the first half of the sentence and listen to the last half, for that's where the real beliefs are.

Up until now, most of what readers have been asked to do throughout this book is internal. Even if this is as far as you go, if you've done the work, you can't help but have new and exciting ideas about pregnancy, birth and parenting.

If, however, it's a better birth you want, you will need to act on your newfound perspective. Intention without action isn't worth a hill of beans. All mothers *intend* to make the safest choices for their babies. The ones who *intend*, but *act* contrary to all **evidence of safety,** have contributed to the current birth statistics that have been outlined here. Few set out to be an unnecessary cesarean, a figure in the outrageously high US mortality rate or a victim of any one of the preventable postpartum problem figures. They just intended to have a great birth. *If you want a great birth, you have to plan the way mothers who have had great births planned.*

It is your actions other people respond to, not your ideas, desires or hopes. If your actions serve no meaningful purpose, the results you seek will not manifest. To create the birth you want, your behaviors must constructively reflect the outcome you want to create. Better choices backed by actions bring results. Intention without action is just wishful thinking, and the odds are against your wishes coming true if you are a healthy woman being obstetrically managed. As another old saying goes, "Wish in one hand, spit in the other, and see which one fills up first." Ok, I changed one letter, but the message is still the same. (Ick!)

By now, if you've been doing the work, you will have identified changes that could be made in your pregnancy, birth and parenting plan that would improve your experience. Have you made those changes? Are you thinking about it? Have you dismissed them?

Take the following test to see where you stand:

                                                              Yes   No

1. Do you take every opportunity to watch
   crisis oriented birthing programs?
2. Would your local fast food delivery person
   notice ...maybe call to check on you...
   if you missed a 'usual' order?

Yes   No

3. You have a case of munchies.
   In the fridge, your choice is a carton of
   cottage cheese or a tub of pudding.
   Do you reach for the pudding every time?
4. Are you still seeing a caregiver that keeps you
   waiting for two hours at every appointment?
5. On the internet, you find a website where women
   post their birth stories. Do you dismiss the stories
   of painless, orgasmic 2-hour labors as unattainable,
   as you dish with friends who tell you how it <u>really</u> is?
6. Has your due date 'changed' because
   your ultrasound says so?
   (How many times has your conception date changed?)
7. Do you spend more time watching TV
   than reading about better birth or taking classes?
8. Are the only books on your shelf
   the ones your doctor gave you, or
   'what to expect' and 'girlfriends guide'?
9. Do you keep candy in your purse, desk, or glove box?
10. Do you spend more time on your make-up than
    on your relationship with your baby's father?
11. When you envision your birth,
    are you surrounded by masked strangers?
12. Are you suspicious of mothers who seem blissful?
13. Do you feel that you'll never have a wonderful birth
    because _____ (fill in the blank with any
    prenatal test scare)
14. Are you afraid birth will be the most excruciating
    event you'll ever experience?
15. Are your days full of worry that
    'something' unspecified will go wrong?
16. Do you feel ill equipped to be a mother?
17. Are you more concerned about appearances
    of competence than actually learning competency?
18. Is your goal to just get by for another month?

19. Do you find yourself afraid to
    ask questions of your caregiver?
20. Do you find yourself saying 'yes'
    to prenatal tests, interventions or plans you
    don't want and for which you question the need?

If you said 'yes' to any of these you have plenty of
company...women who had exactly the kind of birth they *didn't*
want, but didn't do a thing except wish for a different outcome. If
you said 'yes' to less than half of these questions, you need to
decide on at least 10 new actions if you want to change the course
of your pregnancy outcome.

If you said yes to more than half, you need to rethink *everything* to
have a better birth.

You've bought this book and come this far, so part of you must
want a great birth. What is holding you back from making it a
reality? Translating your new insights and awareness into
meaningful action is the only way to get what you want.

Commit to measuring your progress by results, not intent. It's
natural to be inclined to make excuses, to put off actually facing
change. I've made it an art form in my daily life. At least I
recognize it...half way to solving it. If you also have this
tendency, it's not unique to you.

The difference is that I can put off the treadmill as long as I can
deal with the consequences of not being able to wear the clothes I
want. A pregnant mother is on a clock and the stakes are much
higher than what to wear.

It's not unusual to defer responsibility, either. Our society is full
of the victim mentality and blamers, illustrated by our
astronomical malpractice rates and ridiculous lawsuits. It's is not
ok, just typical. In this instance 'not my job, not my fault' is not

an option. You grow this baby, you birth this baby, you need to raise this baby. You and your baby are your only priority.

I'm not interested in helping you make a birth wish list. There is no point in me giving you new insights into the nature of birth if it stops there. In fact, it's supremely frustrating and sad for me when that happens.

I want to help you have a better birth! I want to be one of the diligent people that have been trying to improve birth outcomes in America! I want fewer babies to die, fewer children to suffer the consequences of errant technology and I want mothers to be happy about being mothers. I want pride restored to the most important people in our society doing the most important job in the world. Mothers! Knowing there is a problem is only part of the solution. Understanding how to fix it is part of the solution. We've had those two parts for decades. But the problem does not solve itself. Action is the final component. Action on the part of childbirth educators and authors hasn't raised the bar very far yet because mothers are so willing to settle for second best.

When mothers get fed up, when they stand up and yell "We're mad as hell and we're not taking it anymore!"...only then will birth on the whole improve. It starts with you. Do you and your baby deserve better? Make it happen.

I want to assist you in getting past 'typical'. I want to make it impossible for you derail the grand design of Nature with excuses. Putting this information to work for you means measuring progress by results.

Now, because there are no do-overs, if this is your first baby, that means all you have are *other people's results* to assess where the actions you have in common will probably lead. I have included relevant data and resources throughout the book for you to follow up on so you may asses your own situation. I don't know what choices are best for you, but I want to help you figure out what choices are best. Self-evaluation is the only evaluation that matters. The only way to determine where you are and where you're going is to assess feelings and facts. Neither has a thing to do with 'intending' to do anything. Talk is cheap. A healthy pregnancy, peaceful pregnancy and good birth require investment. Good parenting requires investment of self. Anything worth doing well, does.

Your midwife doesn't care that you intend to stop smoking if you keep on smoking. Your body and your baby don't care what your intentions are. If you keep smoking, your body reacts to your actions, not your intentions. Your baby reacts to your actions, not your intentions. Your midwife must react to your actions.

Expect more of yourself. Stop making excuses about why your expectations of a great birth are being run off into the ditch and do something about it!

This commitment means not making excuses for, or taking excuses from, other people, either. If you decided you will expect better treatment from other people, measure that treatment by their actions, not their words.

For your doctor to tell you she has every intention of 'letting' you have a natural birth means <u>nothing</u> if she's treating you like a sick person and talking about inducing you based on irrelevant findings from a routine ultrasound. Are you going to spend your entire pregnancy letting machines and tests tell you how you *feel*? Dismissing your wise body and built-in mother's intuition because a test, <u>known</u> to be *highly unreliable*, says something different?

It's time to put your foot down! You must commit to this plan with action or it won't work. Start requesting documentation of safety and efficacy before consenting to any test or intervention. A good doctor will welcome this. It's called informed consent and it protects them as well as you. A bad doctor will pay lip service, maybe even treating you condescendingly or lying. Until we sort out the good from the bad, unfortunately, that means checking and double-checking. Again, good and trustworthy caregivers will not take offense at this.

Decline testing for the sake of testing. Decline interventions that don't benefit <u>you</u>. Yes, this means doing your homework. You will be paving the way for the women behind you, healing the wake of the women before. Eventually, when outcomes improve and more women are telling wonderful stories instead of sad ones, this will be unnecessary.

Change caregivers if your current one is threatened by you being a partner in your own pregnancy decisions. If you are told you have a condition for which you need a particular test, intervention or cesarean, look up the condition. Ask to see the evidence indicating you have it. Know what 'normal' is for <u>you</u>.

If your doctor starts taking surgery at 30 weeks because your baby is breech and he says there no way to turn a breech or deliver breech safely, <u>look it up</u>. If a doctor lies to you, even once, it's NOT OK. Before 34-36 weeks it means absolutely NOTHING to you if your baby is butt first, and after that there is an 85% chance you can persuade the little thumper to move. You still have time to find a new care provider. It doesn't matter if you are two weeks away from birthing or actually in labor. You don't have to put up with unacceptable treatment from anyone privileged enough to be allowed at your baby's entrance into this world!

You can ignore the truth—actions do speak louder than words— but that won't change it. When people show you who they are, believe them. The number one job of a mother is to protect her baby from harm. You accepted that job the instant you decided to be pregnant.

It's a gift to be entrusted with a tiny new life to love and care for. It's an honor not to be wasted. Living a life of no regrets means standing up for what you know in your heart is right and not making excuses.

"Intending" to have a natural birth is not the same as doing the work. "Intending" to mother-feed is not the same as doing it. "Trying" means you give yourself permission to not do your best. "Doing" means you prepare, you educate (both yourself and others), you commit, you do. You do, even if it means changing strategies mid-stream to ensure you'll have the tools, the support and the environment to get the results you want.

We plan every detail of our weddings, from the guest list to the menu. We arrange everything months in advance, we comparison shop. We map out a course for college. We plan a schedule that will advance us toward a goal and we make sacrifices along the way. We sometimes have to get creative in ways to pay for it.

Birth requires the same dedication, the same love. We cannot put off thinking about it until the last minute, expecting someone else to take care of everything. Well, we can, and we have...it's what has created the mess we have now.

No one loves your baby more than you. It's not someone else's job to make everything all right. It's an impossible expectation to think someone else can put your baby's needs before their own. Heck, there are a lot of parents that aren't willing to do that, who expects a stranger to?

How much time have you got left? You get one chance at this first face-to-face meeting with the one you'll love beyond reason until the day you die. What are you doing to make it a cherished memory instead of a lifetime of regret? Every decision you allow to be made for you, every purposeless decision you make throughout your pregnancy, is another wasted moment.

Be committed to a better birth, do what it takes to create it and you will have the most rewarding experience possible.

A month from now, you might have read all the books listed in the appendix and have become enlightened, but if you don't do anything with your new-found knowledge, it means squat. Better birth doesn't happen by osmosis.

If you know the elements of a better birth, yet you do nothing about it, you don't get a better birth.

If you know what makes birth into a scary, dangerous, medical event and you do nothing about it, you get the ride you bought a ticket for.

You can tell yourself, "well, I know all this to be true, and I really want to have a homebirth, but I'll do it next time" know that is highly unlikely to happen. You have a 1 in 3 chance of ending up with surgery, which, contrary to evidence though none-the-less so, affects future pregnancy expectations. Even if you don't end up with unnecessary surgery, surrounding yourself with a crisis orientation while you are in the highly suggestible state that is birth will reinforce the idea of 'birth = crisis'. A multitude of iatrogenic or nosocomial complications will give substance to every subconscious fear you have about birth. Home birthing moms hear stories constantly that begin with "I could *never* have had my baby at home because..." with some awful account of an event in which birth was messed up by something a doctor or other staff did.

One woman at a conference I attended did have a homebirth after a hospital birth. She summed up her experience by saying that her decision was like saying "Well, I'd really like my first sexual experience to be with the one I love in a sensual, loving environment...but I'd rather be raped first." Both the same physical experience, but not the same emotional experience at all.

She's not the only woman to liken a hospital birth experience to rape. Women's stories are full of feelings of powerlessness and violation.

The difference between healthy mothers and babies having nightmarish births and those who have the dreamy version hinges on what they <u>do</u>. Fairy-tale birth mothers don't just think about how to create better birth, they make it happen. They actively avoid what they don't want and they work towards what they do want. They approach motherhood the same way. To have what they want, they do what it takes.

Letting someone else have control over your pregnancy and birth does ensure there is no pressure to be accountable for results. Some people prefer the option of blaming others. I would think doctors would discourage this dependency instead of fostering it, but that doesn't seem to be so.

Thus far we've explored what the overall problem with current standard of care is, how it could affect your birth and what role your subconscious core beliefs play in what reality you create. You now know why other people do what they do and why you do what you do. You know that *knowing* better, combined with *doing* better means *having* better. You are moving in the right direction if you get beyond intention, into action.

Nothing will improve for you until you make tangible changes. To get healthy results instead of unhealthy ones, do you need to make some changes? Do you want step-by-step instructions on what to do with what you are discovering? We'll get to how to prioritize your time and energy. For now, just recognizing that you won't *have* if you don't *act* is a big step.

As you create the reality that is your birth, that is your experience as a new parent, through your own actions, the choices will be yours. Your choices will not be the same as mine or anyone else's. We all know what's important. Do we act on it? Do we put our 'money where our mouth is'? Or do we *react*...to circumstances we didn't intend, but did nothing to stop?

Do something different, something important to improve your birth and your life as a new mother. Let change in the world we live in start with you. Changing the world, one baby at a time.

If you start to do different things than 'everyone else'...from choosing to refuse inappropriate technology to choosing a midwife, your odds of a better birth can only get better.

Journal exploration:

It's time to take the opportunity to express previously unexpressed feelings. Write down what would be left unsaid to each of the following people if you were to die tomorrow: your mother, your father, your partner, your baby, your other children (if applicable).

Would you have regrets? What are you grateful for? What might you do differently and how would that impact those above? Would these be the same things you'd say in 5 years? 10 years? 20 years? Look ahead to your old age. If there is something you feel now that you might regret later, do something.

Having identified where you might feel regret, make a list of those possible regrets. For each concern, list a least a couple of actions you can take now that will ensure you never have to feel guilt for not doing what is true to your heart.

Notice "I wanted to but..." or "I wish I could _____ but..." statements. These are excuses. If you want something bad enough, there's always a way to make it happen. The very rare instance of unexpected, uncontrolled outcomes has been blown out of proportion to justify a system that cannot be justified with the facts. I will address the unexpected in it's own chapter. There is no doubt that once in a great while bad stuff happens to good people. For now, know that the vast majority can find a way to make things happen the way they want. Using that very small possibility of misfortune as an excuse not to take charge of better birth is like saying "It's a known fact that people die in choking deaths, so I prefer an IV and will never eat again."

Sometimes just seeing that meaningful change is contingent on being skeptical of 'the way things are' helps us to begin 'examining everything we have been told and rejecting what insults our soul.' Question everything you think you know about birth. Current practice is a house of cards built on illusion and a *willingness* to see only what is displayed.

Question how and where you focus your attention...spend your time. What are your inner tapes? Your self-talk? How do you interact with those to be involved in the single most significant event in your life? Resolve to stop the insanity and *do something*! Intention to have a better birth means nothing without action to create it. This is an opportunity to contribute positively to your world, and all you have to do is take back what is already yours.

Have you familiarized yourself with the concept of comfortable birth without drugs? Do you know how to achieve it? If not, take a Mongan Method HypnoBirthing® class. Have you made out a birth plan of your preferences and discussed it with your caregiver? Do you know what his or her preferences are? Are they evidence-based? Do they match with your preferences? Are they conducive to gentle birth? If not, have you sought out other providers? Why or why not?

Are you healing from a past birth experience? Did you feel powerless? Vulnerable? Abused? Violated? Wounded, physically and emotionally? Did your experience leave you with precious little reserves to be the mother you wanted to be? Have you been told you should just feel lucky? Basically having your need to grieve discounted as trivial? Have you been manipulated so that you feel guilty for being angry, for even allowing your strong mother's intuition to suggest that it's all wrong?

Pushing down those painful feelings only means they will resurface later. You don't deserve to feel bad now and you don't need to feel it again later, maybe in the form of depression or anger, maybe at a subsequent birth. Maybe even misdirected at your baby.

Use any pain that surfaces to get you where you want to be, to give you direction. Consciously creating a better birth can be a healing force. A gentle, natural, safe birth can empower a woman. Empowered women change the world. Allow your pain to be motivation to make birth better, safer, for yourself and for your daughters after you. After your birth, we can be one step deeper into what already isn't working for anyone, or we can be one step closer to healthy, strong moms and healthy, peaceful babies.

Some people are born 'testers'. They question everything. They thrive on being different. They keep doing, adjusting, testing, doing again...until they get what they want just the way they want it. They are unwilling to settle for 'because I said so'. They will not stand for 'good enough'. If you are one of those people, you will embrace what you have learned here and take on the world. Possibly angry at first that you never knew the truth about birth today and no one ever suggested you ask.

Some, on the other hand, don't work without a net. They settle for what they don't want because it feels safer than reaching for what they want. They'd rather check out—playing the game blind folded—than see what they don't want to see, even if it is for their health and well-being. Those of you who prefer illusionary comfort zones to grounded stability in the 'unknown' or the 'different' may have a harder time embracing better birth, because it's uncommonly found around you. You must seek out the components and put them together yourself. It's still attainable...you'll just need to stretch way beyond what you have ever done before. You will be transformed if you take on the challenge for the sake of your baby.

It may feel as if your peace of mind or relationships will be put at risk if you step outside the box. You may feel tension between wanting to maintain the false security of 'sameness' and the excitement of actually getting a fabulous birth. The very act of admitting you want more may rock your boat.

Familiar ideas, even if they are false assumptions, are predictable, like a friend you know is bad for you, but you keep around anyway. Our medicalzed vision of birth makes one wonder, "Better birth sounds great, but what if it's not real? What if I'm wrong? How bad can it get? What do I stand to lose?" In childbearing, obviously the stakes are high. How do you know which vision of birth is real? Which is safe? Test the validity of both. Just because you see birth through culturally imposed blinders doesn't mean what you see is real. Test both visions against FACTS, DATA and EVIDENCE. You will see that you have nothing to lose by checking out what I have been saying. In the years since I have been a childbirth professional, birth has only gotten more dangerous. United States statistics have only declined. Mothers have only become more unhappy. Babies have grown to very disturbed adolescents. I'd like to say it can't get worse, but it can, and it is. However, the good news is that if you make choices based on what we know to be the elements of safe childbearing, if you refute the lies of obstetrically managed birth, if you take the less traveled, unfamiliar path, it *can't be worse* than the familiar.

The bad news is our number one fear as humans is rejection. We measure the results of our efforts by whether the world accepts or rejects us. As mothers, a fear of death or pain ranks right up there in the first three contenders. Results would suggest they aren't #1 or #2, for if we feared death the most, women would not choose to birth in the hospital...one place she will most assuredly feel pain and is most at risk because of it. If the number one fear was pain, coupled with baby's safety, women would seek out alternatives in such numbers that we practitioners would be teaching several full classes every single day and midwives would be swamped.

As the number one fear, fear of rejection, of being odd-man-out or being seen as weird, keeps us doing things that are harmful to us, just because 'everyone else does' it.

What if you face your fears? What if you make choices your friends don't understand? What if you are willing to believe in painless birth? What if you are willing to validate the safety of homebirth? What if you take a chance and 'fail'...what if something goes 'wrong'. New choices can't get any worse results than the old choices are getting us. Not to mention that the choices I advocate are proven by science to result in safer, shorter, more comfortable labor with stronger bonding between mother and infant. These choices I advocate are proven by science to yield smarter, healthier babies.

"Something"...countless 'somethings' go 'wrong' everyday in hospitals. No one suggests that these women 'failed'. Why are the standards different for women willing to make choices based on fact instead of fear? This double standard makes women feel as if they are putting themselves out on a limb, even though the opposite is true. Are you willing to stick your head in the sand and hope for the best? Do you hope that if you avoid exposing yourself to new and different ideas about birth that they go away and your birth will magically be different than all of the women making the exact same choices? Are you sticking with a false sense of security at the expense of your hopes and dreams?

Is an unwillingness to put energy into constructive action towards better birth justified? OR is it unreasonable fear paralyzing your actions? Allow yourself to feel the fear—and do it anyway. Don't let fear be a convenient excuse to be a spectator at your own birth. You have another life to consider. You don't have the right to hide behind fear.

However seemingly illogical your mind may want to make the facts of gentle birth, they are the facts. Gauge success by the birth data.

You deserve to feel pride and strength in your accomplishment of growing a human being and bringing him or her into the world. Make the effort, be persistent, and take back your birth. Better birth won't happen to you by accident. It will happen only because you make it happen. If you do, there will be no regrets, no shame.

Work from where you are now with a clean slate. If regrets or shame have plagued you from a previous experience, work to release or reframe those experiences so that you can be present in the now for this baby.

You cannot have an unnecessarily traumatic birth if you haven't made choices that support unnecessary trauma. Your choices will support a traumatic birth or a better birth. You decide.

Unavoidable trauma is a rare occurrence. Expect normal, accept the unexpected. Manage what you are presented with. The more we take charge of creating better birth, the easier it will be to see that what we expect from birth now has been created and is not the birth experience Nature wished for us.

Journal exploration:

Write a letter to your baby. Explain why you are making choices you are making. Do you find any excuses in what you might say? Are there really options you just aren't willing to look at for one reason or another? What reasons to you give to justify the sacrifices your baby might be asked to make for your decisions? Ask your baby if these are the choices he/she would make if he/she could. Go into the still, wise self with three deep breaths to release tension, then write the baby's response with the non-dominant hand.

AGONY OR ECSTASY

Perception is reality. Events are neutral until we assign meaning to them based on our perceptions.

I was first introduced to this concept through my husband, a quality manager in the automotive industry. If the customer perceives a problem...even if no problem can be found in design or function...there *is* a problem. The customer's perception is the quality department's reality. Period.

The filters thought which we view the world alter our personal perceptions. This fact is immutable. Perception *is* reality. A dozen people can witness one event and every one of them will recount a different version of events.

Two mothers can have experiences seemingly exactly the same from the outside, but have completely different internal interpretations of the value attributed to their experience.

> "THERE IS NOTHING EITHER GOOD OR BAD, BUT THINKING MAKES IT SO."
> *William Shakespeare*

In one video I use in my childbirth classes, one woman in labor using self-hypnosis looks like she's sleeping. Another woman in labor is howling down the hall. The birth process...the muscles involved, the action of the muscles, the birthing hormones, etc...is the same for all normal births. These two mothers are experiencing the same physical stimuli, the same sensations and functions, yet they have assigned very different meanings to their experience, thus creating different realities.

Every event in our lives is neutral, in-and-of-itself. Our interpretations are a choice. Some people *tend by nature* to always see the positive, some the negative. Some circumstances <u>seem</u>

quite negative by their very nature, though we see examples all around us of people who have taken tragedy and turned it into opportunity. Christopher Reeves comes to mind.

It is vitally important to acknowledge that perception is reality when speaking about birth because birth is such a powerful, personal, defining moment in a woman's life. Each woman, as a unique individual, has unique perceptions, and will assign unique meaning to what takes place during her birth. Failure to understand this fully has made dialog about better birth more laborious than it needs to be. If the reader has visited birth related message boards on the internet, the truth of this has already been made apparent.

The plethora of bad birth programming on cable also illustrates this point. I find it very difficult to watch these programs because they make me so sad and angry. In one show I watched, three of three births ended up surgeries. All complications were predictable, all preventable...caused, not encountered.

One mother was induced, labeled 'overdue' via ultrasound. The induction failed, the baby went into distress from the induction agents. Considering ultrasound is known to be an inaccurate way to assess due dates, and it is also know that inductions agents like cytotec and pitocin carry substantial risk to healthy mothers, this is not surprising.

One mother was doing great until her Dr. decided she wasn't progressing 'fast enough' as per 'Freidman's curve'. Dr. Freidman himself has said it's disturbing that his assessment tool is abused in such a way, but it is none-the-less. The mother's doctor broke her water...again, known to be useless in substantially speeding up labor but to carry many risks. The baby's cord washed down out of the birth canal with the tide of water rushing out, the technical term being 'cord prolapse'. Emergency cesarean.

The last mother was also doing quite well, until the nurse suggested that if the mother didn't get "her" epidural now, she couldn't have it later. The nurse assured the mother that labor would get much worse, that she shouldn't 'be a martyr', and that she might as well get the epidural now.

The mother, under such duress, decided to go ahead and get it. The baby went into distress, again, common and foreseeable. The mother was assured that the epidural had nothing to do with the series of events as she was whisked off to surgery.

In every case, cause and effect was predictable and obvious. In every case, the parents were assured the interventions had *nothing* to do with the complication. In every case the parents were thrilled that medical technology had 'saved' their baby. And I was furious at the injustice they'd unnecessarily endured!

This vision of birth is so foreign to what I know birth to be that I cannot fathom why anyone would willingly put themselves though this unless they were sick or injured.

Our perceptions, thus our realities, were dramatically different.

Another example is somewhat singular to HypnoBirthing.®

Many women would say that if they could envision the perfect labor it would be as short as possible. With HypnoBirthing® very short labor is becoming common. Often labors are between 2 and 4 hours and painless. Sometimes though, mothers labor for hours painlessly, not even realizing they are in labor. Or, they may realize they are in labor, but so comfortable, they go about their usual business. Then, when the fetal ejection response (1) is triggered, the baby seems to move down quite suddenly. For some women this is uncomfortable (others actually find it enjoyable), maybe even painful, but of very short duration. The intensity may only last for a couple of surges, but it takes the mothers quite by surprise. Once the discomfort is felt, there may be fear that it will be so for hours more. Not realizing that birth is imminent, the mother tenses up, engaging the fear/tension/pain cycle. It will not hinder her labor ...the baby is nearly out at this point, but it will alter the experience of the event for the mother.

She may feel disappointed, even angry. If she had plans to labor in a birthing tub, surrounded by loved ones, aroma therapy, soft music and candles, her expectations have been dashed, especially if labor was so fast all she had time to do was kneel to catch a baby that was nearly falling out of her.

She may feel as if she's been 'hit by a truck' with no time to emotionally assimilate what was happening, finding herself suddenly with a newborn in her arms.

Someone who enjoyed such an experience, or someone who would like to, might respond with "Your birth was only an hour and your upset?! I'd love that!" Never the less, for the mother who was overwhelmed, the perception is a negative one.

Some women have been able to reframe their experience into something more positive eventually, but the fact remains their initial reactions were partly due to expectations lost, which changes the lens through which the event is viewed.

Pain is perhaps the most subjective reality of all, especially in labor. So, must pain be inherent in labor and birth?

What's Pain Got To Do With It?

There is no doubt that painful birth has been the experience of thousands...maybe millions...of women. So prevalent in our society is this concept, that it is taken as a given that birth must be an excruciating ordeal.

Let them cling to the notion that suffering and birthing are two sides of the same coin. I want to explore the possibility of painless birth...without drugs.

Wait! I'm not crazy! Years ago when I first read about painless birth my reaction was also "Yeah, right!" but I've changed my beliefs regarding birth and pain. I hope I can help alleviate the fear for the reader as well.

Even in my midwifery training I learned that pain in labor is essential for both physiological and psychological reasons. I still believe that in certain instances pain is beneficial. It can be a great communicator, both guiding and warning.

I accepted without question that birth was painful. Still, I felt that it was manageable when weighed against the harm drugs posed. When I gave birth to my own daughter in 1991 labor was definitely not painless. It *was* bearable. I've certainly felt worse, before and since. Birth was a breeze compared to pathological pain such as a kidney infection, a ruptured ovarian cyst or a broken arm.

My own birthing experience, combined with the first hundred or so births I witnessed, reinforced my belief. I did see a couple of women give birth painlessly, one even orgasmicly. However, I felt that they were lucky or somehow different from the rest of us. Maybe they had a high tolerance for pain, I reasoned.

I viewed natural birth as an accomplishment to be proud of. I marveled that there were women who trained incessantly to be thin or to climb mountains, surely enduring more pain for longer periods than what labor would require, only to demand to be numbed on the first labor twinge. I felt it quite ironic that empowerment seminars with fire walking and river rafting were all the rage, yet women's built opportunity for enlightenment was numbed with drugs. What I see now is that my belief colored what I saw, so that what I saw supported my belief.

There are known variables that contribute to pain in labor including positioning (of both mother and baby) tension, environmental factors, obstetrical management and a multitude of other things under the control of the mother. Could it be that a mother's <u>choices</u>, in pregnancy and during the labor and birth, had any impact on her experience? Absolutely.

Once I attained certification as a Mongan Method HypnoBirthing® practitioner and heard firsthand stories of quick and easy births over and over again, I knew for certain what I had hoped was possible. Birth isn't the problem. The obstetrically managed births, known for decades for higher morbidity and mortality rates as well as epidemically high, unnecessary surgical births, are.

It was finally the second birth of my best friend that left no doubt in my mind that my past ideas about pain in birth had been wrong.

I hoped that HypnoBirthing® would work for her. Her first birth was textbook, 12 hours of labor with 2 hours of pushing. It was hard work, and it was painful. It was emotionally difficult for me because I love her and hated to see her in pain.

When I attended her HypnoBirthing® two years later she was radiant. She was calm, relaxed and retained her keen sense of humor throughout. From the time her water broke and labor kicked in, to the time her 10 lb. 4 oz. son was in her arms, was an hour and a half with a 13-minute second stage.
As beautiful as that was, the amazing part was that she had broken her tailbone 4 days prior to birth. She never once felt pain from her injury. She beamed, "It's over already? It was so easy!"

When I believed it, I saw it. Once I saw it, I felt compelled to understand it better.

Is pain inescapable in labor?

In early attempts to let women in on the secret of comfortable birth, I asked parents in my classes if labor *has* to hurt. The responses have been consistent, likely thoughts the reader may have, so I will address them.

Labor must be painful. It's Eve's curse.

This belief is often attributed to the Bible, Genesis 3:16. The word translated as "pain" or "sorrow" is the Hebrew "etzev".

This same word is used 16 times throughout the Bible. Nowhere else is it translated as 'pain'. In fact, in the very next verse, Genesis 3:17, it is accurately translated as it is in all other instances, as 'toil'. (2)

Even if pain and suffering in labor were punishment for Eve's sin, isn't the purpose of baptism to cleanse away sin? Wasn't the purpose of Jesus dying on the cross to atone for the sins of the world? Many women giving birth quickly and comfortably are non-Christian. Why would they be able to birth comfortably, but the faithful suffer? How does this reasoning make a 90% epidural rate ok, but not a relaxation method for more comfortable birth?

Contractions hurt...everyone knows that!

Who is 'everyone'? Obviously not HypnoBirthing® women! Obviously not blissful homebirth mothers.

The uterus contracts painlessly in it's normal functioning at times other than during birth. During menstruation, the uterus contracts, the cervix opening to allow the contents of the uterus to pass. Most women will not experience pain during this process. The uterus contracts painlessly during the Braxton-Hicks contractions of pregnancy. The uterus contracts painlessly during orgasm.

Every muscle in the body functions by contraction and release. No other healthy muscle, going about it's normal function, hurts. A malnourished or dehydrated muscle hurts. An injured muscle hurts. Normal function such as walking, flexing a bicep or the beating of a healthy heart does not hurt.

Something huge is coming through such a small opening!

The uterus is the size of a pear before pregnancy. At term, it has stretched to accommodate the baby. Being pregnant isn't painful. There are normal discomforts as the body adjusts, but most women would not judge it painful.

The cervix has stretch receptors in it that signal the brain to release endorphins. These are the body's own strong painkillers. The cervix thins as it opens over the baby's head, as a turtleneck sweater pulled over a head. This means there is 'extra material' to work with, so to speak as it goes from very thick and soft, to paper thin, disappearing as it is taken up as part of the uterus, which it is.

Viewing images of crowning in class invariably causes wincing. Again, we look to the amazing design of women to understand why this part doesn't have to hurt.

By childbearing age, the genital area is comprised of many folds of skin. During birth, like with the 'extra' thickness of the cervix, these folds are 'taken up'. They smooth out around the baby's head until they are gone completely...like an accordion. This built in 'give' is why episiotomies are so rarely necessary.

Painless Birth—An Old-New Concept

Earlier, we explored choices in childbirth classes. A little history may shed light on how long the concept of painless birth has been around.

Between the early 1900s and the 1970, three doctors tried to help American women give birth naturally and comfortably.

In 1913 Dr. Grantly Dick-Read asked a woman he'd just attended in birth why she has refused chloroform for the relief of pain. Her reply was "It didn't hurt. It wasn't mean to, was it, Doctor?"

Other similar experiences caused Dick-Read to question what he'd learned about birthing. He concluded that what made these painless labors different was the absence of fear. The idea of the fear/tension/pain cycle was born. By the 1950's Dick-Read had published several books on the subject. (3)

In the 1940's Dr. Robert Bradley became a natural childbirth proponent, coming to many of the same conclusions that Dr. Grantly Dick-Read had. From Dr. Bradley's work came his book Husband-Coached Childbirth and Bradley® Childbirth classes.

Dr. Bradley was very interested in hypnosis and originally promoted his 'method' as using hypnosis. However, during the 1950s and 1960s hypnosis was controversial. Eventually, the emphasis on hypnosis was dropped and put on "deep relaxation" instead.

During the 1950's, Dr. Ferdinand Lamaze witnessed painless birth in Russia. He documented what he felt were the essential components for a comfortable birth. In the early years, Lamaze was unabashedly about self-hypnosis, but possibly meeting the same resistance as Bradley, his 'method' was termed "psychoprophylaxis"...or 'mind prevention'. The original intent was painless birth.

Not only has the original intent been abandoned, but Lamaze™ International's (5) current objectives are often ignored by practitioners as well, either because they are at the mercy of the institutions in which they work or they simply do not personally agree with those objectives. In fact, right or wrong, anything contradicting current obstetrical management (6)...much of which is the *origin* of pain...will be excluded from discussion.

Many nurses, and doctors, object to teaching painless childbirth on the premise that if we say it's possible, women who perceive birth as painful will feel like 'failures'.

This is like saying that if women have painful periods, they should feel like failures for not menstruating painlessly because most women do. Pain is a subjective experience. Perceptions differ. There are too many variables in birth, and in the choices that women make, to ensure that every woman have the same exact experience.

Apply this logic to any other situation and it becomes ridiculously obvious it's flawed. Say, a friend and I have two garden lots. My lot is sandy, hers rich and fertile. I have slugs and bugs, she has no pests. We have the same tools and the same seeds, but my climate is cooler for more of the year. If we plant gardens, can we expect the same results? What if I procrastinate and plant a month later than I should? What if I am guided to fertilize and choose not to? What if I let deer come in and trample what *is* growing?

A Rose by any other name...

One mother of the 50's who had benefited from Dr. Grantley Dick-Read's work decided it was time for women to take back their births. Her name is Marie Mongan and she is the originator of a program utilizing the necessary components of a gentle birth...HypnoBirthing®.

As the name implies, HypnoBirthing® is unabashedly about self-hypnosis. Mongan has chosen to educate people about what self-hypnosis actually is instead of cloaking the method in alternative language.

Misconception still surrounds the word 'hypnosis'. It isn't something someone does *to* you. All hypnosis is self-hypnosis. Anyone can and does access this state several times a day. Falling asleep or waking up, driving, reading or even watching TV, our brainwave pattern is the same as in 'hypnosis'. Advertisers know this and use it to their advantage. Commercials slip information into our subconscious constantly. If we *are* in a state of hypnosis when a commercial comes on for a flame-broiled burger, why don't we all rush to get one?

Because no one will do something against their own values while "in hypnosis". Those whose only exposure to hypnosis has been stage hypnosis have probably seen participants do outrageous things, however, stage hypnotists purposely *choose* people who might act outrageously anyway if asked after a couple of stiff drinks.

Back to the burger...
If I am a vegetarian and a commercial comes on for a burger, I'm not going to instantly desire seared cow. I might go to my freezer for a veggie patty. However, if I'm already thinking a burger sounds good, I'll probably get up and go...or at least the thought will stick with me until the next time I drive by the burger place.

The common thread

As briefly mentioned earlier, in the 1970's Dr. Herbert Benson studied a state he termed the 'relaxation response'. He acknowledged that this relaxed state carried many labels, one being hypnosis. If the *word* hypnosis is objectionable, the physiological state and brainwave pattern characteristic of hypnosis, and the relaxation response, has also been called biofeedback, prayer and meditation. No matter what name it goes by, what's important is how the mind affects the body.

Benson's main concern was relieving stress. He recognized that modern day humans spend far too much time engaged in a "fight or flight response" which you may have heard of. His contention was that our modern life kept us in this state continually, harming our health. We now know this to be true.

In birth 'methods' that actually result in comfortable, shorter, natural birth, the interruption of the fear/tension/pain cycle was integral to the method. What I found interesting when I read Dr. Benson's work (7) was that the essential components in what he termed the "relaxation response", the opposite of the "fight or flight response", were what made up the working 'methods' for painless birth.

The four elements

If we look at what is required to elicit the relaxation response, we can see why some methods may have worked when they were developed, but no longer do.

  1. A comfortable (and safe) environment.

Dr. Lamaze's concepts did not translate to American hospitals where the limbic system, the primitive part of the brain that conducts birthing, interpreted strangers and unfamiliar odors as signals to 'fight or flee'. This also explains why homebirth mothers usually consider their births more manageable.

Also, husband's were not allowed in the delivery room, as a rule, until Husband-Coached Childbirth. The painless births that Lamaze saw in Russia included labor support. Just this one component has since been proven to improve outcomes (8) yet it wasn't until recent years that American women had even heard of the term "doula".

2. A mental device—a sound, word, prayer, fixed gaze or focus on breathing.

The counted breath and focal point of Lamaze™ is one example of this. HypnoBirthing® uses deep abdominal breathing which holds a relaxation trigger in and of itself.

3. A passive attitude—not worrying about performing well and the ability to put aside distracting thoughts.

Again, harder to achieve in a setting where everything down to whether or not you pee enough is obtrusively assessed.

4. A comfortable position.

When Lamaze's methods were brought over from Europe, this was not even an option in American hospitals...all women were laid on their backs, the most uncomfortable position imaginable for birthing.

Before the routine use of non-medically indicated technology, Lamaze™ might have helped many women despite less than ideal conditions. A mother may not have been comfortable in the hospital, but she might be attended by the physician she'd had since childhood. She might not have been allowed a comfortable position, but if she were able to focus intently, she might be able to block uncomfortable sensations. As birth began to revolve around the convenience of staff and the use of technology, mothers would have had a harder time adapting. As these mothers experienced painful labors, the mothers and those attending her made the sweeping assumption that Lamaze™ "doesn't work", never considering it was the adaptations that rendered it ineffective.

The importance of deep, slow breathing for relaxation is now widely recognized. The success couples experience is due to their dedication to being informed consumers and reducing interventions to only those that are medically indicated. Bradley,® ALACE and BirthWorks™, indeed most independent classes, help many women in the same way but may or may not teach techniques that trigger the relaxation response. HypnoBirthing® does teach such techniques along with wise consumerism.

New Choices

If our only choice in labor really was torture or being numb to the most important event in a woman's life, it would be quite understandable that women would disconnect. The spin that has been put on this normal process is that no drugs=pain, drugs=no pain with some serious misrepresentations. It's human nature to not look very deeply into those misrepresentations if we believe that it will take away our salvation.

Now that we know that we don't have to make a choice between suffering in labor or our babies well-being we truly have options. HypnoBirthing® has revived the concept of comfortable birth, now supported by the science of evidence based care. Those willing to conquer the fear our culture has falsely instilled in us will change the face of what it means to birth safely...gently and with dignity. We'll see it when we believe it. Perception is everything.

Everyday, in every circumstance, including the birthing of your child, you have the power to choose your perceptions. There is neither 'good' nor 'bad' sensation until you assign meaning to it. Your response to labor is not a function of physiology, but how *you* choose to perceive labor.

I am not suggesting that all labor is painless—only that *normal* labor can be. Obviously, if illness or injury should become part of the experience, pain may be an important communicator. Also, if your birthing choices include things that cause pain in labor, realistically you may or may not be able to reframe the sensation until the pain-causing elements are eliminated, either by actually removing them or by using self-hypnosis to mitigate their effect.

Do we know what causes pain in labor? Without a doubt. Anything that creates tension, fear, or disruption of the primitive birthing brain. Strangers, unfamiliar scents, bright lights, constant interruption of the mother's efforts, unnatural positions and alteration of the birthing hormones with artificial chemicals. In short, most of what is considered usual at the typical American birth today. No wonder women have a hard time accepting the idea that labor doesn't have to be painful!

If you have had a past negative or painful birth, the good news is you can choose to learn from that event, making different choices this time. Only you can decide how to use your experience. Will it continue to hurt you everyday, affecting each subsequent birth, or will you refuse to carry it beyond this day?

Emotional pain is a filter in itself. Though it may seem that it is never ending and deep, there is another side eventually. There are inspirational stories to draw from...concentration camp survivors, mothers who have lost children to drunk drivers who then went on to save other's children, and John Walsh, who lost his son Adam to murder but went on to help others. Through unspeakable pain, these individuals have made the choice to use their experiences in a positive way.

Even if it doesn't seem possible right now, there will come a time when that choice is yours. If you are pregnant again after an unfortunate outcome, as far too many wounded mothers are, it might behoove you to be courageous and seek help now before the past affects the outcome of the present.

Ultimately, how you perceive pregnancy and birth is your choice. The birth shows where strangers attend mothers in strange environments meant for sick people are alien to me. I choose to see pregnancy and birth as natural, physiological events until there is reason to believe otherwise. Fortunately for me, science backs up my belief. It's painful for me to see other people's distorted perception of birth portrayed as reality when I have seen and experienced something so radically different, especially when it's contrary to every bit of evidence as to what makes birth safe.

I understand 'perception is reality' so I recognize that the choices made within such a reality make sense to those making them. It just makes me sad that anyone would choose it.

Our personalities, experiences, beliefs and attitudes powerfully influence the interpretations we assign to birth; those interpretations, in turn, determine how we will respond and how others will respond to us. This is neither good nor bad—it simply *is*. All of us view the world through our personal filters. Filters may be healthy or distorted; constructive or destructive. To make our own best decisions, we need to recognize what our filters may be so they don't distort perceptions critical to our safe birthing decisions.

There is no question that our filters include perceptions passed down to us from mothers before us who processed their own experiences through their own filters, as well as from medical personnel who view birth through the filter of pathology. A woman raised to be afraid of birth as a medical event...virtually all US women...will come to birth afraid. Fear creates pain.

If this view were reality, it would stand to reason that everyone would experience it, which we have established is not so. If there are mothers who choose a joyful experience, maybe you can consciously create a joyful reality, too!

We are products of both conscious and unconscious input. What matters is not whether that input was beneficial or not, but how we choose to let it affect us now.

Maybe it's not other's perceptions that brought us to see birth as scary or dangerous. Maybe you have actually had an unfair and horrible birth. Allowing your current reality to be affected by past events allows the past to dictate both your present and your future.

In order to ensure that *this* baby and *this* birth, are not disrupted by the *other*, past experience, learn about what went wrong. Is it preventable? If not, is it a repeating sort of problem? Is it reasonable to be concerned this time, or is an unreasonable fear clouding your perceptions. Know your filters so you can compensate for them. Accepting accountability for that which you can control makes what you *can't* control more acceptable.

Some people adapt to stress gracefully, others come unglued when faced with the same pressures. How do they differ? One sees an opportunity, the other an obstacle. Their perceptions, their filters, determine the quality of their experience. One parent, faced with prenatal test and interventions may decide that even if the chance of something going wrong is small, they couldn't live with themselves if their child developed a problem that might have been prevented. This is actually often suggested to them by the physician who wants to do the testing. "Well, if it were *my* child and I could have prevented such-and-such, I couldn't live with myself." No matter if the condition of concern is likely to be minor and the treatment actually more dangerous.

Another parent might weigh the risk and benefits just as carefully and see things completely opposite. If the condition of concern is equal or lesser than possible complications resulting from the testing or treatment, this parent may say to themselves, "Of course I would feel horrible if something bad happened, preventable or not, as any parent would, but I'd feel *worse* it I were the one to *cause* it by taking the riskier action."

In the five years it took for my husband and myself to get pregnant, we did a lot of research on healthy pregnancy and safe birth. We decided that if we only got to do this once, we didn't have room for error in our choices.

After our homebirth, one family member said to another, "It's a damn good thing everything turned out okay! If anything had gone wrong, I'd never forgive them!" If anything *had* gone wrong, which I knew to be unlikely, considering statistically I was certain we'd made the safe choice, I'm sure we would have felt sufficiently bereaved.

However, knowing what I knew about those statistics, had we opted for a hospital birth and something had gone wrong, which was much more likely, I would have felt *worse* because I would have felt that we knowingly put our child in danger. Ironically, we would have gotten sympathy for an unexpected outcome for the socially acceptable choice, though we didn't get support for the wonderful outcome of our socially unacceptable choice, no matter how well educated we were on the matter.

This family member loved us very much, but often, when someone else's filter is drastically different from our own, the behaviors resulting from their filters are labeled strange. Our filters were simply different. From my moderate standpoint, I might form similar opinions about unassisted birth.

I support parent's right to choose it, knowing that the odds are with them, but I wouldn't do it. No one is wrong, just viewing birth though a different lens.

A common misperception is that if one person's perception is right <u>for them</u>, the other person's must be wrong. Nothing could be further from the truth. Clearly, the perception of reality is not the same, but the reasoning behind decisions could, in fact, be very much alike. They start out with divergent filters, so their eventual reality outcome will be as well. What matters is whether or not their filters result in an outcome that is beneficial *to them*. That can only be determined by each mother, each parent, alone.

218

I know faulty assumptions resulting from my own filters have led me down unproductive paths in my own life. I'm sure if you think about it, there are times when your own filters have led you to faulty assumptions...quite likely regarding pregnancy and birth.

This is only a bad thing if you fail to *investigate your assumptions before beginning to treat them as truth.*

The behavior of most parents, physicians and nurses would make perfect sense if the initial assumption of birth as a painful, dangerous, medical event were sound. Current obstetric management can be viewed as a test of the validity of that assumption. If pregnancy were dangerous, routine medical testing would improve outcomes. It hasn't. If birth were a medical disaster in waiting, routine medical intervention would not disrupt the process. It does. If technology were integral to the process of birth, routine technology would improve outcomes. It hasn't. If birth were inherently painful, all women would suffer without medicine. They don't. The initial assumption is proven faulty.

Continuing to behave under a faulty assumption perpetuates the perception of a reality with no basis in fact. This is illogical for parents who desire comfort and safety for their birth.

Have you made assumptions without testing their validity and then acted on those assumptions as if they were irrefutable truth? Is the consequence of this behavior that your birthing reality is based not on fact, but on a fear-based, untested perception?

If you accept the assumption that normal birth is always painful, you might disregard evidence to the contrary. This assumption will affect your opinion of women who choose to give birth at home without drugs. Your assumption may cause you to make decisions that aren't in your best interest, or that of your baby. Other women, making the same assumption, may demand their epidural at the door. Suppose that, she too, has failed to test the initial assumption. Both of you have made faulty initial assumptions which neither has tested for truth or reliability. You may be operating under sound logic from your perspective, but starting wrong and thinking right can still result in huge mistakes. Your fear-based thinking is more likely to result in major complications, which will reinforce your fear...a self-perpetuating cycle. Sadly, this is where we, as women, are today. This is the cycle I want to help you break so that you, too, may experience ecstatic birth.

Unfortunately, our thinking about ourselves is most distorted by our *unconscious* filters. Pregnancy, birth and mothering are areas where we tend to be less objective or realistic than any other area of our lives. We completely negate the ways in which we contribute not only to our own experience of the world, but the world itself though our children. We have more resources and knowledge than our parents and grandparents had, which one would think would mean we would strive to do better by our children. Instead, I hear all the time, "It was good enough for me!" This is a defensive statement and proof of 'settling'. "Good enough" parenting. Don't our children deserve for us to reach? Much of the reasoning behind why our ancestors did things was not based on fact. Granted, there is often wisdom to be found in 'old wives tales', but it's time to use what stands up to scrutiny and discard the rest.

It is most difficult to see our own complicity in birthing events when fixed beliefs are involved. Most of the beliefs we have about birth are fixed. Consciously or subconsciously the decision has been made to stop seeking, receiving or processing new information, making these beliefs very dangerous. If you are accepting the belief as fact, you will no longer subject it to debate or modification. From this head-space, you will not only miss new data, you will fail to see important changes in yourself or others that could negate the fixed belief. When the beliefs are ones you have about your own abilities or limitations, either real or imagined, they become limiting beliefs. Limiting beliefs run rampant in the childbearing year.

One area where this has given me fits for years is 'pushing'. For a dozen years I would instruct the parents in class to use 'physiological pushing'. This is not what most women learn in their hospital class. They learn what is called 'purple pushing' by those of us trying to abolish this practice. It is unnecessary and harmful.

'Physiological pushing' basically means you do what your body tells you. It is also called 'breathing the baby down', or 'nudging the baby out'. This doesn't mean that you never push, but that you only do if it feels good and is productive.

The natural progression of labor usually has a resting phase after full dilation is complete, yet women are instructed to begin pushing, and pushing hard, as soon as someone declares it is time through a vaginal exam. This is akin to being told to defecate or regurgitate on demand. Both of those functions require an internal reflexive prompt, as does 'pushing'. If the reflex is not there, it is a non-productive action and wasted energy to try to force it. Women being instructed to push with no urge need to be told to 'push like you're having a bowel movement' because it's the only frame of reference they have. Women who push as their bodies tell them would find that instruction ridiculous! When you feel the need to bear down, it's unmistakable, irresistible, and nothing like a bowel movement! An entirely different set of muscles is involved! When women do bear down, they don't hold their breath for longer than about 6 or 7 seconds, nor do they normally push three times during a one- minute surge. Holding the breath for 10 seconds, several times consecutively, restricts the baby's oxygen.

Women in coma have given birth vaginally with never even pushing once! The uterus does all of the work.

However, my clients were telling me that the doctors and nurses wouldn't 'let' them conduct second stage this way. When I began teaching HypnoBirthing® I would get reports that the labor went fine...up to that point.

Recently, it was published that what teach has scientific validity (finally!). So, I began giving a letter to my students describing what I was teaching and why, and I attached my sources. [1]

Having gotten this far in the book, you may have already guessed how much the facts changed the belief.

One nurse angrily asked me, "You don't *really* tell them they don't have to push do you?! They **have** to! The babies won't descend if they don't!" Despite the fact that I gave her all of the information that I shared here, her mind was made up.

Another nurse who taught childbirth education classes (in hospital) agreed, insisting that because forced pushing speeds descent, the doctors insist on it and she didn't feel it was fair to teach something that doctors wouldn't let the parents do. I feel differently...if I don't teach it, parents can't choose it. If I teach it, providing all of the benefits and evidence along with the detriments to their other choice, and they **choose** to birth with a caregiver who ignores science in an institution that doesn't honor their choice, then they have made a conscious decision to suffer a perineal laceration and to put their baby into fetal distress.

Forced pushing only speeds decent if the integrity of the pelvic floor is compromised because someone has sliced it wide open. In that instance, yes, pushing hard will shoot that baby out. However, in a normal (read: natural) birth, think of it this way...if you have a ring on your finger and your hand is swollen, if you pull on the ring with all of your might, what happens? The tissue

---

[1]Feb. 2002 issue of Journal of *Midwifery and Women's Health Obstetrics and Gynecology* 2002;99:29-34

ahead of the ring gets in the way. Or, think of a Chinese finger trap puzzle. The harder you pull, the more it's stuck.

Pushing hard against healthy, uncut pelvic floor muscles tenses the muscles and makes 2nd stage *longer*. Women who breathe their babies down may only feel like bearing down a few times and 2nd stage is routinely shorter with these women...often only 15 minutes or so.

If practitioners don't 'allow' passive descent because they 'know' it doesn't work (contrary to common sense, scientific evidence and the experience of women doing it) they will *never* see it.

These erroneous beliefs cannot be changed if they aren't acknowledged. If you don't acknowledge and identify your birth related limiting beliefs, they will actively threaten and undermine your attempts toward better birth. Often, it is when you are facing a challenge that a limiting belief will rear it's ugly head, creating doubt about your ability to cope, proving fatal to your efforts. Birth is nothing if not a challenge. Neglecting limiting beliefs allows them to persist. You must confront them and eliminate them now if you want to optimize your best birthing reality.

Your objective here is to ferret out beliefs...beliefs you hold to be true and accurate, perhaps self-evident, thus treating them as fact. You no longer challenge them, if in fact you ever did. You 'know' this negative self-perception or belief about birth to be accurate so you simply accept it. Many of these are probably products of a distorted cultural or personal filter.

Some of these beliefs may go back as far as childhood—possibly back to your own birth. Others may be more recent or even adopted from someone else. Your limiting beliefs impact your ability to achieve your goal of better birth. Not identifying these beliefs means you are defeated before you start.

Journal Exploration:

What are your limiting beliefs about your ability to birth joyfully? Here are some common ones to help you recognize the sort of thing you might be looking for:

- *Birth hurts, everyone knows that!*
- *Maybe some women can do it without drugs, but I can't even deal with a hangnail!*
- *Some women just get lucky and have easy labors.*
- *Why get my hopes up? Something could go wrong at any moment.*
- *I couldn't do it last time, why would this time be different?*
- *My body has failed me before, I should just plan on the worst.*
- *I don't deserve a comfortable birth, it's God's will that women suffer.*

You will know limiting beliefs by the finality of language such as, "always", "never", "everyone" as well as by their rigidity. Any belief that disallows new thinking or ideas is likely a limiting belief. If it has gone unchallenged up until now, it threatens your ability to create a better birth if you fail to address it.

Do you have fixed beliefs about:

- *Doctors*
- *Midwives*
- *Homebirth*
- *Nurses*
- *Hospital birth*
- *Birth Centers*
- *Your mother's birth experience*
- *Your friend's birth experience*
- *Your partner*
- *Your ability to mother (or father)*
- *Babies*
- *Pregnancy*

- *Labor*
- *Birth*

By examining the idea that certain limiting beliefs may be causing you to think and behave in ways that are not in your own best interest, you can transform you birthing possibilities. You control your attitudes and perceptions. You control what sort of birth is attainable for you. That's empowerment!

Do the required work in order to verify that your perceptions are grounded in fact. Challenge the views you hold about your mother-self and the act of giving birth instead of blindly accepting the limited perspective that holds you, and millions of other women, back and puts you at risk.

Perception is reality. Allow your perception to be grounded in fact, not myth or someone else's history. If you are using this book properly, you have already made some cognitive shifts...maybe even some spiritual shifts. Every experience, every new bit of input, can change us...better us. Let yourself be open to the growth that *is* motherhood.

Notes on Chapter Nine

1. Term coined through the work of Dr. Michael Odent to describe the rapid descent a baby will make in a completely relaxed mother who is following her instinctual prompts.
2. http://answering-islam.org/Index/L/labor.html
    www.geocities.com/Wellesley/Atrium/5148/bible.html
3. HypnoBirthing® A Celebration of Life, Marie F. Mongan,   M.Ed., M.Hy., Rivertree Publishing
4. An independent Study Continuing Education Program from Lamaze™ Internations, The Lamaze Philosophy of Birth, Judith Lothian, RN, PhD, LCCE, FACCE
5. A Guide to Effective Care in Pregnancy and Childbirth, Enkin, Deirse, Renfrew and Neilson, Oxford University Press, 1995
6. Obstetric Myths versus Research Realities, A Guide to Medical Literature, Henci Goer
7. The Relaxation Response, Herbert Benson, MD, The Mind/Body Institute, Associate Professor of Medicine, Harvard Medical School, Harpertorch, 1975
8. Doula Can Improve the Heath of Both Mother and Newborn, www.mercola.com/2000/oct/1/doula.htm

PART FOUR
EXTERNALIZATION

BY NOW YOU SHOULD HAVE ENCOUNTERED NEW IDEAS, TESTED THEIR VALIDITY AND EXPLORED YOUR FEELINGS ABOUT HOW IT RELATES TO YOU. NOW THAT YOU KNOW YOU CAN CREATE BETTER BIRTH FOR YOURSELF, THE NEXT STEP IS TO SEEK OUT OPTIONS AVAILABLE TO YOU,

VARIABLES AND OUTCOMES

We'd all like a guarantee that our lives will go as planned. We don't get one in life, and unfortunately, we don't get one in birth.

We'd like to think that bad things don't happen to good people who do all the 'right' things. Deep down we know that's unrealistic.

So far, I've put the emphasis on how much control parents, especially mothers, have over the baby-growing and baby-birthing process. It would not be fair to imply they control all outcomes, all of the time.

However, neither do doctors or hospitals. Somehow, we've gotten the impression that if we take all the prenatal tests and make sure we are in the hospital, everything will turn out right. We know this is not a reality based on fact. Even so, none of us is immune to this thinking.

At the very beginning of a midwifery apprenticeship, at one of the first births I attended as an observer and assistant to the midwife and first apprentice, when I was approximately 7 months pregnant, something went dreadfully wrong. A tragic and rare occurrence, the mother suffered an amniotic fluid embolism, a rare situation, neither predictable nor preventable, (1 in 50,000) in which amniotic fluid is forced into the bloodstream somehow. The mother was transported to the hospital via ambulance, accompanied by the midwife. The rest of us followed close behind.

When we arrived we were told both mother and baby had died. I remember thinking, as I stood there in the hall, that it just couldn't be...we were in the hospital. They were supposed to save her. That's what hospitals *do*.

The next couple of months were difficult. I had not lost faith in birth or in my midwife. I knew there was nothing that could have been done differently.

However, in the midst of our grief for this wonderful mother, there were people with their own agenda trying to get the father to sue, trying to have criminal charges pressed against the attendants, trying to make it seem as though the fact that this was a homebirth was somehow relevant to this outcome. (Even though the same problem had happened to two other mothers in the previous year at two different hospitals a few hundred miles apart.)

In one, the mother and baby were also both lost. In the other, the baby was saved...only because the embolism occurred *during* a cesarean and the baby was already half delivered.

My first reaction, standing under those bright lights with my own baby furiously kicking from the adrenaline pumping across the placenta, was that the hospital could fix anything. That's what they are there for...emergencies. This expectation we have is not realistic, but I understand how alluring it is.

It is this mind-set that causes a cesarean mother to choose to have another cesarean well before her due date for all subsequent babies after losing her first baby. Sent home from the hospital with the first baby despite her concern over 3rd trimester bleeding, the first baby died. Doctors, hospitals and technology didn't save her first baby, and in fact were responsible for the catastrophe and then performed surgery to cover their butts, knowing there was nothing to be done for the baby. Yet deep down in the parents hearts, there was a hope that doing the same thing over-and-over would produce different results. Of course it *did*, but not *because* of the technology, rather, *in spite of it*. The unfortunate event was non-repeating, but we attribute this God-like capability to always control life and death to our physicians.

We expect perfection that Mother Nature doesn't even promise. What of the mother who has a baby with several congenital abnormalities incompatible with life? Again, routine technology didn't predict or prevent it and could not fix it. Yet, with the idea firmly entrenched that modern medicine can give us perfect offspring, would it seem logical that this mother would ascribe the health of her subsequent children to the medical establishment?

Even though, again, the condition was non-repeating and the odds were overwhelmingly in favor of normalcy after suffering such an unlikely, unlucky and heartbreaking outcome with a first baby?

Why is it that if midwives encounter similar situations to doctors, the doctors want them prosecuted...but want immunity from prosecution for themselves?

Nature has a plan. For the most part, she wants the majority of us to survive and perpetuate our species. Sometime, however, 'stuff' happens. Sometimes we can determine a cause, sometimes not. The sane way to deal with those times is to prevent them when they are likely to occur, which is very rarely, but not to use pliers to remove slivers.

Think of how often we hear of women and babies dying in the childbearing year. Not often. We've already established that here in the US it does happen, and far more often than elsewhere. If we adopted maternity care similar to the top 5 safest countries in which to birth (Hong Kong, Sweden, Japan, Norway and Finland), we'd hear about mother or baby deaths even less often. Obviously, prevention and management are only going to be required in a small number of cases.

"It's not an insignificant number if something is wrong with your baby" is often a comment used to manipulate parents who rely on the weighing of risk and benefit ratios in their decision making process.

No, it's not insignificant if it's your baby. No more insignificant than when a mother dies from an unnecessary surgical delivery, yet that hasn't stopped obstetricians from supporting elective cesareans. It's no less tragic when a baby dies from a hospital acquired infection that would not have happened if the baby had been born into the home in which his mother had lived, producing antibodies to pathogens she was exposed to in order to keep him safe. Yet, physicians would have us birth our babies within institutions for sick people, where antibiotic resistant organisms are a huge concern. If we are going to use the above argument in keeping babies safe, let's at least use some consistency!

We face challenges and the unexpected every day in our lives. Most of us do not live in constant fear of what *might* happen or what *could* go wrong. If we did, we wouldn't eat...we might choke. We wouldn't drive...we might be in an accident. We wouldn't take a bath...we could slip and fall. If we looked up the mortality rate for such accidental deaths, we might just find that birth is safer than things we do each-and-every day without a thought. We don't live 'just in case' lives. We take reasonable measures to avoid trouble and cope the best we can when it finds us anyway. We wear seat belts and we learn CPR. We manage.

Acceptance of this fact...taking responsibility for that which we control and accepting that which we can't...is what helps people navigate hard times.

It is inevitable that tough times will befall some people some of the time...in pregnancy and birth as anywhere else.

With some of the challenges of birth, it is sometimes not the particular circumstance that's upsetting, but a violation of expectation. As with the mother who expects to go to the hospital to labor three hours to labor three days instead. Or, the mother who expects no pain, but through no fault of her own ends up having a variable in her birth that makes pain unavoidable. And, the mother who eats well, gets lots of rest, carefully chooses a holistic caregiver...and ends up with a transport for a cesarean for a very real, unavoidable, unpredictable complication.

When expectation has been lost, there is grief, even if the outcome is as joyful as a live, healthy infant. As with any loss, we need to honor the feelings, not discounting disappointment or pain, then work through them and then make a decision to desperately try to hang on to what's lost, or embrace what we have left. Only in gratitude for what we have, can we grow and heal. We have a choice to choose peace.

The deeper losses, those of pregnancy loss or the loss of hope of a whole and healthy child, involves the same process at a much more profound level. Still, acknowledging grief and choosing to use it in a positive manner is possible. Truly, it is when we hurt the most that we are capable of anything. Many a children's hospital, cancer program or other worthwhile 'movements' have been built on a mother's grief. My own work toward better birth grew out of my desire to help other mothers have what I thought couldn't due to infertility, and then secondary infertility.

What we are focusing on here is realistic expectations and emotional reactions when our expectations are not met.

Isn't it easy to see how this concept affects other people? It's always easier to give a friend advice.

Try advising yourself as if you were your own best friend, which you should be. It can be as easy to be your own best friend as your own worst enemy by simply choosing to do so.

Assess your pregnancy progress and birth plans based on results, or projected results based on the probabilities laid out by statistics. These are the best predictor of future outcomes.

Ask yourself:

1-Is your 'best friend' (you) helping you and your baby remain as healthy as your circumstance allows?

2-Is your best friend keeping you from making unwise choice?

3-Is your best friend creating opportunities for you to have a better birth?

4-Is your best friend supporting you emotionally, mentally and spiritually?

5-Is your best friend ensuring your relationship with your partner and your caregiver nurtures you and your baby?

6-Is your best friend requiring you to be your best mom-self for your baby?

7-Does your best friend allow peaceful 'down time' for you do bond with your baby and reduce stress hormones?

8-Does your best friend provide balance and structure between work, growing a healthy baby and planning for the changes that will take place with the baby's arrival?

From this objective standpoint, are you really your best friend? Would you keep another person in your life if they treated you the way *you* treat you?

If another person were not treating you with the love and respect you could cut them out of your life. When the person who should be your very best friend...you...is not, it's a different story. With great patience you must educate and motivate yourself to treat yourself better and make your own best choices.

What happens to you affects your baby, so you need to be his or her best friend and advocate too. You must treat yourself with care now and in the early years of motherhood. As my husband is fond of quoting, "If momma ain't happy, ain't nobody happy."

That is not permission for selfish behavior to the detriment of your child or partner. It's a simple principal of supply and demand. You can't nurture others if you don't first nurture yourself and allow other people to love and nurture you. In pregnancy that may mean interviewing care providers until you find one who will respect you, your intelligence and your choices. In birth, it may be insisting that your preferences be respected unless true medical indication prohibits it. In the first weeks of motherhood, it may mean putting a sign on your door telling visitors to come back when you and baby aren't resting.

Mothers deserve respect for the awesome job with which they have been entrusted. It is our duty to commit to doing it well. From the moment a woman commits to the journey of motherhood, she needs to be replenished. She is literally giving of herself. If she doesn't require the most of herself and those around her, who will?

As your own best friend, how can you create your own best birth?

First, apply everything you have learned from this book so far. It's not enough to just read it. If I told you that in 6 months I was going to take you to the middle of a lake and make you swim back to shore, but you didn't know how to swim, would you prepare? Or, would you just hope for the best?

If you only read a book about swimming, how prepared would you be? If you read a book and took lessons, how prepared would you be? If you read a book, took lessons and practiced for a few months, how prepared might you be?

I'm leading you to data, but I can't make you think. If you just read these words but don't apply the knowledge, you are no better off than when you started. Expect more from yourself and you will be amazed and pleased at how well you do.

Second, commit to *resolve*, rather than *endure* what's not right about where you are. The longer you put up with elements of the typical obstetrically managed birth, the less likely you are to change it later. You must resolve to direct the greater part of your problem-solving energies toward your pregnancy and birth. It's your only priority right now. Deadlines and commitments in other areas of your life cannot compare with the life of your child. The birth of your baby, because it is a memory charged with emotion, will be a defining moment in your life, more so than any other event.

I tell the parents in my classes that the 'what if' game is a very useful tool in removing the last resistance to actually moving toward better birth. I've already given an example of how I used it during my own pregnancy.

We've all played the 'what if' game. The problem is that we don't play it <u>right</u>. We don't follow our 'what if' to the logical and true conclusion. Since our fears are almost always worse than reality, our 'what ifs' paralyze us, making us very ineffective friends to ourselves, indeed.

Playing this 'what if' game allows us to work through our fears. What if the mysterious 'something' *were* to happen? What if something *is* wrong with the baby? Take any fear and make it *specific*. Research it. Find out if it's a reasonable thing to be concerned about or if it's an irrational fear.

Irrational fear is fear that is disproportionate to the actual risk. What is the actual incidence of the thing you fear? If it is fairly common, how often is it really a problem? Compare it to something that carries the same risk as in the choking example...is *that* something you are afraid of? Is it a variation of normal or a true complication? Are you at risk for some reason, or is this an equal opportunity complication? If you alone are at risk, is there anything you can personally do to lower the risk? Are there minimally invasive options to invasive intervention that might be suggested?

Most of the things parents toss into our 'what if' games in class are usually non-issues for normal, healthy mother-babies. By illuminating the shadows with the light of knowledge, we can play the 'what if game' more constructively. We can move past the debilitating fear of the unknown.

By taking the time to consider, research and actually answer the 'how', 'what if', 'why', and 'what' questions you can assure yourself that things are not nearly as overwhelming as you first imagined.

Maybe your fear is a cesarean, which is a reasonable concern. Instead of allowing your fear to manifest into reality by feeding into it, throw light...knowledge...at it. What are the primary reasons behind unnecessary cesareans? Fictional cephalo-pelvic disproportion (CPD)? Failure to progress (FTP) that is really failure to be patient? Questionable fetal distress, or distress caused by inappropriate technology that was ostensibly used to prevent cesarean? An emergency surgery due to pre-eclampsia from a low calorie, low salt diet that was prescribed for 'gestational diabetes' that could have been avoided by simply not eating sugar (or not taking the test if a woman is not actually at risk!) Fill in the blank with any avoidable unnecessary cesarean set-up.

What are the real, unavoidable indications for a cesarean? A transverse baby who can't be convinced to move to a favorable position? Pre-eclampsia due to liver compromise or naturally occurring high blood pressure? Actual, pre-existing diabetes? Conjoined twins, a mother's malformed pelvis, a baby with hydrocephales, cord prolapse not caused by artificially rupturing the membranes or a placental abruption. Yes, bad things do rarely occur.

Can any of the bad things be prevented through excellent self-care or minimally invasive technology? Which are predictable? Treatable? For the complications that do require a necessary cesarean, how can you lessen the physical challenges or emotional trauma that can accompany surgery?

Play the game to it's logical conclusion. Deal with what you can, figure out how to manage what you can't.

Your fourth responsibility as your own best friend, is do deal with any emotional issues in a timely manner. Believe me when I tell you that your *child's* childhood is no time to deal with your *own* childhood baggage. Children, yes even babies, press our buttons. Oh, not intentionally, at least for the first couple of years, but push they do.

If you have unresolved emotional conflicts, relational problems or an inability to distinguish frustration from anger, you may be apt to 'cumulatively react' to your baby's needs as expressed through his or her crying...the only mode of communication available to an infant at first. Likewise, you may react to your partners differing communication style inappropriately. Before baby, different ways of relating may not have been a problem, but after baby, there is so much more to communicate about! Miscommunication, non-communication, making assumptions or taking things personally can create huge problems in a relationship that was stable to begin with...it will most certainly end a relationship that wasn't. Now that you have created another human being that is part of your familial relationship, you have an obligation to try harder to make your union strong. Fluctuating hormones and sleep deprivation are common in the first weeks after the baby is born and tend to exacerbate any tendency to over-react if it's already present.

Invariably, at six weeks postpartum, I get calls from mothers in the midst of a meltdown. Baby has a growth spurt, mom may feel either isolated, if she's staying home, or conflicted/overwhelmed if she's going to do work other than mothering. In a moment, she looks at Dad, whose life seems not to have substantially changed and realizes...her life will *never* be the same. (Of course this is her perspective, which is her reality, though if there is good communication she will realize Dad's life is probably going through changes as well) Life will never even be remotely similar to what it was before baby.

Mom is a completely different person. Her self-perception has shifted and her social standing has changed. She now must think for another human being, anticipating every mood and eventuality, indefinitely. She may get 'touched out'. There are countless factors involved in how a parent's life changes. If unfinished emotional business and/or inadequate communication between partners is added to the mix, it's no wonder so many marriages fail soon after baby arrives.

Parents are planning (minimally with a 4 to 6 week series of 2-hour classes, usually) for the birth, but not for life with a new family member... with individual and distinct needs.

Get closure on issues of a parental nature. Will you parent the way your parents did, or your partner's? A combination...or neither? Do you hold resentments against your parents-or his? What do you know about mother-baby feeding, circumcision, vaccination, healthy sleeping arrangements for baby, discipline? Do you both agree on your options? Is your relationship well-grounded and healthy? Are forgiveness, apologies or confrontations required to get past certain issues?

Refuse to allow unresolved issues to burden your relationship with your baby and your baby's other parent. Whatever it takes to start out fresh, do it. Your baby deserves a clean slate.

Finally, have integrity in your agreements with your self and others. If you've make promises to yourself, take steps to keep them. Now is the best time to break any bad habits you may have developed when it comes to commitment. Actually, bad habits in general. Children are mirrors, reflecting back to us both the best and the worst of ourselves.

Children are especially aware of broken agreements, spoken or unspoken. When you make the decision to bring them into the world you automatically became their safe haven. Make sure that you are. You agreed to be their protector, their provider; to teach them and to learn from them. You made a commitment to raise them in a stable environment and to put their needs before your wants. If you didn't make those commitments you had no business creating a life. Children are not a lifestyle choice. They are human beings with needs that are yours to meet. Putting anything above that responsibility tells them, loud and clear, that they are not your priority. Whether you intend it or not, they feel rejected.

That means childbirth classes come before cable and books on better birth come before a new spring wardrobe. It means you pay out of pocket for evidence-based care if you have to, even if it means downsizing a little or sacrificing some indulgence.

If you've been unreliable before, you can no longer afford the luxury of selfishness or procrastination.

As a parent, you must work as hard as you would expect anyone you might hire as a substitute parent, and then some. Treat your new role of MOTHER as if it matters...*because it does!*

Parenting is, to a large extent, a learn-as-you-go process because you never know what lessons your little one has in store for you. Making a commitment to learn the basics will put you ahead of the game.

Giving special significance to this job above all other concerns, not later, but now, shows you respect your unique status and approach your responsibility in earnest.

If you just sort of decided you wanted a comfortable, safer birth, but you never get around to finding a class, how effective have you been?

Contrast that attitude with the parents who drive two hours each way to attend ten to twelve hours of instruction. The difference in the outcome that could be expected should be obvious.

Do you have a conviction that you deserve the wonderful births that others have? Are you and your baby worth the effort required to get it? Remember, the primary difference between the fairytale birth-ers and the nightmare birth-ers is that the fairytale birth-ers were willing to do what the nightmare birth-ers *weren't* willing to do.

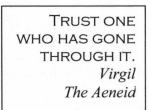

TRUST ONE
WHO HAS GONE
THROUGH IT.
Virgil
The Aeneid

Don't sell yourself short, settling too early and too cheaply. Your pregnancy will keep advancing, your baby will keep growing, your due month will keep approaching—whether you are doing something to optimize your outcome or not. Don't promise yourself you'll do better tomorrow. Start <u>now</u>. You must be serious about having a better birth and mothering experience or you wouldn't have come this far into the book. Make better birth a priority and you will be far more likely to have it.

I'm not suggesting that just because you are now willing to reach for better everyone will be willing to hand it to you. You will still face obstacles. It may even seem like there are more than before at first. Anything worth having is worth working for.

A comfortable, safe birth and healthy, whole mother-baby are definitely worth having. Keep your path clear and you can make it through a few thorny parts.

Birth and early motherhood are not to be feared, just carefully, purposely and lovingly navigated. The experiences you are about to undergo are transformative if you allow them to be...if you consciously take your turn at empowerment and even enlightenment. Standing up for yourself in pregnancy gives you strength to carry with you to your birthing. The rite of passage that is birth gives you the courage to love without reservation. Mother love equips you to manage your new and ever changing life.

The tools you've learned thus far have helped you to ground yourself if you've consciously applied them. These baby steps should have minimized or eliminated many of the impediments to better birth.

Your grounded-ness stems from certain life decisions that are part of your very being. You may not consciously be aware of what these are, but they guide your actions daily. You may have made a life decision that you would protect your child with your own life. You may have decided nothing is more important than your baby. Choices you make spring from these decisions. What are your personal commitments to parenthood?

Journal Exploration:

Without taking anything for granted, write down your conscious parenting decisions. For example:
I will respect my baby's dignity, treating him or her with kindness and patience.
I will be the best parent I can be, learning what I don't already know.
I will not harm or allow others to harm my baby, as protective as a mother bear.

Whatever these commitments are, they guide your behavior all of the time. These are your convictions. These are the things you will not compromise. For instance, if a mother were to list the last one, but she lived in an abusive relationship, it's not really a <u>conviction</u>, but rather an <u>ideal</u> she's striving to attain, or she would not compromise it.

You may be very proud that you are already living your life with your head, heart and hands. Or, you may be disappointed in yourself if you are failing to live up to an ideal. Where are these incomplete places? How can you fix them? What is your individual standard of adequacy? How will you deal with set backs and how much effort are you willing to put forth for the sake of your baby?

If you set unattainable goals for yourself, of course, you are putting yourself at a disadvantage. Likewise, if you don't require much of yourself, problems can manifest there as well. Be realistic in your expectations and take motherhood empowerment one step at a time. Just don't mistake procrastination for caution—you have only weeks left in which to work. There's no better time to demand excellence of yourself. No one else can do the work you are doing.

Are you living in a comfort zone? Have you avoided reaching for that which is not already comfortable and familiar? Have you adapted to acceptance to avoid exploring and expanding your boundaries?

Staying in your comfort zone now can be hazardous to your health. You are the sole agent for change in your birth. If you don't take action toward better birth, no one else will. If you want events to progress more safely and comfortably than everyone else's births, you're the one who must take action.

It's not enough to change your thinking, or even change what you feel...you must take action on those shifts. Remember, do what everyone else has been doing, get what everyone else has been getting.

If you want that safer, more comfortable, dignified birth, you must ask yourself everyday, "What am I doing to make my birth better?" Then, do something!

If no one else has noticed your newfound strength, maybe you're falling short of what I'm trying to convey. Stepping into your mother-self creates obvious changes not just in your decisions, but in your very stature, your demeanor, your speech.

You stop 'going with the flow' and become passionate about mother-love. You are your own barometer of excellence. You know if you are being true to yourself or not.

How you handle the bumps and jiggles that crop up along the way also helps you assess your progress.

Not every decision you make, when you are new to decision making, will be great or even good. Others may not be willing to meet you where you are. By now you should be committed to working it out and finding solutions when you make a wrong decision for yourself, making a wrong decision right.

The stakes are high...the quality of life for you and your family. Your baby's life. Your life. Your hopes and dreams.

You have the skills to simply 'survive' a bad experience, but why should you settle for survival when you can have joy and wholeness in body, mind and spirit?

This isn't just your life we're talking about, but a new human on the planet. By extension the lives affected include, a father's life, as well as the lives of grand parents, siblings, and teachers; friends your child will eventually have and so on. If each birthing woman made better birthing choices we could save our government billions of wasted health care dollars, allocating them instead to care for the sick, injured and elderly. Watch 'It's a Wonderful Life' now instead of at the holidays and take note of how many lives just one person touches.

The danger component has been overemphasized for far too long, but now that you know that, you can move ahead with purpose and knowledge, creating a better birth...a better life.

The only promises that are for sure are the ones mothers make to themselves. The trick to managing special circumstances appropriately is being well grounded in the control you do have, but being flexible when the unexpected occurs. Your birthing and parenting convictions are what keeps you on track.

SAFETY FIRST?

People will treat us the way we allow them to treat us. This includes your partner, your caregiver, and eventually, your child.

When preparing for a better birth, this concept is primary. The provider/mother relationship is all too often based on inequity.

It is, in fact so commonly extreme in severity that we can't even see how distorted and unhealthy it is. Your relationship may not fall into this category, which makes you the most fortunate among women. Unfortunately, I hear stories every day of women who are not so lucky.

Even if you feel this irrelevant to your experience, please read on. We will discuss how this same concept is at work in other relationships, including relationships with those you probably won't meet until you are in labor.

If you are going to have a better birth, you will have to negotiate, not with one person, but with many, unless you are birthing at home with a midwife. In that instance, negotiations will be one-on-one, for the most part. At most, one or two apprentices could be involved in your birth, but only if you agree to the arrangement. At home, you always have the final say in what you do and where you do it, unless there is a compelling reason to do otherwise, which the midwife always explains to the parents.

People learn by trial-and-error, reward and punishment. We do what rewards us and avoid (or try to) what doesn't, particularly what harms us. Except, in the US it seems, when it comes to pregnancy and birth.

Consider the following illustrations:

Upon hearing that I was planning a homebirth, one father exclaimed, "That's just nuts! We were so lucky we were in the hospital! When they broke her [his wife's] water, the cord came out before the baby and our baby could have died! We were lucky we didn't need a cesarean!"

He's right; they were lucky that they didn't need surgery. Cord prolapse is very serious and most often does require surgery to save the baby's life. How they managed a vaginal birth without surgery is a mystery...unless it was an occult prolapse wherein they were able to push the cord back far enough to proceed. However, his baby would not have been in danger if it weren't for the unnecessary use of a dangerous intervention, amniotomy (breaking of the bag of water) which is used so often in birth that people consider it a 'normal' part of labor.

In the last several months I've heard of two different doctors in two different areas of the country tell women that their vaginas were damaged so badly with their first births that they wouldn't be able to have vaginal births for current babies. One doctor said this during a *news* program, detailing the extensive damage done to the pelvic floor with natural birth, advocating elective cesareans.

What I want to know is what they are doing to those poor women to cause such damage, because it certainly isn't part of natural birth! If a doctor is incapable of helping women deliver over an intact perineum or butchers her so badly her bottom is then useless for the most important task it was designed for, she needs to find a new doctor! Yet, the women in these instances didn't even *question* their doctors!

During that same time frame, a fellow childbirth practitioner had a client who was told by her doctor that she would need a cesarean because she had hemorrhoids! It's a sad state of affairs, but there are surgeons out there looking for a reason to do surgery using the most inane excuses, and women are letting them get away with it!

Doctors do these things because they can...because no one is questioning safety, efficacy or even the nonsensical nature of some of these recommendations. By allowing dangerous practices to continue unchecked, we give them permission to continue. As a society we have made a collective agreement that substandard care is okay, and that we will defend it to our very deaths.

I would like you for a moment to consider a situation that strikes me a similar.

For years, smoking was socially acceptable without question. Manufacturers touted cigarettes as beneficial! Celebrities promoted smoking. Doctors even encouraged women to smoke to help keep weight down!

Eventually, some people questioned the safety of voluntarily inhaling thousands of poisonous chemical compounds. Some people were connecting the dots between cigarettes and cancer, asthma and emphysema deaths. These people voiced their concerns. They were ignored at first. I remember the acrimonious reaction to these discoveries and announcements. "My gramma lived to be a hundred and smoked every day of her life!" or "My brother has asthma and he's never smoked!"

The evidence continued to mount. Some people quit, others rationalized. "Smoking is the only thing that calms me down." I've actually heard that recently—even though it's a well known fact that cigarettes are stimulants, not relaxants. However, smokers perceive relaxation...and as you now know, perception is reality.

In any event, smoking continued as a socially acceptable practice. "If you don't like it, no one is forcing you to light up." smokers persisted. To each his own. Even if smoking was dangerous, smokers were only hurting themselves. It's their body. (Full disclosure: I smoked for 10 years before I got pregnant.)

Except when it isn't. Next we learned about second hand smoke and how smoking affects babies before birth. Some smokers refused to believe the research. Some smokers got more considerate. Some started to see the common sense in the idea that if you pollute your body, you will get sick. Now it wasn't just your own life you could affect, but your family and even strangers.

Anti-smoking movements coalesced. Smoke-free establishments become common. The idea spread and smoke-free towns were next as people demanded that the effects of smoking not be imposed upon non-smokers. Understandably, people that had smoked for years while it was socially acceptable were irate that all of the sudden they were outcasts.

Emphasis was placed on the amount of money smokers cost our government in a variety of ways.

Whistleblower lawsuits followed when it was revealed tobacco companies knowingly and willingly contributed to the loss of billions of governmental health care dollars.

Ad campaigns focused on lost wages from smoking and how smoking impacts the work place through increased sick days lost. Insurance rates were raised for smokers.

Are you wondering where I'm going with all of this? How women give birth and parent is a personal choice. It also ripples out into a larger cultural context that affects us all.

The evidence against medically managed birth for healthy women is abundant. Yet, it persists because we allow it. Unless and until it is challenged it will continue...because it can.

Almost all of the societal effects of smoking can be applied to the mismanagement of healthy pregnancy/normal birth and low breastfeeding rates.

I have heard it said that a parent is only as happy as their unhappiest child. I would suggest that could be extrapolated to society-at-large.

When mothers reward, accept and validate unacceptable conduct by continuing to see a care provider who abuses his authority, they are assuring that bad behavior will repeat. There are plenty of compassionate and competent care providers out there. Reward them. Soon enough manipulative tactics and inappropriately applied technology will be as taboo as smoking has become.

Relationships are mutually defined. Obstetricians are the most sued profession because they have taught the birthing public that legal action is the only recourse available to rectify a bad outcome. In a power-over situation, the powerless will seek retribution in a way that gives them their power back, even if it's only momentary or superficially.

This problem is magnified in that many times, when parents decide they will no longer put up with offensive behavior from a provider, their attempts to find a replacement are futile. The other providers support poor behavior by making it difficult, if not impossible, for parents to switch. Add to this the limitations of HMOs and it seems parents are between a rock and a hard place. Is it any wonder they are angry enough to seek punishment when their instincts are proven correct and something bad happens?

We have also meekly accepted that the costs of birth require a substantial loan. We pay for the abuse!

You may never have considered that you were negotiating and creating the relationship that exists with your caregiver. After all, you may only see him for 10 minutes once month.

Now you know. Because you are aware of how your own action, or inaction, contributes to the relationship, you can choose to change it if you need to. You are the only one responsible for this relationship since you can't change a person who doesn't want to change. And why would a doctor want to change the current system? They think it's working for *them*!

> (WOMEN) KEEP TRYING TO CHANGE THEIR CAREGIVER WITH EVERY VISIT...INSTEAD OF CHANGING CAREGIVERS.

I see mothers all the time who realize this intellectually, but just keep trying to change their caregiver with every visit...instead of changing caregivers. Repeating behavior that didn't result in the desired outcome, and then expecting a different outcome from the same behavior, is insanity.

Women keep going back to the same doctors that lied to them and whose abuse to their bodies resulted in lifetime consequences. If you don't expect people to treat you with dignity and respect, they won't. Plain and simple.

I cringe inside when I hear birth stories full of statements like, "Then *they* broke my water" or "Then *they* put cytotec on my cervix to induce me". Where is personal accountability here? Not to mention, *informed consent*.

It is the law that parents <u>understand</u> and consent to any procedure. It is a right that carries responsibility. In order to consent, we must know if we are getting all of the information we need to decide.

If not, (and it's obvious that in most cases patients are being woefully misinformed or under-informed by the amount of harmful intervention in birth today) doctors have taken on that responsibility themselves...which is when a lawsuit is warranted.

I have yet to see an epidural consent form (1) as follows commonly used:

EPIDURAL CONSENT FORM

1.   I authorize the performance upon _____ (patients name) of the following procedure _____ (elective epidural)   performed   under   the   direction   of _____(physician's name).

2.   I consent to the administration of local anesthetics, narcotics, 'caine derivatives and/or other medications into the epidural space.

3.   I understand that the following risks, among others, are possible complications as reported in the medical literature:

- o   Failure to relieve pain.
- o   Hypotension (low blood pressure).
- o   Postdural puncture (spinal) headache which may require medical therapy.
- o   Persistent area of numbness and/or weakness of the lower extremities.
- o   Temporary nausea and vomiting.
- o   Breakage of needles, catheters, etc. possibly requiring surgery.
- o   Hematoma (blood clot) possibly requiring surgery.
- o   Infection.
- o   Rapid absorption of local anesthetics causing dizziness and seizures.
- o   Temporary total spinal anesthesia (requiring life support systems).
- o   Respiratory and/or cardiac arrest (requiring life support systems).
- o   Back pain.
- o   Fetal distress resulting from one of the above complications.
- o   Permanent paralysis

o   Increased cesarean rate, increasing the mortality rate
o   Neurological damage to my newborn
o   Epidural fever for my newborn (requiring a spinal tap, etc.)

4.   I consent to the performance of procedures in addition to or different from those above, whether or not arising from presently unforeseen conditions, which the above named doctor or his associates or assistants including residents, may consider necessary or advisable in the course of the procedure.

5.   The purpose of the procedure, possible alternative methods of treatments, the risks involved and the possibility of complications have been fully explained to me. I fully understand the administration protocols of an epidural. I understand that no guarantee or assurance has been given by anyone as to the results that may be obtained.

Equal time to equal risk?

A VBAC consent form details the horrors that could befall a woman choosing this option, which is actually *less* dangerous than the procedure—the cesarean—that precipitated it. Inductions are often done without informed consent as to the probable complications associated with pharmaceutical induction agents...including the fact that they are *not* FDA approved for non-medially indicated inductions due to the substantial risk associated with them. (2)

As it stands now, a parent must sign a waiver if they opt against many standard, yet unproven, interventions, but not interventions proven dangerous and/or of no use! This gives the impression that one thing is safe while another is not. Of course, this is the intent. It is subtle manipulation in action.

Analyze your own relational behavior with your caregiver. Is this a mutually respectful relationship? Is there adequate time to communicate your needs at each prenatal visit? Do you understand and accept your caregiver's limitations? Is your doctor capable of assisting a woman in birthing over an intact perineum? Does your midwife have a good working relationship with local medical personnel so that transport, should it become prudent, would be smooth? (Keep in mind all variables. I know many great midwives with wonderful outcomes who have made every attempt to establish working relationships with other professionals, but have been met with less than warm responses...to say the least.)

You can determine whether, or not, the things people do are working for you. *You* can change the relationship—either the agreed upon dynamics with the one you have or actually changing to a different provider. *You* are the only constant in this event.

Starting today, this minute, by internalizing this concept, *you* have the power. It may not be easy, but you have to decide that you and your baby are worth the trouble.

How you respond to a caregiver's treatment of you governs the tone of your relationship. Their response to you is equally important. Resistance to your insistence of respect is a warning sign. When people get their way by controlling and manipulative tactics, they have just been rewarded for that behavior.

Notice how you feel after your next visit with your midwife or physician. Were they attentive or indifferent? Preoccupied with your chart or inquisitive about your life as it related to your health? Were your questions answered to your satisfaction? Was your caregiver supportive and encouraging if you sought out a variety of sources of information about your care? Pay attention to body language—did words and actions seem to be consistent? What did your mother's intuition say? If you had a similar interaction with your life partner, a sibling or co-worker, would it be positive, negative or neutrally acceptable?

This works both ways, of course. Doctors and midwives, are your clients pulling their weight in the relationship? Or, are they coasting, expecting *you* to be responsible for *their* health? Do you know if your client is still smoking, drinking or taking drugs, and if they are, do you fail to say anything or demand better? If so, you have just agreed to clean up after her mess. Failure to do so, even if it's not humanly possible, means she will place the blame on you. You've set it up that way. Give her the names of three other providers willing to take that risk by putting up with such behavior and cut her loose. Don't give her a false sense of security by implying it's no big deal because you want to be politically correct. When that security is shattered, she won't blame herself...she'll blame you and she'll expect you to pay her for the pain and suffering she caused herself.

I've heard providers say that they can't demand more from their patients, or that it's financial suicide say 'no' to a client when they demand elective cesareans, non-medically indicated drugs or even antibiotics for viral infections. Even though the doctors are well aware that prescribing antibiotics for a cold will do nothing about the virus and contributes to astronomical problems with antibiotic resistant organisms.

As if doing what they've been doing is working? If it was, malpractice suits wouldn't be putting them out of business. Hmmm...let's see, dropping a client who might, in a lifetime, contribute a few thousand dollars to the doctors bottom line, or setting up the perfect conditions for a multi-million dollar lawsuit? Which is financial suicide?

Relationships within families and social circles also change when women start redefining what is acceptable to them regarding their birth. Many women intrinsically feel comfortable with the elements of a safe birth...good maternal nutrition, midwifery, natural childbirth, homebirth and breastfeeding.

They would choose midwifery and breastfeeding because it makes sense to them right down to their bones. They are sure enough about their convictions that they could change care providers—if they had support. They go home from a visit with a midwife excited, only to have their husband 'put his foot down' and insist on all the bells and whistles of a medically managed birth.

This relationship needs redefining. Communication needs to be clear and explored in a calm environment. It took loving cooperation to get the baby in there, that's what it takes to birth it gently.

Mothers need to actively listen to what their partner is saying. Usually, a father's objections to unfamiliar birth options are just that...objection to the unfamiliar. They have grown up with all of the fear and misconceptions about birth that women have...with no intimate knowledge of women's 'mysteries' or inner knowing. They want to protect their partner and baby. Machines and external references to the unknown feel safe to them. In return, fathers must listen to what the mothers are trying to say, instead of insisting on the last word when they know little to nothing about the subject.

Agree to learn about your options together. If one of you has more knowledge about safe birth, help educate each other. Tell him you are perfectly willing to do things his way if he can demonstrate that his way is supported by evidence. Heck, give him a monetary incentive for doing the research if you have to!

Tell him Jock Doubleday will pay $25,000 to any person who can prove "hospital birth to be safer, in any category (i.e., infant or maternal mortality or morbidity), for most mothers and babies than home birth with a trained midwife in attendance". (3)

In situations where mothers have lovingly shown fathers (and grandparents!) the merits of homebirth, those who were resistant have subsequently become the strongest advocates!

Early in my teaching career, there was a mother who wanted a homebirth. She had strong faith in the birthing design of women. She had two previous births that were somewhat traumatic. She had a strong intuition that the complications she experienced were iatrogenic and she was right.

The father feared for his wife's safety, but attributed the problems in the previous births to *birth*, not obstetrically managed birth. He was a loving and wonderful husband, willing to learn all he could, but just could not get 'on board' with the idea of homebirth.

He was willing to compromise by getting a monitrice (or doula) to stay at home as long as possible, going in to the hospital for the actual birth.

Throughout that birth, he was very sweet, asking often if it was time to warm up the car. He repeatedly suggested, maybe it was time to get going. She labored beautifully. He wanted to help her birth her way, but it was obvious he was nervous.

She went in to the hospital at 7 cm dilation, had her baby and returned home after a few hours of observation.

With the next baby, he was more willing to consider homebirth, and did extensive research. His confidence grew as his wife's gorgeous belly grew. Their homebirth was a family event, full of love and support. They've gone on to have another baby at home since. The initial resistance of the father and medically oriented family members has melted away.

Mothers have interviewed HypnoBirthing® practitioners thrilled with the prospect of comfortable, fast labor, only to have their siblings or parents influence them against it later.

This might be due to their own ignorance about safe birth, or it may be that they see an alternative approach to what they might have done as threatening. This would be especially true if they have seeds of doubt about their own choices.

Parents must be patient, but firm, about their choices in this circumstance. If others can contribute in a positive way, let them know you are grateful for their help. If they are not supportive, ask them what they actually know about the options you have chosen. You know they have your best interests at heart, but are their ideas based on fact? If they make claims, assertions or statements, ask them to substantiate them. You'll find, after having gone through this book, that their concerns are most likely based on unfounded fears and *beliefs* they regard as facts. Take the time to help them though these issues the way this book has helped you. If they are unwilling to explore their beliefs, you may have to limit the input you are willing to accept from them.

Besides family, friends and even strangers may inundate you with horrible stories, criticism or unsolicited (and bad) advice. It's okay to politely stop them, thank them for their concern and inform them that you prefer not to hear such negativity. Pat your belly, smile, and tell them "especially with little ears listening". If you can educate them and get them beyond their own fear, wonderful. If they are simply acquaintances and not worth the time and effort it would take, let them deal with their own birth issues on someone else's time.

Your commitment to positive action must come from a place of strength. If you have self-doubt or fear because you haven't come to terms with the truth about birth, you won't have the ability to stand your ground. If you haven't worked through your fear by now, you may need to go back and see if you've been completely honest with yourself in previous journal explorations. Programs for better birth have encountered situations in which women claim they 'don't work'...when the women have never even opened the book or done the work in the class! Talk about denial! How is the class supposed to work? Magic?

If you don't face yourself, you can't face the problem with any hope of resolution. You must do the work and do it deep.

If you have done the work, those around you must be clear that you have not adopted your new birthing attitudes for shock value or because it's "in". You are now making decisions for the safe arrival of your baby. You are making decisions that ensure you and your baby are treated with dignity and respect for a healthy, happy outcome.

Don't be tempted to play the victim. I have heard "I really wanted a homebirth, but..." followed by some lame excuse that blames a husband or insurance company, followed by a sad birth tale, all too often. Once, a woman who had expressed interest in homebirth before becoming pregnant, insisted once she was pregnant, that she had chose a hospital birth because her *husband* had diabetes! How is this relevant? Well, the logic was that homebirth would stress him out and stress altered his blood sugar levels, so it was for <u>his</u> safely, you see, that they needed to be in the hospital.

The funny thing is, she came up with this bizarre rationalization as if it matters to me where she gives birth! I do get *exasperated* when I encounter situations like these. It's inconceivable to me that women intentionally (for once someone has suggested the risk, it takes intention to avoid looking into the claim, either to prove it wrong or prove it right) and willingly put themselves and their babies in harms way under the delusion that they are doing exactly the opposite.

A mother who really wants a homebirth (or any other birth) will find a way to make it happen. If you don't want one, fine! Say so. You are responsible for your own decisions whether you face that fact or not, which includes the outcomes attached to said decisions.

This responsibility extends to the hiring of a monitrice or doula as well. Your relationship with a labor support person needs to rest on the same principals of trust and good communication that all of the previously discussed relationships rest.

There is one relationship that may end up as part of your experience, if you choose a hospital birth, that cannot really be assessed beforehand. This would be with the nurses that will assist you throughout most of your labor.

Most of the time, you will not meet the women (or men) you will share your labor with until you are admitted into their care. Negotiation of these relationships occurs in an accelerated fashion, with unique stressors providing a great degree of difficulty.

In labor, at some point, you are in a very suggestible state akin to self-hypnosis, whether you use a method like HypnoBirthing® or not. It is a natural state-of-grace we get if we go with the flow of labor. Even if we don't, we reach it eventually...through exhaustion if we have entered the fear/tension/pain vortex.

The vast majority of nurses are kind souls who care very deeply about women and babies. Because of the very nature of their work in places of the sick and injured, they view birth as pathology...or potential pathology. They may care very much, but they still operate under their fundamental wrong beliefs about birth.

Open-minded nurses working from a neutral paradigm, as well as nurses hostile to all new and different concepts, are working in obstetrical wards all over the country. You have to be ready to deal with what you get.

I have met nurses who were downright abusive, brusque and rude. I have also met angels of mercy with midwives hearts, so kind and compassionate I have waited for them to come on duty before taking a labor support client into the hospital. These nurses follow protocol—just barely. They bend the rules when they can, pleading your case and stepping in with non-interventive labor support techniques if they see you need help or are heading in the direction of cascading intervention.

Some nurses do everything by the book with no regard to common sense. One nurse, after a birth I attended as labor support, kept insisting after the birth that the breastfeeding mother needed to switch her baby to the other breast to avoid sore nipples. The mother explained that she had been nursing children continuously for the last 6 years and sore nipples were not an issue. The nurse just did not comprehend that the mother didn't *get* sore nipples, or it seems, that she could have lactated continuously through three children, and got noticeably agitated that the mother was not following her instructions.

The best way to enter this relationship is with positive expectations...with contingencies for negative reactions. Dad or a birth partner can plan to run interference if it becomes necessary. That's one reason it's important for him to be as educated as you are. Otherwise, he'll have no recourse but to acquiesce to authority. Feeling unsure, he could end up an accomplice to your misery.

In writing your birth preferences, also called a 'birth plan' use positive language, thank them for sharing your birth and let Dad briefly explain your birth philosophy. If you are met with an arrogant attitude of 'Okay, if you think that will work...but call me when you want to beg for your epidural', you know you need to make a strong stand for your birth.

If a nurse dismisses your preferences, ignores your requests or makes fun of your plans, politely remind her that unless there medical indications to alter them, these *are* your intentions. If she is still recalcitrant, ask for another nurse. Nurses are people too, with all of the same tendancies of anyone else. There is the possibility that someone with that negative attitude could act vindictively. It's rare, but it happens. You can't know if it will happen to you until it's too late. This may be a day-job to her, but it's the birth of *your baby*. You deserve to be treated like the Goddess you are!

Journal Exploration:

How healthy are your relationships with those persons involved in your pregnancy and birth?

Yes   No

1. Do you feel your partner controls your birthing choices?
2. Is your relationship with your caregiver more like parent/child than equality between adults?
3. Do you and your partner, parents and friends argue over your safe & gentle birth choices?
4. Do you find yourself apologizing to your care provider for what should be reasonable expectations & requests?
5. Do you feel that during your pregnancy you have made more concessions and compromises than anyone else?
6. Do you frequently make excuses for your partner & care provider when discussing their involvement in the direction your birth path is heading?
7. Do you feel your emotional needs are either not being met or are being played upon?
8. Do you feel that choices made by others regarding your pregnancy and birth are-or may be-cheating you out of joy in your experience?
9. Do your pregnancy/birth discussions with your partner (your care provider, your family, your friends) leave you frustrated, exhausted or afraid?
10. Do you feel your wants and needs are not a priority to your caregiver or partner?

                                                              Yes   No

*11. Do you have ideas about how you want your pregnancy
and birth to be that you don't share with your partner or CP*

12. Do you feel devalued?

*13. Do you secretly believe other people are leading
you to a less than desirable birth experience?*

*14. Do you see negative patterns to your relationships
with those in your planned birth party?*

*15. Do you feel afraid to be vulnerable in any of
your birth related relationships?*

*16. Do you feel you are the only one willing to <u>work</u>
for better birth?*

*17. Do you feel emotionally detached from those who
will be a part of this most emotional event? Including your baby?*

*18. Do you feel you've had to give up dreams, or expectations,
of a better birth to keep peace in your relationship with your
partner, cp, family or friends?*

*19. Are you just coasting along, not making waves,
hoping for the best?*

*20. Are you seeing your cp just because you started out
there, or because someone you know did, rather than finding
someone you really like or are comfortable with?*

How many of these did you respond 'yes' to? If there were very
many, you have serious inventory to take. Are your 'yes-es'
confined to one particular person, or many? Do you see a pattern
of acquiescing due to a fear of authority or a fear of hurting
someone you love?   How can you establish (or reestablish)
healthy boundaries? How might requiring more of yourself and
others alter your relationships?

No one likes change. The people around you are no different.
When you begin to relate differently to them, they will try to
revert to old patterns. They may be angry. They may make
assumptions and take things personally. They may insist these
notions of painless birth are the illusions of fringe groups and that

the idea that obstetrically managed birth in America could be less than ideal is just so much garbage.

Any attempts to create doubt or guilt, or to put you on the defensive need to be seen for what they are...desperate. There may be a manipulative attempt to dissuade you from this 'craziness'. To bring you back in line with what 'everyone else does'. There may be accusations that you are being selfish, reckless or difficult.

Stand your ground, Mother Bear. With scientific evidence and common sense behind you, ask them to prove you wrong. They won't be able to, and in the process of trying will end up educating themselves. There are plenty of supportive resources for evidence-based care and the midwifery model. Find them and you will also find other souls committed to excellence...like yourself.

While you are examining other people's motives, examine your own. Remember the rule of reciprocity. What comes around goes around. If you have loving support and a care provider who is open to change, do you show gratitude? Do you have unhealthy behaviors for which you are rewarded by others? Are you holding yourself accountable for your actions? Be willing to put our own behaviors and motivators under the same scrutiny of inspection you apply to others in your quest for your best possible birth.

Notes on Chapter Eleven

1   I first found this at: www.gentlebirth.org/archives/epdrlrsk.html with no source or author given. I would like to credit the author in future editions of this work. Please contact me if you are the creator.

TO FORGIVE (NOT FORGET)

Birthing should be our most fond memory in life. We are meeting this new little being that will (or should) help us think, feel and act as better people in the world.

Instead, far too many women feel anger and resentment regarding their births. Women's souls are wounded every single day when violated and dis-empowered during their births. Babies suffer innumerable indignities in a system that views them as commodities instead of tiny beings with feelings.

In reading this work, there undoubtedly will be women who have 'stuffed' their 'unacceptable' feelings who now see clearly that those deep emotions are justified.

Anger and resentment—no matter how warranted—won't change the situation for the birthing mothers to come. These feelings are not helpful to the poor mothers who struggle with them.

The only way to rectify the situation, healing the hurt and helping our daughters, is to take back your power from those who have damaged you. It's time to take back our births!

That may sound like a battle cry, however, I don't feel women are yet in a place for a warrior approach. Angry books like *Silent Knife* (*1*) and *Immaculate Deception* (*2*) are the words of warriors, vital and important, that have galvanized many women...but not enough.

Besides, not every woman has a warrior spirit. Not every woman is strong enough to claim her anger. Countless women have been convinced they have no right to be angry, while others are simply unaware of how much has been stolen from them.

Still more feel the pain of knowing deep in their bellies that something wasn't right about their births, but feel powerless against the priesthood of medicine.

Their trepidation is well placed. Fighting back has been fruitless so far. The powerful are only using more force to keep their power.

Though the situation is said to be a 'health care crisis', the headlines may give us the first clue that what we face isn't so much about health care as it is about money, and it isn't so much about women as it is about OB-GYNs. "Fed-up obstetricians look for a way out", says USA Today, while the subtitle to the Nightly News explains, "Doctors say malpractice insurance rates are forcing them out of business." (3)

Before we can begin to understand why this situation is not a crisis, but an opportunity, we first need to look at the current general understanding of the problem.

The American College of Obstetricians and Gynecologists (ACOG), a trade organization akin to a union for obstetricians, (4) has issued a national "Red Alert" on the condition of obstetrical care in America. They are correct, it is scandalous that we have some of the highest cesarean rates and some of the poorest outcomes for both mothers and babies.

However, that isn't the concern of ACOG regarding the "Red Alert". They are referring to obstetricians inability to make money because medical liability rates are so high that doctors are simply unable to practice anymore. The contention is that fundamental problems with the medical liability system are to blame...if doctors weren't sued so much, we wouldn't be in such a mess. This, they explain, jeopardizes the availability of physicians to deliver babies in the US. Their solution is not to determine *why* obstetrics is the most sued profession, but to lobby nationwide damage award caps. For the average person presented with this version of the story, maybe that solution makes a lot of sense.

This is a band-aid solution to a hemorrhage. Sure, it would make malpractice rates more affordable for the doctors, but the root cause of high malpractice isn't addressed. What *is* the real reason for high malpractice suits? Are lawyers running amok? Is the inappropriate use of technology causing more harm than good? Have OBs implied an ability to "deliver" what Nature cannot—perfection—and are now reaping the results of such hubris? Is it due to generations, now becoming parents, raised on an attitude that abdicating responsibility is a way to free one's conscience? What about true malpractice? In cases of true malice or negligence, what recourse should a parent have?

The model for reform that AGOC proposes has origins in California, where we are assured it 'works'. Works for whom? Are we to assume for mothers and babies?

In California at Madera County Hospital, during a three-year experiment in which midwives managed the vast majority of births, the neonatal death rate was reduced to less than half of what it had been for the obstetrician managed births. The California Medical Association opposed the program and it was subsequently terminated. OBs again assumed control of births, and over the next 2 ½ years neonatal death rates tripled. (5)

Poor outcomes provoke lawsuits. Is it any wonder California would initiate tort reform to place a ceiling on damages that can be awarded to parents who see no alternative but to seek compensation for their pain and suffering that was, in all probability, avoidable? Are we to believe that *parents* consider such reforms "successful"?

The tort reform proposed is predicated on the assumption that the United States is one of the safest places to give birth due to the plethora of modern technology used. Which you should now know is not true. If it were, simply limiting the dollar amount parents of damaged or dead children could collect would be a workable solution. If the resolution of our 'health care crisis' only means making sure obstetricians are adequately paid, then certainly ACOG's recommendations are the answer. If, however, the objective is to make maternity care in the US safer, as the ACOG spin implies in the media coverage, first we must address the false assumptions the public has about the state of US obstetrical care.

Some people might be surprised to learn that there has been no reduction in the maternal death rate in the U.S. since 1982 (6) when many of the current routine interventions came into common usage, or that most birth technology is not only *not* useful to healthy mothers, but in some cases proven harmful. (7 8)

It seems to me, an educated lay-person, that even if the problem *were* as simple as outrageous insurance premiums due to out of control litigation, the solution would be to find out why there is a problem and fix it.

So, *is* ACOGs solution to reduce cesareans by adopting the proven midwifery model of care?

No. In fact, ACOG resist well documented proposed improvements in US maternity care that might effect the financial bottom line of their members.
The problem is far more complicated than doctors facing high malpractice rates. While targeting the real source of high malpractice is imperative to the solution, it is *not* the solution.

It has been argued by some that lawsuits are not the appropriate way to solve the dilemma of negligent or abusive practices. It is too little, too late. Not only that, but it punishes the competent OBs (and their clients) as well as the incompetent. All of this is true, but what is the alternative?

We need to become knowledgeable consumers for the sake of our babies. We need to move from a system that punishes everyone, to a system that rewards the greater good.

The ultimate solution needs to incorporate all of the above elements: revamping US maternity care to mirror successful midwifery systems already in existence, establishing cooperative care with ethical and competent obstetricians, and helping mothers to understand the powerful position they occupy in this new triad so that they can affect change before, instead of after, damage occurs. We also need to just accept the fact that doctors are people and people do, on occasion make mistakes. Somehow, our culture has gotten the idiotic idea that if something bad happens to them, someone always owes them money. Doctors have bore the brunt of this thinking and it must stop.

So much of the technology that is used inappropriately is used in the name of defensive medicine. Sometimes bad things just happen. Sometimes bad things even happen because parents make bad choices.

The erroneous beliefs of our birthing system also support a group of professionals whose service is integral to the future of safe maternity care, yet changing how we see birth would necessarily, and substantially, change how we view the profession of obstetrics. A collaborative relationship is imperative for safe and effective care.

Hospitals should be available in the capacity that hospitals are available to people in all other areas of healthcare....for the sick and injured. Meaning that only medically indicated technology would be covered by insurance and government programs. Any technology or treatment not scientifically proven in efficacy or safety could still be accessed with the same ease as now, but would be paid for by the parents out of pocket.

As it stands now, I'm appalled that more mothers will get c-sections than breast cancer (9), yet we have no celebrity spokesperson or national cesarean prevention month. Current unproven obstetrical practice continues unchecked.

With some adjustments to the current system, cesarean rates would go down, more women would start to tell of their empowering, joyful births as precious few mothers do now and mothers could bond with their babies more fully which would lead to higher breastfeeding rates. The amount of money our country could save in healthcare costs from these changes is staggering.

Supporting all safe options in birth is important in a free society. Just as important is ensuring that all options are safe. Our babies depend on us to make decisions for them that will determine the quality of their lives. The least we can do for them is know what the truth is and be clear on why we are making the decisions we do. Is it from a place of informed consumerism and honesty...or fear and misinformation?

An even harder question is how we can change a system that doesn't want to change?

I say it begins with forgiveness. I don't believe all of this is happening because of some sweeping generalization that all obstetricians are bad. I do think many of them are very afraid. They understand how powerful mothers could be if they knew that they held all the cards. By keeping women afraid, they make themselves indispensable, and, so the thinking goes, if they can limit damage awards or restrict the availability of the competition, (10) they can remain 'safe'.

Success is based on results. Their strategy is not working. Their fear of lawsuits, and the defensive medicine that stems from that fear, is only drawing to them more of that which they fear.

It's time to stop this madness. We need to call a truce amongst all parties and devise a plan that will work for everyone.

I propose that the only way to do that is through forgiveness. Anger, blame and mistrust are only hurting those that harbor and feed them. They change who we are, how we perceive the world and how we relate to others. They will become all consuming if we allow it, poisoning our relationships with our partners and children.

These ugly emotions, no matter how justified they may be, affect us physically as well. Anger and fear both trigger the fight or flight response. Stress hormones, like adrenaline, flood our bodies. These stress hormones do cross the placenta and affect the delicate balance in the baby's brain development. These hormones in birth are counter-productive to birthing hormones, creating pain.

Despite the known effects of stress, mothers are 'tested' incessantly with very little positive return on the effort, (11 12 13) quite possibly causative in the rise in postpartum depression due to the stress it creates.

In reality, some postulate, what we seem to be seeing is actually post-traumatic stress disorder (PTSD), not postpartum depression (PPD). Would that be a reasonable conclusion to draw? Let's look.

PPD symptoms: (14)

> Persistent sadness or depressed mood, loss of interest in ordinary activities, including sex, decreased energy, fatigue, lethargy, sleep disturbances (oversleeping or insomnia), weight gain or loss, lack of concentration, feelings of guilt, hopelessness, worthlessness, suicidal thoughts, irritability and agitation, excessive crying, aches and pains that don't respond to treatment, drug abuse

Some PTSD symptoms: (15)

Inability to control emotions, difficulty managing anger, self-destructive or suicidal thoughts/behaviors, chronic pain, sexual dysfunction, panic, chronic guilt, shame and self-blame, feeling that you are permanently damaged, feeling ineffective, feeling nobody understands you, minimizing the importance of trauma, adopting distorted beliefs about the perpetrator, yourself and what actually happened, idealizing the perpetrator, inability to trust, despair, hopelessness

Not only are the PTSD symptoms eerily similar to the PPD symptoms, but the symptoms listed under PTSD that are absent from the PPD list are actually common to women suffering from PPD. (Whew!) Aside from the research suggesting an overabundance of pitocin (synthetic oxytocin-a nearly universal, and usually unnecessary, obstetrical intervention) has something to do with PPD, the victimization that PTSD sufferers endure is strikingly similar to women with PPD.

I also have to wonder how much misplaced anger plays into PPD? How many have heard new mothers exclaim, as I have, that they are mad at their babies for 'what he did to me' or 'what she put me through', because they erroneously attribute their problems to the birth of that baby. What they are *really* angry about is the obstetrical management of their birth that made it traumatic.
Between the anger, the disconnect that occurs with the disruption of birth hormones in medicated/obstetrical births and sleep deprivation, is it surprising that we are seeing more child abuse as well? Motherhood is challenging enough without added stressors and removal of nature's coping mechanisms!

Since perception is reality, the victimization so many women feel in their births transfers into all areas of their life. (16) This feeling of powerlessness elicits fear. Fear is often experienced as anger. This means millions of mother's have a perception of reality altered by these emotions, to which others react.

A central moment in the life of a woman...that of birthing a child, an act of co-creation with the Divine, is now contaminated, eroding the quality of your emotional and relational life.

In order to ensure that your relationships with your partner and baby (or babies) are not compromised, you must realize that just because you have a right to be angry doesn't mean you have to be. Women who have been harmed by their perceived protectors, maternity care providers, must have the courage to cleanse their hearts and minds of resentment and anger.

Learning how to counter the fight or flight response with the relaxation response early in pregnancy will help you become familiar with the physical difference in how these two responses feel and can only benefit you and the baby.

You cannot give pure, unconditional love if what is in your heart is contaminated by negative emotion. Your baby deserves unadulterated love. You deserve to feel that love for yourself. Forgiveness is the key.

This may seem difficult if your idea of forgiveness requires that the party who hurt you feel remorse over their deed. "Forgiveness" is not contingent on 'closure' and acceptance of responsibility by another party.

First of all, as we've already established, you can only change yourself. You can't change a person who doesn't want to change. Our obstetrical system—and the people within it—don't want to change. Why should they? They have the 'market' monopolized. They have legislation in the works that allows them to cause unlimited damage with impunity. They are accountable to no one and are self-regulated. They aren't required to justify 'standard of care' with evidence, nor are they required to explain why *standard of care* is *substandard care*.

Second, the primary motivational factor in obstetrics is fear. Fear of litigation and fear of 'something going wrong' (which leads back to the first fear) due to a mindset of birth=pathology.

Finally, the rest do what they do because of this belief that birth is a dangerous medical condition. Why would they apologize to anyone if they honestly feel they are just helping? They are doing the best they can with what they have.

As we established early, every action that comes from a faulty core assumption is then flawed to its very core. The facts prove the limiting beliefs—the core assumptions—are wrong, but don't confuse them with the facts. We've already seen you can't change a belief with facts.

No one is going to apologize for the unnecessary deaths of mothers and babies. No one is going to apologize for cystocele, rectoceles or the divorce resulting from a failed sex life stemming from an unnecessary episiotomy. No one is going to apologize for the brain damaged babies suffering 'birth trauma' that had nothing to do with Nature's birth design. It's unrealistic to expect an apology for the hysterectomies performed as a result of the use of pitocin or cytotec. It's simply not going to happen.

Some care providers honestly don't understand the depth of your suffering. Some make a very conscious choice not to see it. Sadly, some don't care.

Regardless, forgiveness isn't about them. It's about us. It's about healing ourselves, choosing to let go of the anger, and accepting responsibility for our own complicity in the hurtful event. It's about refusing to allow the moments of a single event to destroy every moment that follows. It's about putting safety first.

Forgiveness means letting go of expectation that the other party be involved in the healing, but more than that, it means forgiveness of self if we are to own our contribution to the painful birth experience.

That does not mean placing blame on ourselves. It means accepting that you made the choices you made in your birth. If anyone 'did' something to you, face the fact that you allowed it. You chose the consequences when you chose the birth location, the care provider and each intervention.

It may not be fair that bad things happened, especially if you are thinking "...but I didn't know I <u>had</u> a choice!" Unless your last birth was more than 10 years ago, the information has been easily available. Up to 20 years ago, it was available to motivated seekers. It took a choice to not know.

I am aware that it's not easy to accept this idea when we've been conditioned to decry such a comment is 'blaming the victim'. A 14 year-old incest survivor is a victim. There may be a handful of other situation in which a mother has no control, no choices, no options. Mothers of 30 or 40 years ago, before the research and the information age may have been victims. Everyone else made the choices that led to the consequences.

Every non-medical intervention—from breaking of the water to giving medication to cutting healthy tissue for no valid reason—is legally considered assault if you don't give consent. Anything inserted into the vagina is legally rape—unless you consent.

Think about how often we don't recognize this when it comes to birth.

"I wanted a homebirth, but my husband wouldn't let me."
"I wanted a midwife, but my HMO won't cover it."
"Then my doctor broke my water." (or "gave me" or "made me")

Some readers may conclude that by this assertion even more obstetricians should be sued. This would be a faulty conclusion!

The cycle will never stop if we keep trying to solve the problem with a hammer when we need a screwdriver. Lawsuits are not the answer. Taking back our power with forgiveness and empowerment is.

Real forgiveness is not about 'them'; it is about *you*. Forgiveness is about how you will react to an event or behavior...how you will choose to feel. It means doing what you must to preserve your own emotional well-being. It means not giving away your power. It means releasing fear and negativity and refusing to carry what belongs squarely on someone else's shoulders. It doesn't matter if they agree to pick up the load or not. What matters, is that you put it down and walk away. If you don't you allow the other person control over your life each and every day.

If you understand that you don't need the other person's cooperation—that they don't need to apologize or even know about this act of forgiveness—you can turn a painful memory to impetus for positive change. It's about you, not them. It's your choice. It's a birth-day gift to yourself and your baby.

Journal exploration:

The current birth environment is rift with abdication of responsibility and blame. In this exercise, identify those situations that created anger, resentment or frustration in a past birth or your current pregnancy. Once the origin of the trauma is identified, love yourself and your baby enough to let it go. By forgiving yourself and others, you can empower yourself in your current pregnancy instead of letting past events control this outcome.

Start by looking for 'blaming' statements in your own situation. These may be similar to the earlier ones in bold. For doctors and other caregivers, this type of statement might include, "The client insisted."

Realize that others in these situations may have chosen different problem solving techniques and achieved different outcome. All of the sample statements required compliance on the part of another.

Write down as many possible options for each situation as you can think of, with the benefit of hind site and knowledge you may not have had at your disposal at the time of the event.

Now, forgive yourself and the other party for the interactions so you may release negative emotion. You might do this by writing a letter and then burning it. IF it's safe to do so, you may wish to converse with the other person in a constructive way to ensure learning by all parties. You may choose to channel emotion through art, or have a written 'conversation' with the other party, using your left hand for their 'voice' and your right hand for your own 'voice'.

You may visualize the other party sitting in front of you while you tell them everything you need to say. You may also use the CD for release in the Better Birth Pack, take a HypnoBirthing® class, which includes a release of past negativity, or see a certified hypnotherapist.

If the event is one that has changed how you relate to your child or partner, make a conscious effort to heal those relationships, even forging new bonds of love and trust if necessary.

If you allow the feelings of anger to consume you, control you, eat at you, you are only punishing yourself for the transgressions of another.

When you are in pain, possibly suffering from PPD or PTSD, it's hard to believe in the 'what comes around goes around' theory. You may feel totally justified in judging another, and may feel that there is no way they have regrets or feelings about the event too if they aren't acting the way you think they should. It truly is not your place to judge, but it is up to you to be the better person and trust that a higher power, however you conceive of it, will sort it all out in the end. Surrender your burden.

You and your baby are worth whatever it takes to rise above the pain and move ahead. You must have the conviction to create what you want and eliminate what you don't. It's not your concern how this will or won't affect anyone else but you. Realize that circumstances are different now and you are in control.

Notes on Chapter Twelve

1   Nancy Wainer-Cohen
2   Suzanne Arms
3   USA Today, Monday, July 1, 2002, *Feb-up Obstetricians Look For a Way Out*, Rita Rubin
    NBC Nightly News with Tom Brokaw, May 8, 2002, *Some States Facing ob-gyn shortage*
4   What Every Midiwife Should Know About ACOG and VBAC: Critique of ACOG Practice Bulletin No. 5, July 1999, "Vaginal Birth After Previous Cesarean" by Marsden Wagner, MD, MSPH. "ACOG is not a college in the sense of an institution of higher learning, nor is it a scientific body. It is a "professional organization" that in reality is one kind of a trade union. Like every trade union, ACOG has two goals: promote the best interest of its members, and promote a better product (in this case, well-being of women). But if there is conflict between these two goals, the interests of the obstetricians come first."
5   *Reclaiming Our Health*, John Robbins, 1996, pg. 24
6   The Safe Motherhood Quilt Project, www.rememberthemothers.org/inamay.html
7   *Expecting Trouble: The Myth of Prenatal Care in America*, Dr. Thomas Strong, New York University Press, 2000
8   *A Guide to Effective Care in Pregnancy & Childbirth*, 2nd edition, Enkin, Keirse, Renfrew, Neilson, Oxford Medical Publications, 1995
9   1 in 4 women will end up with a surgical birth, 1 in 10 women will be victims of breast cancer. 31 women per 100,000 cesareans will die, 26/100,000 per capita will die from breast cancer.
10 *The Official Plan to Eliminate the Midwife*, www.goodnewsnet.org/safety_issues01/rosenbl11.htm
11 *The Tentative Pregnancy*, Barbara Katz-Rothman
12 *Journal of the American Medical Association*, 1999, 282-147 Thomas Pickering, MD D Phil, FRCP, Director of Integrative and Behavioral Cardiology Program of the Cardiovascular Institute at Mount Sinai School of Medicine, New York
13 *Expecting Trouble...*, Dr. Thomas Strong
14 Effects, Symptoms and Treatments of Postpartum Depression, Lori Ramsey, www.thebabycorner.com/pregnancy/info/preg0123.html
15 Adapted from the PTSD Workbook, Mary Beth Williamson, Ph.D., LCSW, CTS, Soili Poijula, Ph.D., New Harbinger Publications, Inc.
16 *Birth as An American Rite of Passage*, Robbie Davis-Floyd

PART FIVE
REALIZATION

ALL COMPONENTS COME TOGETHER IN THE REALIZATION OF YOUR OWN BEST BIRTH! YOU'VE DONE THE INNER WORK AND YOU'VE SET UP THE SUPPORTIVE CONDITIONS FOR YOUR BIRTH IDEAL TO MANIFEST. THE COMBINATION OF MOTHER'S INTUITION, WOMAN'S WISDOM, NATURE'S DESIGN AND APPROPRIATELY APPLIED TECHNOLOGY COME TOGETHER IN THE BEST WAY POSSIBLE.

In Control

"If you buy the ticket, you take the ride"

Over the years I've seen numerous parents make the effort toward better birth with a strong desire and heartfelt changes, only to have it come apart at the seams. Why? Two reasons, mainly.

One, they are making decisions they know with their heads are right, but their hearts still aren't in it. Beliefs, unconscious fears and faulty assumptions lay in wait for a moment to spring up. Modern obstetric care seems to have a justification for everything, which gives ample opportunity for doubt to creep in.

A mother is encouraged to have an ultrasound at 8 weeks. She's hesitant, having heard their could be risks to early ultrasound including increased miscarriage, but her nurse-midwife tells her that they have to determine a due date. Not knowing that a.) a due date is irrelevant at this point b.) a due date should really be a 'due month' and c.) this will do nothing to change her care, she agrees.

She is told there is 'something possibly wrong with the yolk sac' and she will need another ultrasound at 12 weeks. If there is 'something wrong with the yolk sac' she will probably miscarry. If she doesn't, a resulting anomaly could be serious enough she might be counseled to abort. If she chooses not to, nothing can be done to rectify the situation. So, either way, her care doesn't change.

It *sounds* as if there is medical justification, but there is <u>none</u>. The only justification is of the CYA (cover your _ss) type for her provider.

Liability is of great concern to the provider. There are certain procedures and protocols (in fact most of those regarding hospital birth) that have *nothing*—<u>not one thing</u>—to do with actual safety and everything to do with the CYA advice of a lawyer. (If lawyers are going to practice medicine, maybe we should just cut out the middle-man?)

A woman had a previous cesarean for a failed induction. Her doctor insists that 'for her safety' they will have to induce this time if she goes past her due date, if it looks like the baby will be big (via ultrasound, of course, which can be four pounds off!) or if she doesn't deliver during daylight hours.

Despite that fact that none of these recommendations are evidence based, and in fact are refuted by the very study cited as the reason for the recommendations (which, we are being told, says VBAC is unsafe, when in actuality it says that *chemically induced or augmented, obstetrically 'managed'* birth is unsafe) the mother is convinced that she should concede. After all, it *sounds* like there is a medical indication. Again, it's CYA –not mom's concern.

Just this week a birth story passed my desk of a woman who was induced because her doctor thought she 'looked ready' and by ultrasound her baby looked to be about 8 ½ pounds, which he deemed to be getting 'too big'.

After sufficiently frightening her with dire predictions of a stuck baby, she consented to an induction. The parents felt the doctor was wonderful throughout the whole pregnancy and didn't feel they were pushed into induction at all. As far as the parents were concerned, the doctor was just doing his job and looking out for their best interest. Never mind that induction is notorious for ending in unnecessary cesareans without improving outcomes or that ultrasound is notorious for being highly undependable at weight estimation.

Her baby was born after a difficult labor (again, a known consequence of induction) weighing in at only 6 pounds 10 oz., under 19 inches long, with an estimated gestational age of 35 or 36 weeks. This prematurity was not only preventable, but caused by the doctor. The parents will be lucky if there are no developmental delays for their child, which is the reason we purport to try to <u>prevent</u> premature births.

Another case of preventable prematurity touched on earlier was the woman with twins. Her doctor had warned her throughout her whole pregnancy that she should expect to deliver early. By the time she was 30 weeks along, she was told she 'might not make it to next week'.

Always, the parents are making decisions based on one source of information that is hardly unbiased. It sounds as if there's medical justification, but is there? In pregnancy more than anywhere else it's important to seek out other sources of information and second opinions, yet it is precisely here that such investigation into your own health and well being is most discouraged. Why?

Chapters leading up to this point have laid out a plan for avoiding the pit falls the above parents encountered, so you are one step ahead in this area. But what of those parents at the beginning of the chapter who tried so hard and were still sabotaged? What is the other reason the best laid plans were laid to waste?

They were trying to fit a square peg into a round hole. This behavior comes from underlying fear, the 'just in case' mentality, but it's the act of trying to make the medical model fit the midwifery model—or maybe even thinking that it's *possible*—that creates problems.

It sounds something like this..."I know birth is a healthy, natural process, but [now ignore that and listen to what I really believe] we want to have our first baby with Dr. So-and-so, just in case something happens." Thus, ensuring 'something' will happen, simply by the law of probability.

It usually plays out something like this:

Mr. & Mrs. Anybody are enlightened and intelligent expectant parents. They have read a dozen books and are in an independent childbirth class. They learn about informed consumerism, evidence-based care and the consequences of inappropriate birth technology.

They make a birth plan. They outline all of the things that are important to them. They take it to their doctor, who barely glances at it and says "Yeah, sure, whatever you want...as long as there are no problems." Sounds reasonable so far, right?

Mr. & Mrs. Anybody know that midwives encourage ambulation (walking in labor) so they ask if that would be allowed for them. "Sure, we want to have you up and about...except for when we need to have you on the monitor, or of course, after you've had your pain relief."

"We won't be using pharmaceuticals." Mr. & Mrs. Anybody remind him.

"Huh?" He looks up from their chart. "Oh, right. Ok, if you say so." He says with a grin.

Midwives provide perineal support, will he? "Of course," he says "unless I see that you really need an episiotomy, at which time I assume you want me to do one instead of letting you rip wide open."

"Certainly!" Mrs. Anyone agrees. He must make that determination. After all, that's why they hired him.

"We'd like the cord to stop pulsing before being cut." The parents request.

"Sure," The doctor amiably replies, "not a problem! Unless, of course, the baby needs to be resuscitated or you are hemorrhaging or something." He says in an off-hand manner as if it happens all the time.

"Of course." The parents say weakly, growing pale in the face as they picture these complications that must be so common that the doctor would mention them.

If 90% of communication is what is between the lines, these parents should be running, not walking, to the nearest exit. Instead, they tell themselves what a good thing it is they chose this doctor who will "let" them do what they want in labor. They have the 'best of both worlds' as far as they are concerned. They push down the feelings of unease that struggle to be acknowledged.

He tells them he is scheduling a triple test for next week, a gestational diabetes test for the week after, and an ultrasound for the week after that.

"We'd like to avoid further routine prenatal testing." The parents again must remind him.

"Of course you do!" he agrees. "I wouldn't suggest these if I didn't think they were important. You see, I'm concerned about your fundal height. The baby might not be growing as well as I'd like, so we need to have that ultrasound (not adding that repeated ultrasound is implicated in intra-uterine growth retardation—the condition he supposedly is looking for). The triple test is probably not really necessary, but it's just a simple blood draw, no problem at all really. Not invasive. No reason not to do it if we can save you heartache down the road (no mention of the fact this test has a high rate of false-positives that could result in immeasurable heartache). Gestational diabetes is treatable. If you have it, wouldn't you want to know so that you could prevent the high rate of stillbirth that occurs with diabetic mothers? (Again, no explaination that the high rate of still birth is with women who have a pre-existing condition or history of diabetes in the family, who may be exhibiting signs or symptoms of manifesting the condition, or that the American Diabetic Associating advises against routine testing of healthy women because there is no improvement in outcomes). If you were my wife, I'd want you to have it."

He's been so cooperative, they go along with it. [I'm resisting the urge to add my own snide comments about his cooperative and congenial nature here.]

One test leads to another. He may even agree that some of the tests aren't necessary...unless. Somehow, there is always a reason, that seems legitimate, to have them done. Each ten-minute visit with Dr. So-and-so builds their relationship on trust and full disclosure [not!—sorry, that time I couldn't resist!] They may get their dream birth, but I wouldn't bet on it. Even if a couple has avoided the vast majority of unnecessary technology though pregnancy, the caregiver who misuses or overuses technology will find a way to justify his presence at the birth somehow by the time all is said and done.

You buy the ticket, you take the ride. As Nancy Wainer-Cohen says "If you don't want surgery, don't go to a surgeon."

It's not fair to the surgeon to expect him to practice midwifery. He's not a midwife. He's not trained in normalcy and he's not geared to sit around doing nothing until he's needed. The medical establishment is based on pathology. He's trained to *do something*...<u>anything</u>!

Going to a hospital and hiring a doctor, but telling them "I'd like it to be as close to a homebirth as possible" (something they hear all the time) is an unrealistic expectation.

Remember, they don't believe homebirth is safe, despite all the contrary evidence that it is. If they did they'd be doing them. You aren't going to change their belief system in the short time span of your pregnancy, so why would their behavior change? You have not altered their underlying assumptions about the very nature of birth and you won't because all around them they see 'evidence' to support their belief. Birth is a very scary event in the hospital. When I have done a string of hospital labor support gigs without homebirths to balance them out, I've started to doubt the safety of birth. I can't blame them if that's all they see. I agree...Yikes! However, I take issue with the fact that those same people will avoid viewing several midwife-attended homebirths or reading any evidence that contradicts their paradigm. It may be true for *them* that birth is dangerous—perception is reality—but as a whole, it isn't supported by fact. It's very difficult for someone who has only operated from this fear base to just let you go happily about your birthing business.

To be insistent that you want all of the amenities of home to fit into the routines and schedules of the hospital and doctor is going to mean behind your back someone is going to be saying "If they want a homebirth so bad, why don't they have one?" I've heard it...I'm not joking. Quite frankly, they have a point.

In some areas, free-standing birth centers fill the gap. The word FREESTANDING is vitally important here. If a birth center is contained within a hospital, or affiliated with a hospital or medical practice, it's most likely obstetrics as usual with pretty rooms and nice ladies.

Have you made out your birth plan? What are the details of your perfect birth? Take a moment, close your eyes, breathe deeply and imagine the perfect birth (the Better Birth Pack has a visualization for the perfect birth).

Where did it take place? Who was there? Does this picture tell you anything about unconscious beliefs you didn't even know you held?

In composing your birth plan (worksheet in WW companion book), what was important to you and why? How does your care provider feel about birth plans? Some online OB message boards are accessible to the general public...it makes for interesting reading about how they really feel. Some just dismiss them. Some are outright hostile to the idea. Some comment that a substantial birth plan is a sure cesarean. Would that be the fault of unrealistic expectations? Or, perhaps these couples are treated differently for expressing their wishes? Both, I believe. What might seem totally reasonable for a home or (freestanding) birthing center birth just doesn't translate well to an institution whose very existence is antithetical to the idea of natural birth.

Unfortunately, at this moment in history, we must pay very close attention to whether the words and actions of our health care representatives match.

There are too many caregivers who have made it abundantly clear that they *will not* change—but they don't want to see that effect their pocketbook so they say what they think you want to hear.

Admitting this ugly truth is cause for some caregivers to protest that advocates of safe and gentle birth are making parents distrustful of their caregivers. This again would be a classic case of shooting the messenger. This book would not exist if these things, sadly, didn't happen all over the country every day.

I am not fostering distrust. What I am encouraging is a healthy discernment. Parents have a right to verification of safety and efficacy. There are caregivers out there who practice more safely than current 'standard of care', which, I will repeat, has been established not by medical evidence, but lawyers. As consumers ask more questions and demand better, more physicians will join those pioneering souls. Until that time, I'd wager that the *good* doctors would be willing to answer a few more questions than usual. The bad doctors don't even have to worry about going hungry...there are millions of women convinced that birth is something it isn't, not to mention the millions of women who don't <u>want</u> to put any effort into their health or their children, as evidenced by the child abuse, neglect and abandonment we see on the news daily. Remember, I'm not forcing anyone to have a great birth...I'm only guiding the ones who are willing to work for it.

Physicians have given consumers no other option. The situation is similar to the innocent priest turning a blind eye to the sexual abuses within the church and protecting the perpetrators. As long as bad doctors are allowed to abuse technology and poor outcomes on the whole are acceptable, parents can sue...or let their voices be heard through their wallets. Short of a whistle-blower lawsuit for the billions this out of control situation is costing the US government, these are the only ways care will improve.

If there is a shift in what parents are willing to accept, good doctors are rewarded. The others can choose to follow or not, but at least it won't be at the expense of you or your baby.

This is not fostering distrust. It's forcing accountability. It's not expecting doctors to be something they aren't or hospitals to do the impossible by being 'just like home'. Hospitals are *not* home. They are places for the sick and injured, filled with highly skilled professionals, that must run efficiently to be effective.

You must decide what you really, truly want if you are going to be able to take steps to get it. You must be specific and you must ask yourself every step of the way if your decision to do this or that to gain your objective is based on fact.

Before now, you may not have thought you had a legitimate chance of having a safe birth that was comfortable too. For a very long time the desire to have a gentle birth has been placed in conflict with the desire for a safe birth (purposely, I might add, because the two are not mutually exclusive by any stretch of the imagination). Mothers have been asked "Are you concerned about a 'good experience' or a live baby?" The two are *very much* <u>interdependent</u>!

Now that you know that, you may still be unsure about how to recognize and articulate exactly what it is you want. If all you've been offered is one of two options, how overwhelming to suddenly realize you can have it *all* if you want.

None-the-less, indecision creates inaction. Inertia. Inertia leads, unintentionally, to undesirable results. Since you probably know exactly what you *don't* want, start where you are.

You don't need to limit this exercise to just your birth. Extend these ideas into early parenthood to give you a head start on what reality you are creating there.

Journal Exploration:

On the left, make a list of what you don't want. For every item on the list, create a positive affirmation on the right. For example:

I don't want a cesarean!   *My body is designed, and I am capable, of birthing gently and comfortably.*

Then, for each item, list something that you are doing (can do or will do) to manifest what is on the right instead of what is on the left. For instance, "I will interview caregivers until I find one who supports my efforts in word and deed."

Our brains have difficulty with "negatives" so use positive language in your right hand column. What do you see in your minds eye if I say "The child did not fall down the stairs." Or, "The dog did not chase the cat." First you probably saw the child fall down the stairs or the dog chasing the cat before you could negate it. Again, for the above example, "I won't let anyone cut me!" is not appropriate, first because of it's negative language, but also because it's absolute. Always keep in mind, the message is not to avoid technology at all costs, but only inappropriate technology that carries more risk than benefit.

You'll only get as much as you ask for and no more, so ask for the moon. If a series of events outside of your control alter what is possible, you are still striving for your own best ideal, but you need to identify what you want, make a plan for how you can make it happen and put the effort toward the desired outcome. No one else will do any of this for you. The world in general doesn't care if you have your ideal birth. Your childbirth educator shouldn't be working harder or putting more hours into your birth than you are. Your caregiver certainly won't put more time and effort into you birth than you. They shouldn't have to. It's your baby, your body, your life, your responsibility.

Having said that, be careful what you wish for. Your subconscious mind can take you very literally sometimes. If you keep telling yourself that all you want is a fast labor, you just may get a half hour birth that hits hard, fast, and furious.

You may think that's what you want, but mothers who are in the midst of a precipitous (very fast) labor don't *know* it's only going to last a half hour.

Fear that the intensity could last indefinitely can engage the fear/tension/pain cycle, turning what might have been one painful contraction in a nearly painless birth into many in a painful one. If you still think your idea birth is fast, you may want to add 'comfortable' to your list of wants...and then plan to have your baby at home with a skilled caregiver so that you don't end up birthing in your car on the freeway with the help of a 911 operator. See what I mean about thinking this through carefully?

Also, remember that this ideal birth you'd like to plan has a time limitation. You have nine months or less to optimize your health, choose a caregiver that will contribute to your experience without contaminating it, decide on birth location and become educated on the postpartum issues that round out the 4th "trimester" of your childbearing year. Take the time to learn about the seemingly endless decisions you'll face after the birth. These can't wait until the last minute.

In order to avoid regret over any of these decisions, use the same tools you have learned in this book to create your birth. Many of these first decisions are often not made in conscious awareness. A great deal of myth and misconception surrounds each of the ones I've mentioned and I've only touched the tip of the ice burg. The subjects are too vast to elaborate on here, but I have given them a space in WW, the companion book to MI.

The moments immediately following birth are primary. While it's true we don't bond with the first object we see like a gosling, the first interactions are vitally important to the developmental changes meant to occur within the mothers birthing brain and the baby's. Neurological connections are being made now, including the number of new brain cells being produced through a complex mix of baby's first interactions, protection from chemical alteration and the presence of certain substances within the mother's milk. (1)

Yes, mothers who are drugged during birth or who don't breast feed love their babies. The bond is different, however. (*Please* note: I did *not* say 'less'...only different.) Mothers who have done it both ways attest to this. We aren't being honest with ourselves if we insist "I had narcotics in labor and bottle fed artificial baby formula and my feelings for my baby are <u>exactly</u> the same as a mother who had no alteration of brain chemistry and who makes a life-sustaining substance from her own body for her baby every moment of every day!"

The irony is, the mothers who would say this are the same ones who complain that it took them months to fall in love with their baby and that this bonding thing is all a farce in the very next breath. They'd rather blame nature than admit they started out at with a deficit they must compensate for. If they haven't done it another way, they can't possibly know if there is a difference, which mothers who have insist there is. Science says there's a difference. Nature provided us with the same chemicals and instincts for the protection of our offspring as were provided to other mammals. Other mammals will reject their offspring, refuse to protect them, even attack them, if the first moments of birth are disrupted and nursing of babies is prevented. This is biology, not an opinion.

Baby's first days, weeks and months lay the foundation for how they will learn, how they relate to the world, how big their brains will be, what disease they will be susceptible to and even how fat or thin they will be as adults. These are not things to be taken lightly or to 'worry about later'. (2)

There is a window of opportunity, from birth to three years, that never, *ever* opens again. It would be devastating to learn the ramification of careless choices too late.

This requires prioritizing, focused intent and adaptability to manage in a timely fashion. You must discover what's meaningful and important—not just in the short term, but the long term over a lifetime.

· What do you want for your child? For yourself? Not in vague terms like "I only want her to be happy." What would happiness mean? How does it feel? It sounds like a simple question, but to one person happiness is security, while another is adventure. A

155 pound four year-old didn't suddenly expand when he turned four. Certainly, what the child eats *as* a four year-old and the amount of movement he engages in, supports his overweight condition, there is no doubt. The anguish the mother of this child feels and the health problems this child faces very likely has it's roots in the very first substance that child was given...either sugar water or formula. Does that mean that all formula fed infants will be fat adults? It depends on if the rest of their life contributes to the original damage or not. It depends on genetics. It depends on a lot of things, but giving our infants nothing but the equivalent of baby junk-food through the most highly formative period of their life ensures they have three strikes against them. This has become such a huge problem (pun intended) that we have children getting gastric by-pass surgery.

· How do you get to where you want to be? If happiness for you is a close knit, loving family, sitting around the fire playing games on family game night, you must build that brick by brick. Do you think you will have a close relationship if your child has spend 80% of their waking hours with someone else?

· If you had your ideal, how does it differ from now? How can you make it happen? Are your proposed parenting choices propelling or impeding your efforts?

If you can't answer these questions right this minute, you're going to need to peddle faster. You have serious work to do. Your birth is not something you can 'plan' to coast through...parenthood even less so.

Reach for the sky, keeping your feet on firmly planted on the ground.

It's ok to admit you want this once in a lifetime event to be peaceful, comfortable and empowering. "Safe" fits into all of those. If you have one of those exceedingly rare complications of pregnancy, your field of possibilities may narrow, but it should not be obliterated.

Keep in mind that many variations of normal are now used as excuses to cut babies out, even when outcomes haven't improved with the effort. If you want to keep your vision of a better birth in mind, you have to know the difference between a variation and a true complication. You have to know if something like a malpresentation is preventable, fixable or workable. You need to be willing to get a second opinion on subjective things like 'too big' of a baby, 'too small' of a pelvis, 'too much' water, 'too little' water. You must be knowledgeable about things like fundal height so that if you are told it's too high or too low you know what simple things, such as the baby's position, can affect it. You need to be aware (and believe!) that being pregnant 42 or even 43 weeks is perfectly fine as long as you and the baby are healthy and that there *are* non-invasive ways to assess fetal well-being.

Don't depend on luck when it comes to your life or that of your baby's. Knowing *why* you want something is as important as knowing *what* you want. "I want a natural birth" can mean you want your baby's brain free from chemicals that may alter his brain structure. It may mean you want to feel the strength, pride and sense of accomplishment a natural labor rewards one with. It could just mean you are afraid of surgery. Move toward something you want, instead of running away from what you don't.

To some women 'natural' encompasses, albeit by stretching the limits of the English language, any tool that keeps them comfortable, while other women—believe it or not—would rather feel pain. There are payoffs for all of these women for the experience they choose.

The following conversation has taken place with countless variables. Twins, breech, cesarean, induction, you name it. I'll use VBAC for this example because it's a hot topic in the news these days.

Childbirth Educator (CBE): In considering your birth preferences, have you decided what's important to you for this birth?
Parent: I want a vaginal birth, if at all possible. Recovery was very hard after my section and I didn't feel really bonded with my baby for nearly a year. I got depressed and everything.
CBE: What efforts have you made toward that goal?
Parent: Well, I've talked to my doctor about it and he encourages it, as long as nothing goes wrong. I'm just not sure I should get my hopes up. I mean, my OB is really nice and all. He wants this for me as much as I do. But, the cesarean for my last child was because the induction didn't work, and my doctor says if I go past my due date, he'll have to induce me, or if the baby gets to big, he'll induce. It's hospital policy that if I don't go into labor during daylight hours while the anesthesiologist is there, or if I'm in labor but it doesn't look like I'll deliver before he goes home, that they will just do the cesarean.
CBE: How would you feel if this birth were to be similar to your last birth?
Parent: I just couldn't stand it! If I get that depressed again I'm going to ask for an anti-depressant, even if it means I have to stop breastfeeding, if I even <u>can</u> breastfeed. It was so hard before. But, I'd deal with it, you know. You have to. You just wonder if there was something you could have done different. You know, disappointed, but you have to do what's best for the baby. That's all that matters...a healthy baby.
CBE: So what you really want is what is safest for you and the baby, preferably emotionally satisfying as well?
Parent: Yeah. I'm just afraid I won't meet all of the conditions that my doctor feels are important for our safety.
CBE: Would those be the conditions you just mentioned?
Parent: Yes. Plus, he says I have to have an epidural because if there is an emergency, they don't want to have to wait to place one. And, of course we have to have continuous electronic fetal monitoring in case of uterine rupture.

CBE: So what do you know about each of those interventions and their affect on labor? What would have to happen for you to be able to avoid those interventions that are known to increase surgical deliveries without any demonstrable benefits to outcomes with their use. (3)

Parent: I don't know. I guess I don't have a choice. My doctor won't do it without all of these conditions. I think it's hospital policy or something. (sounding distraught) See! I knew I couldn't do it.

CBE: Why would you feel a sense of failure on your part? Are these conditions in your best interest and based on fact? Do you have control over any of these conditions?

Parent: (perplexed) I don't know. I guess I don't have much control, if any, over them. But they must have these rules for a reason. I know my doctor wouldn't do it if he didn't have to. I mean, he's helped a lot of women have VBACs, so they must be Ok.

CBE: What percentage of his VABC mothers actually have vaginal births?

Parent: (sounding angry) I don't know! A lot, I'm sure. He's a very good doctor! What do you think I should do? (crying)

CBE: You have hard decisions to make. I can help you access the information you need to make evidence-based decisions, but you have to do the work and make the hard choices.

Parent: Do you think my doctor is a bad doctor? (sounding defensive)

CBE: My job is to help parents make their own best decisions using the latest scientific literature available. I don't know your doctor. I only know what the evidence says. In order to help you clarify if you are on the path to have the birth you say you want, why don't you tell me how you would feel if your dream of a natural birth were realized?

Parent: Proud of myself. Happy. Strong. Capable. I assume physically better. Glad that I did the best I could.

CBE: So, You'd like to feel whole, proud, fulfilled, strong and empowered?

Parent: Yes! Then I could connect with my baby better. Maybe I could feel like I didn't fail as a woman and I could concentrate on being a mother instead of dealing with depression and healing from surgery.

CBE: What do you need to do to maximize the possibility of that outcome?

Parent: If it's going to happen, I guess it's up to me. I'll look into those interventions my doctor insists on, and if they aren't in our best interest and based on fact, I won't agree to them. I hope I don't have to, but if he won't work with us, I'll change doctors and find someone who will.

You may have guessed that this fictional account flows to it's logical conclusion, whereas in reality, it usually ends at "I don't know...what do you think I should do?" because the CBE won't take responsibility for the birth. It wouldn't matter if the CBE gave her a point by point strategic disassemble of everything that was wrong with the illogic behind that conversation and a bulleted list of what the mom could do to change it...she still wouldn't do it. I know, I've tried! Silly me, I thought when I was asked for advice I was actually supposed to give it and the people who asked actually asked because they wanted to follow it!

Women know down in their heart what's right. It is their mother's intuition and it guides them well...if they would only listen.

Listen to your heart and the small voice within. Don't be deterred from what you know is best for you and your baby.

Journal Exploration:

Ask yourself the hard questions—and keep asking until the answers are clear. What do you want? Why do you want it? What do you have to do to get it? Are your choices based on fact or belief? Are all of your choices in your best interest and the best interest of your child? What must you do to get what you want? How will it feel when you get it? How will if feel if you don't? How might it affect the rest of your life?

Be specific in defining your objectives for this birth in as many ways possible. You will develop a clearer understanding of what you want. As a result, your choices will be more goal-oriented and your success more likely.

Once you know what you want and how to get it, and have set up your environment to support it, you need to step up and affirm your right to have it. Birth is a rite of passage that is the birthright of every woman. Be willing to allow yourself to say "I deserve this!"

There are, unfortunately, people out there who have a stake in what you think, feel and believe about birth and early parenting. Your thoughts control their bottom line. That honestly, not pessimism.

If you have the strength and resolve to believe you deserve to get what you want, you make possible what others see as impossible. If you make your choices based on fact and stick to your guns, the improbable becomes probable. Then, even if your outcome falls short of your ideal, you can be free of guilt or regret. You will know you have done everything in your power to make your own best choices.

If you've spent your whole life settling for less, it may feel unnatural to take a stance on excellence, consider it your first act of motherhood...protecting your young, ensuring that *your* baby has only the very best.

I'm not talking material goods. I mean the very best of *you*, because you are acting on their behalf as a whole and competent person. It means taking the step from mediocrity to excellence consciously by resolving that *your* child won't have to settle for second best in a parent. Require the very best of yourself.

Consider if you were able to hand pick the parent who would raise your child if you couldn't. What qualities, characteristics and behaviors would you expect? Would it be good enough to just keep the kid alive, or would you expect interaction that would nurture body, mind, and soul? Would minimum contact be enough, or would you want loving contact? Is impatient, distracted communication enough, or would you want respectful, meaningful exchanges?

Do you meet the criteria you would expect of another? Resolve now to do what it takes to ensure the emotional, spiritual and physical best for your child. It may inconvenience some people who might be irritated that you won't "just do what everyone else does". How many of those people love that precious little being growing inside you as much as you do?

Is your sweet baby worth a little extra effort? A little bit of sacrifice? Is your baby worth going the extra mile? How many opportunities do you think you get to impact the world through direct action? It's a wonderful life. Make it count.

Notes on Chapter Thirteen

1   *Mothering the Mother* and *Maternal-Infant Bonding* by Klaus, Kennel &
Klaus. These doctors have done extensive research on the importance of bonding
as well as the mechanisms of bonding and the consequences of disruption of the
process.
    The Scientification of Love, Dr. Michael Odent
2   *Tracing the Roots of Violence*, Robin Karr-Morse and Meredith S. Wiley,
     Atlantic Monthly Press 1997
     Magical Child, Joseph Chilton Pearce, Plume Books, 1992
     The Continuum Concept, Jean Liedloff, Addison-Wesley Publishing, 1995
     Mother Nature, A History of Mothers, Infants, and Natural Selection, Sarah
Blaffer Hrdy, Pantheon Books, 1999
3   ALL OF THE INTERVENTIONS REQUIRED IN THIS EXAMPLE
     NEGATIVELY AFFECT LABOR WITH NO DEMONSTRABLE
     BENEFITS TO OUTCOMES.

DREAM IT, DO IT

By now, I hope you've become convinced that birth can be anything from orgasmic to manageably sufferable and everything in between.

Most of what we experience arises directly from those beliefs and expectations about birth from which we make our decisions. A small percentage of undesirable outcomes result naturally, but far more are happening that are preventable.

The variables are endless, the experience, subjective. The promise of this book is that you can create better birth—better than what our culture at large is experiencing, better than what you would create if all of your actions were dictated by unconscious motivations stemming from faulty core assumptions.

It assumes no choice inherently right or wrong in every situation, only that purity of intent be the assessment tool by which an action in measured.

It passes no judgment on a particular caregiver, action or birth location...only on unsubstantiated claims of safety and efficacy.

Knowledge is power...knowledge of the system, knowledge of the process, knowledge of your self. When I teach a childbirth class, I begin with the question "How much of the childbirth and parenting information you feel you need do you expect to be provided from this class." The response is often 75-100%! This is a totally unrealistic expectation! With an eight-hour investment of their time, they expect to learn what should actually take at least a year!

In compiling this book I had to set aside enough information for space considerations that a whole separate book was born to be a companion to this one.

I do not claim to have all of the answers. I do not expect anyone to substitute my considered opinion for their own convictions. I do expect them to become aware of whether or not those assumptions are based on fact or fiction and are in their own best interest.

I am confident that with Better Birth Basics you can create your own best birth. I encourage you to explore the recommended reading and independent childbirth classes. Some sources are better than others. If a source has a vested interest in influencing your choices, it should be deemed secondary to independent sources. This is an organizational conflict of interest, yet this is the source parent's have singularly depended on for years.

Throughout this book you have eliminated inconsistencies in what you believe you can achieve and what you want to have. You know what is clearly within your control. You know that what you experience in the first few months as a mother is directly related to what you experience in birth. In order to attain the highest success for yourself in birth, you need to assess where you stand.

Journal Exploration:

Rate where you are in relation to your ideal. On a scale of one to ten, with one feeling unsure or afraid and ten being fully confident, decide if your words and actions are representative of your feelings.

On your scale, circle your ideal, place a mark over where you feel you actually are. For example:

□

I know all I can know about prenatal testing   1 2 3 Ø 5 6 7 8 9 (10)
to make my own best decisions about them.

In this instance, I may not feel it's realistic to ever know enough, but in being honest with myself, I admit I haven't really made much of an effort.

Now it's your turn.
I understand the purpose behind routine   1 2 3 4 5 6 7 8 9 10
prenatal testing that I am encouraged to have

I am aware of the accuracy rate of these   1 2 3 4 5 6 7 8 9 10
recommended tests

I am confident my care provider uses   1 2 3 4 5 6 7 8 9 10
technology appropriately

I trust that I am able to give true informed   1 2 3 4 5 6 7 8 9 10
consent for recommended interventions

I have researched all viable options for   1 2 3 4 5 6 7 8 9 10
safe birth locations for my situation, and
have evaluated them fairly.

I know the pros and cons of all of the   1 2 3 4 5 6 7 8 9 10
parenting choices I will face after the birth
(vaccination, circumcision, feeding, etc.)

I am aware of the importance of brain   1 2 3 4 5 6 7 8 9 10
development from birth to three years,
and have done everything I can to
optimize my child's potential.

Continue on your own. Make a list of what you feel are the ideal characteristics of a good parent. Then decide how close you are to reaching your ideal. If you fall short of your ideal, make a checklist of what you might do to bring you closer to your ideal.

How many of these actions can you actually take? How might you have to re-prioritize to make sure they *can* happen? Are your ideals realistic? Have others been able to achieve these ideals and how did they do it? Are their situations similar to yours or can you re-structure your life to be similar to those you wish to emulate? If the circumstances are different and you are unable to make significant changes, are there other ways to make your goal a reality by doing the best you can with what you have?

If there is still a wiggly feeling that resembles guilt, ask yourself if you are being brutally honest with yourself about whether it's a matter of 'can't' or 'won't'. No one is judging you during this exercise. No one can see what's in your heart but you. If your mother's intuition is telling you something, it's a private communication to you and you alone.

If you are doing the best you can with what you have, take pride in that. Do not *compare* yourself with anyone else. Rather, use your perception of others to try to get an idea of how reasonable you are being about your situation.

Remember that often what we think is true about others is only an illusion. All that matters is your own intent; your own motivation; your own assessment of what you are capable of. That inner voice may *not* be guilt...it may be sadness that you cannot provide what you feel best. Or, it *might* be guilt. Is it justified? Do you have options that bring you closer to your ideal, but you aren't choosing them because you are confusing a <u>want</u> with a <u>need</u>? Is this discrepancy something you can live with, or will it tear you apart with every reminder that you didn't rise to your own potential for the sake of your child? People have achieved greatness against seemingly impossible odds. A parent who wants to excel at parenthood is certainly capable if they make it a priority.

Journal exploration:

Another way to see if your words and actions are in sync is to make a list of your priorities, and then take a close look at how you allot your time. Where do you focus your energy?

Your list of priorities might look like this:

My baby
My health
My partner/relationship
My job

Your actual time expenditure might look like this:

My baby: 15 min. prenatal visit, once a month, tests, 2 hours a week of classes, 4 weeks.
My health: healthy meal planning/shopping/preparing, exercise, time alone 2 hrs/wk
My partner/relationship: Too busy. Sunday afternoons we have all day, but we have to do laundry, clean the house, etc.
My job: 45 hours/wk.

By doing this exercise, it becomes very clear where our words and deeds diverge.

Once it's clear where the discrepancies are, you have the choice of reassessing your stated priorities in relation to your real priorities, or you can realign your investment to reflect your priorities.

Preparing--bringing your priorities and your attention together.

Prenatally, this can be put to work by making a birth plan and then ensuring that your actions bring about optimal results. It's imperative to lay the groundwork for your birth preferences early. A caregiver cannot honor your birth plan if you have set up conditions that require the use of the things you say you don't want.

Use a multitude of resources to construct your birth plan. You can learn about your options through a number of places, including the internet, books, and classes. Woman's Wisdom contains an entire chapter on the construction of an effective birth plan, but the following guidelines will be useful:

- **Keep it short.** Midwives, Doctors and Nurses are very busy and often won't even have a chance to get through anything over a page or two.
- **Be polite.** This isn't a list of demands, it's the ideal picture you have in mind for your birth. Request nicely and make sure you thank your birth team in advance for their help in creating this ideal.
- **Be clear that you are flexible.** Again, this is your wish list for your birth, but it's important that you let your care providers know that in the case of true medical indication, you are certainly willing to alter it. You have the right (and responsibility) to understand the rational for any intervention you agree to...this is called informed consent and it is for the protection of both you and your provider. You may ask about the perceived problem, why it is a problem, what the treatment might be, what the side effects are and if there are alternatives. In the event of a time sensitive emergency, you may get an abbreviated reply, so it is wise to be familiar with possible interventions and the medical indications beforehand. *The Thinking Woman's Guide to Better Birth*, by Henci Goer is a good resource.
- **Be clear in your reasoning.** You don't have to fill your birth plan with medical journal abstracts, but be prepared to back up your choices with language they are familiar with from their own periodicals. They have little patience for people who want to go against protocol 'just because'. Let them know that there are solid reasons behind your

choices, that you choices are safe and that they are supported by evidence. Henci Goer has compiled just such a resource in a book with scientific evidence from medical journals called *Obstetric Myths versus Research Realities* that can help you.

- **Use Positive Language.** Fill the plan with what you do prefer, not what you don't want. By keeping the tone of your birth plan positive, respectful and reasonable, you will very likely be able to create a unified birth team and have a safe and satisfying birth experience.

Balancing the external effort with the internal desire is important. The Better Birth Pack includes a CD with a visualization for a gentle water birth.

Your perfect birth visualization might be something completely different. If you choose to construct your own visualization, it is important to make sure that it contains the elements required to elicit the relaxation response discussed previously. If you have set up your environment to support and maintain the relaxation response throughout a normal, natural birth, it's quite possible that a painless birth, or at least relatively comfortable birth, may be expected. However, it's important to understand that going it alone will probably be less effective than using a program that has worked for thousands of women.

This birth belongs to you alone. The events of your birth-day will rest in your heart...either sustaining or haunting. You are accountable only to your own heart...and to your child.

Putting it all together

You've done great work! You should now have a plan in mind and the courage to implement it. Let's get particular about how to put it into action.

First, specifically define your desired outcome in behavioral terms. Not "All I want is a healthy baby", but how you plan to behave your way to a healthy baby.

If your better birth were just a pipe dream, it would be alright to be vague. "I want a natural birth" is wide open to interpretation. If you want it to happen, it's necessary to paint a picture for your subconscious mind and use enough detail so that you can clearly define the required steps to reach it.

For instance, does "I want a natural birth" mean you want a drug free birth? A painless birth? Does it mean you are only willing to commit to draw on your own reserves for a set amount of time before you allow yourself to make a determination that you are willing to ask for drugs? You'll need to define your objective and then figure out how it can best be accomplished. What will you need to do...or not do? How will you know it's happening the way you want before, during, and after? What is the emotional impact of doing your birth, your way?

Next, decide you will evaluate your progress in realizing your dream birth. In the above example, to have your natural birth, where would you have to plan to give birth? Who would you allow at your birth? Which caregiver? Would you have a doula? Is your partner contributing positively to your effort? What needs to be done to get everyone on the same page? What comfort measures will you stock your 'bag of tricks' with?

How do you think you'll behave your way to your goal? How much time do you need to allocate to this endeavor every single day? Create a schedule for yourself in which you can take 'baby steps'.

Idea:

Purchase small children's snap together beads or color coated paper clips. String them end-to-end in mental increments of one bead for each week of your pregnancy, or other workable chunks of time to reach your pregnancy goals. For example, if you use weeks, and you begin at 12 weeks gestation, you will have 32 beads, remembering that 40 weeks is merely and average and that 42 weeks is perfectly normal. Only 5% of women actually birth on their 'due date'.

Approach each week as a celebration, with tangible efforts and rewards for being a part of the procreative process. Each week make a promise to take three actions that would be required to achieve your perfect birth. Use a body, mind, spirit approach. What can you physically do to increase the odds of a natural birth? Stop smoking? Exercise? Visit a nutritionist? Take a pregnancy yoga class?

What can you do to educate yourself? Take a class? Read a book per week? Think about your birth plan and create an outline?

Remember your spirit...honor your role as a co-creator in this most sacred task of creating a human being. You may want to visit a certified hypnotherapist to clear away any trauma from your own birth or a past birth. You may want to journal, forgive a parent or explore your special connection with the Divine through art. Write it down, manifest your reality.

If you have five different bead colors, use them to create a repeating pattern, then use corresponding colors of markers or pens to write down what you promise to do on each week you remove another bead.

In order to avoid getting discouraged, map out only what you control and remain flexible. You control the state of your health (in large measure), your emotions, who you hire or fire in your maternity care, where you will plan to give birth. You cannot control the actions of others (though you have complete control over what you will put up with), you cannot control the weather and in <u>very rare</u> instances, Mother Nature will throw you a curve for which you will have to alter your plans. If this happens, it does not mean all is lost! It means this is your first of many lessons in patience and adaptability that comes with being a parent.

Flexibility requires a good working knowledge of your possible obstacles and resources. Take a proactive approach to dealing with any hindrances that might occur. Set up your environment to support your efforts. Make "Because I'm the mommy, that's why!" your mantra!

Be gentle with yourself, but not permissive. Don't take a guilt trip if you don't meet a goal one week...but also don't allow breaking promises to yourself, your baby and your partner become a habit. Feel good about doing your best as long as you are making positive progress. Have the insight and initiative to take charge of what you have control over and accept that which you don't.

This is a good place to pull your partner in to help you stay true to yourself. Be sure to communicate clearly that what you need is a sympathetic team player...not a warden or baby sitter. If you know someone is keeping tabs on your efforts, you are more likely to self-monitor. However, you don't need someone following you around with a notebook recording each bite you take, stocking the pantry goodies you are trying to avoid, or telling you to get more sleep, then demanding to know why his underwear hasn't been washed!

Taking these last steps may be leaving you feeling empowered, but overwhelmed. Excited, but anxious. It's liberating to know that your options are more plentiful than you imagined, but scary that there are so many choices. Knowing that you are the determining factor in the sort of experience you create can be terrifying as well as exhilarating.

I haven't sugar coated anything. At times the perception may be that some observations are politically incorrect, but we can't afford to step around accountability issues anymore. Too many mothers and babies are suffering.

Even so, you are not being asked to substitute my observations for your own. I'm not in your shoes. All I can do is share the information, which is neutral in and of itself. If you don't agree with the data, it may not seem neutral to you, but apply the standards set forth in previous chapters to test validity.

Only by examining your beliefs—and questioning mine—will you be able to decide if you are part of the silent and exceedingly sad epidemic of birthing apathy that has resulting in unacceptable national statistics and troubling social tribulations.

Midwives often say we birth as we live. I say, it's the other way around. All areas of our life, beginning with our issues of self-worth, are affected by how we give birth.

You may still choose trial and error methods, hoping that you have a nice birth and accepting the penalty for not understanding the game. That's your prerogative. I believe in mothers. I think they will rise to their calling if they know they _do_ matter. Devaluing a mother's contribution has left us with a collective despondency that has left mothers with little direction.

I believe that as we lift ourselves up, we gain momentum. Eventually, as we expect more of ourselves, feeling the joy and deep, deep feelings of love and devotion our biology has provided us with to care for our babies, we will reach a point of critical mass. The positive and far-reaching implications will generate changes in our lives that will transform our communities, our country and our world.

You now have the awareness, knowledge and clarity to make this dream reality. What you do with it is up to you. You can learn from the mistakes of the past, or repeat them. You can begin to see synchronicity or ignore it. You can decide to focus on the positive, or let the negative drag you down. Ignoring that it exists makes you easy prey.

Every choice, every thought, every action, every moment of every day, makes up who you are. You are the only one that will ever be. The baby within you is enveloped physically, energetically, emotionally in what you *are*. You are building the body and brain that will be home to your child's soul for a lifetime. You get **one** chance. You are unique. Only you know what is right for you and what results are acceptable. I hope by now you realize that you have special license to be outspoken, non-conformist, choosy and maybe even a little demanding. You are the only one who can speak for your baby, protect your baby, make life decisions for your baby.

Decide that you have a special entitlement as a mother holding generations within you. As long as what you want or need is in accordance with free will and for the good for all, not at the expense of others, you have a right to it. Remember, *intent* makes the difference.

If you let people intimidate or manipulate you into disregarding your mother's intuition, the valuable insights this book could provide are lost. Live your own best life, create your own best birth, love your baby before all else. That is *all* that is important in this life.

If what you've been doing isn't working, change it. If what you are being told doesn't make sense, challenge it. Reject it if it isn't based on fact or not in your best interest. Policies that help your doctor or a hospital avoid malpractice are not your concern. If protocol and procedure is not for the benefit of you and your baby, why submit to it?

Why be cheated out of video of your baby's first moments because your doctor has a fear of litigation...these are your baby's first moments, never to happen ever again! Condition yourself to question those motivations...where is the concern that the doctor might have reason to fear litigation? Why is it when the hospital tour includes expensive and elaborate security measures, including lock down and baby tagging, parents are in awe, instead of being alarmed that such measures would be necessary?

Choose the right attitude and right behaviors to optimize your best results. Study the successes and failures as you perceive them around you. Emulate the successes. Refuse to repeat failure...as you define it. Seek support for your ideals. Believe all things are possible.

Of course there is no actual 'right' or 'wrong', no 'success' or 'failure' other than your own perception. By success I mean emulating that which is beneficial to you, body, mind and soul. By 'failure' I mean that which harms. I'm not implying you should try to be someone you aren't....only the best *you*, you can be.

I am saying that if you look around you will find women who have had joyful, ecstatic or orgasmic and painless births that can be role models if that is the experience you desire.

There are parents that seem 'lucky' because their children are calm, peaceful, smarter than 'average' or hardly ever sick. It isn't an accident and it isn't luck. We know what parenting skills produce those results in un-compromised children. It isn't that luck *never* enters into the equation, but there is a demonstrable cause and affect relationship to nearly every childhood development or behavior.

What is it those parents are doing? It's worth your time to dissect and analyze their strategies. Do you admire their philosophies? Is there an underlying philosophy that their success hinges on? Do you share that attitude or can you adopt it? Do they have a strong commitment and sense of ethics that you respect? Will they take risks to put their children first? Do your children have the same type of personalities as theirs?

Most likely, they share certain parental characteristics that make the difference between exceptional parenting and parenting by default.

They have a firm conceptualization of what it means to be a good parent and what actions they need to take to be that. They aren't afraid of doing what it takes for the sake of their children's well-being.

These parents are sure of what's right for *their* children and why. They don't care what other parents do because they know only *they* live with the consequences of their actions. They are informed before making decisions, so there is no regret or guilt...only learning. They allow their children to unfold at their own pace, developing their own individuality.

Exceptional parents are passionate about what they do. They know there is no job more important than raising children. They don't just give parenthood lip service. They make a real investment of themselves.

They hold themselves to high standards and speak their truth. They feel no need to defend their actions and value any and all information that might help them grow as parents. They understand the demands required to do a job well and accept them.

They meet challenges with flexibility, accepting input on all viable alternatives and reserve the right to change their minds at any time if new information comes along...and do so without apology for doing the best they can with what they have.

Great parents are willing to face the unknown as an adventure instead of a threat. They are willing to grow. Their maxim is "Change is inevitable, growth is optional." They do not see themselves as the shapers of young minds as much as co-learners. They respect their children from the beginning and demand that others treat their children with respect. They honor what their children can teach them.

Strong ties and deep bonding are important in these families. They *like* being together. The parents enjoy their children's company, and value the need for their time as a couple as well as alone time. They orchestrate balance in their lives.

Effective parenting demands that priorities are set and that self-management ensures priorities are kept. They keep promises to themselves and their children from day one. They make sure their actions match their words...because children understand to their core that people show you who they are. Children internalize what you *do*, not what you *say*. Their concepts of self-worth are built on where they fall on your priority list, and their level of self-esteem determines who they become. Yes, they are born with certain aptitudes, but what they will do with them is shaped solely on whether you nurture or corrupt their gifts.

You make a difference! You are a part of a whole. Do not trivialize what you mean to the big picture, or allow anyone else to do so. Take pride in how you approach this special role you've accepted. It's a gift.

(Almost) The Last Word

Throughout this work I have repeatedly referred to 'evidence-based care'. Yet, the book itself is called "*Mother's* Intention". It may seem that there is a dichotomy here, but there isn't. I do not discount mother's intuition or other ways of knowing.

The reason I have insisted on testing the validity of facts is due to the current hypocrisy in which medical authorities dissuade the use of herbal remedies because 'they aren't approved by the FDA' or 'haven't been studied', yet most of the drugs used in obstetrics have not been studied and are not approved.

This same hypocrisy allows doctors to discount traditional midwives or childbirth educators as autonomous practitioners because they don't have a degree, thus, the claim is, their care or advice is not predicated on science...yet nearly every single thing touted as 'standard of care' in obstetrics today is **disproved** by this science they claim so essential. No science is better than _bad_ science.

The Hippocratic Oath, supposed to be a promise to serve, reads in part:

I will apply, for the benefit of the sick, all measures which are required, avoiding those twin traps of over-treatment and therapeutic nihilism.
I will remember that there is art to medicine as well as science, and that warmth, sympathy, and understanding may outweigh the surgeon's knife or the chemist's drug.
My responsibility includes these related problems, if I am to care adequately for the sick.

Excerpted from the oath written in 1964 by Louis Lasagna, Academic Dean of the School of Medicine at Tufts University, and used in many medical schools today.
Both versions found at:
http://www.pbs.org/wgbh/nova/doctors/oath_classical.html

Dr. David Graham in _JAMA_, the Journal of the American Medical Association (12/13/00) states: "The original oath is redolent [evocative, reminiscent] of a covenant, a solemn and binding treaty." Nearly 100 percent of graduating doctors pledge this promise of harming none...so why are so many being harmed?

This oath is supposed to be our promise that if we surrender ourselves to the physician in our most weak and vulnerable of times, our health and well-being will come before personal profit, establishments, ego or HMO.

Who will require more of these who would take such an oath so casually? It's up to us. We must require more of _ourselves_ so that others will be lifted to their own best self. We must do it for the babies. We must honor those who have not lost site of the greater good.

We have the best resources in the developed world. We can be one of the safest places on the planet to birth. We can make it happen.

AFTERWORD

Writing a book is often compared to having a baby. It's a fair comparison.

It takes longer to write a book...and get it published. Having a baby was easier (in my humble opinion) although both processes are gratifying, as is the sense of accomplishment at the end-result.

During the writing of *Mother's Intention*, birthing stories crossed my desk continually. It would be hard to explain the feelings that surfaced as I saw such vivid examples of what happens when unconscious fear dictates action. I would wonder, with great curiosity, how so many mothers whose conscious impetus was safe birth, would insist that there was no time to take a childbirth class, yet frenetically try to 'tie things up' at work or get the baby's room finished. What could cause a caring mother to make unwise choices, resist information that would help her make safer decisions, and prioritize insignificant and trivial concerns above the baby's birth?

As you've already learned, there is a pay-off for our actions or we wouldn't do what we do. I wondered if all the busy work and avoidance of real issues was a distraction tactic. I marveled that, in many cases, it's not just a matter of avoiding exposure to anything that might contradict a belief, but actively putting a considerable amount of energy into avoiding it!

We've explored why parents do such things in great depth throughout this work. By the time I got to the end—here—I began to wonder how many other factors are involved in the millions of women who are willing to settle so cheap and make motherhood so much harder.

What else could make women choose what they are choosing? Other works have explored anthropological and sociological factors. I've heard theories that there could be women who make the experience as hard as possible to prove a point...either to prove they can endure such an ordeal, or to 'prove' joyful birth proponents wrong.

I would venture a guess that there are many women who have such low self-esteem that they feel they don't deserve a wonderful birth, and others who have such low expectations of themselves that they don't want to consider that birth can be amazing, lest they be unable to attain such a 'lofty' ideal. Maybe such a woman would be so insecure that the fear of not being able to 'do it' means they would just rather not even try.

It seems to me, fear and false birth beliefs are still at the root, but what keeps these beliefs alive?

They are actively fed. Consider the example of artificial induction of labor mentioned throughout *Mother's Intention* and the cavalier attitude about it that sabotages an enormous number of parents with the best intent.

Say a woman goes in for a prenatal visit near the end of the pregnancy and during the visit she is given her routine (worthless and dangerous)[2] internal exam which may seem unusually uncomfortable. She may or may not be aware of what has happened, but her care provider has just 'striped her membranes'.

(She also may not know he has a golf outing planned for the weekend--or a New Year's party, or a vacation scheduled--and

---

[2]Expecting Trouble, Dr. Thomas Strong, New York University Press
Obstetric Myths versus Research Realities: A Guide to the Medical Literature, Henci Goer, Bergin & Garvey
A Guide to Effective Care in Pregnancy & Childbirth, Oxford Press
http://www.ican-online.org/resources/wp_pharma.htm
http://www.hencigoer.com/articles/elective_induction/

wants to get this labor started so she won't have her baby while he's away.)

Parents *may* question the wisdom of rushing Mother Nature for convenience, but are often told, "Sure, there could be a small amount of risk...as there is in anything...but we do this all the time and rarely encounter problems."

If she has agreed to the procedure, Mom probably was **not** told that it could likely result in premature rupture of her membranes, or that it increases her chance of infection.[3] Neither would she probably be told that if she fails to go into labor after the water breaks, she will be on a clock to deliver within 12 hours because her caregiver would be concerned about...are you ready for this...infection. The next step after this seemingly innocuous intervention is probably going to be one of two drugs, neither of which is approved by the FDA for elective labor induction.

So, in the next day or two, her water might break, and she may have surges...or she may not. But she will definitely now be in the hospital, with fingers in her often to assess her (slow) progress. Of course it's 'slow'...she probably wasn't quite ready. Even if she was, it will seem 'slow' to her caregiver, because now he's got to wrap this up before his engagement (and that threat of infection...that wasn't there until he put it there).

As he suggests cytotec or pictocin, he will downplay the risk because he wants her 'compliant'. He may or may not give an

---

[3] "Techniques for induction of labor may be divided into surgical or medical. Surgical techniques include stripping of membranes or amniotomy. Stripping of fetal membranes involves bluntly separating the chorioamnionic membrane from the wall of the cervix and the lower uterine segment. The efficacy of induction of labor by stripping membranes has not been established. Risks include potential infection, bleeding from previously undiagnosed placenta previa or low-lying placenta, and the accidental rupture of membranes." **www.medical-library.org**

actual risk factor to the intervention except to say that it's 'small'. He's probably right. The odds may be in his favor that nothing bad will happen. It could be that there is a 75% chance that all will go well, which is only a 25% chance that something will go wrong. (these are arbitrary figures)

What he fails to explain is what the odds are that this intervention will lead to another, which could lead to any number of serious problems, and ultimately unnecessary surgery. Nor will he be pointing out that although 25% is low, the rate of complications associated with this cascade of interventions was <u>ZERO</u> before he purposely injected them into the situation. Or, that even if she avoids surgery, pitocin may turn her labor into a nightmare from which she begs to be rescued.

How many parents buy what he's selling? Probably most. The caregiver is banking on the fact that the odds he's playing with your baby's life are in his favor, and he's right. Sort of.

Moving ahead to the probable conclusion of a safe delivery, let's imagine (it appears) we have a healthy mom and baby. Everyone is happy that it all turned out, and the belief that concern was unjustified is reinforced. Mom and baby need to stay in the hospital a few days, instead of being able to go right home (which is where they would have been better off all along), exposing them both to a hospital-acquired infection.[4]

At home, the baby is unresponsive to normal stimuli. "What a good baby!" everyone exclaims. The baby may not be interested in nursing, either because the jaundice from the pitocin makes him sleepy, or because of the narcotics, starting a vicious cycle ending with inadvertent weaning and much frustration.

---

[4] http://www.gentlebirth.org/archives/nosocoml.html

These problems could have been avoided, but since they weren't, they need to be managed without causing more damage. They **can** be overcome, it's just going to take a lot of effort to make it work.

In our culture, mothers are encouraged to be content with this. It's a 'good birth', if the mother and baby survive...bonus if they do it without getting cut. Even though the ecstasy of birth and deep bonding have been lost, if the parents are happy with what they have, that's good enough. I do support the right of mothers to have the birth they want...as long as it's not to the detriment of the baby...I just find it incredibly sad that 'good enough' is all they wish for themselves.

Deep down on a soul level I think we know when we've been robbed of our bliss...or we've voluntarily given it away. I can't imagine a bigger disservice to women than letting them think that's all there is!

When all is said and done, the parents are so glad that they got to have their baby before their doctor left town instead of having his back up, who is known to be quick with the knife.

Why is there such gratitude that their caregiver cared so little about them that he was willing to leave them in the hands of a colleague he's reasonably sure will harm them? And, who was so self-absorbed that instead of putting *the one and only birth of their baby* first, was willing to introduce a number of potentially very harmful interventions to ensure he wouldn't miss a minute of his own plans. Why isn't this questioned? It's a blatant disregard of the 'do no harm' oath!

What if the other probable outcome happened, instead of this 'good' one? What if the interventions lead to a surgical birth as so many of do?

Still, 'As long as everyone's ok now...that's all that matters' is what we've been conditioned to say, in order to not make the mother feel what, by now, you know we *can't* make a mother feel. Why (Oh, why?!) doesn't anyone question this line of reasoning?

Essentially, women's feeling are devalued by this type of comment hundreds of times a day. Most of those mothers are women who avoided the information you've just read with a 'see no evil' attitude, thinking nothing bad could happen to them if they just closed their eyes to reality. *Please*, don't be one of them.

> WHEN YOU WANT
> TO BELIEVE IN SOMETHING,
> YOU ALSO HAVE TO BELIEVE IN EVERYTHING
> THAT'S NECESSARY FOR BELIEVING IN IT.
> *Ugo Betti*
> *Struggle Till Dawn*

Selected Bibliography

Many books have shaped my thinking over the years. Some are noted in the chapters in which I reference them as well as here. This bibliography is intended only as a recourse for those readers wanting to follow up on any of the areas that have coalesced into this work.

Baldwin, Rahima, *Special Delivery: A Guide to Creating the Birth You Want for You and Your Baby,*
Celestial Arts, 1986

Benson, Herbert, *The Relaxation Response, revised ed.,* Harper Torch, 2000

Benson, Herbert, *Beyond the Relaxation Response,* Berkley Books, 1985

Blaffer Hrdy, Sarah, *Mother Nature; A History of Mothers, Infants and Natural Selection,* Pantheon Books, 1999

Brookfield, Stephen D., *Developing Critical Thinkers: Challenging Adults to Explore Alternative Ways of Thinking and Acting,* Jossey-Bass, 1991

Brookfield, Stephen D., *Becoming a Critically Reflective Teacher,* Jossey-Bass, 1995

Chilton Pearce, Joseph, *Magical Child,* Plume, 1977

Cohen and Estner, *Silent Knife: Vaginal Birth After Cesarean and Cesarean Prevention,* Bergen and Garvey, 1983

Cohen, Nancy, *Open Season: A Survival Guide for Natural Childbirth and VBAC in the 90s,* Praeger Trade, 2000)

Dilts, *Changing Belief Systems with NLP,* Meta Publications, 1990

England, Horowitz, *Birthing from Within,* Partera Press, 1998

Enkin, Keirse, Renfrew and Neilson, *A Guide to Effective Care in Pregnancy and Childbirth, 2nd Ed.,* Oxford University Press, 1995

Frye, Anne, *Understanding Diagnostic Tests in the Childbearing Year, A Guide for Givers and Receivers of Health Care in Childbearing, 5th ed.,* Labrys Press, 1993

Frye, Anne, *Holistic Midwifery: A Comprehensive Textbook for Midwives in Homebirth Practice, Vol, 1,* Labrys Press, 1995

Gaskin, Ina May, *Ina May's Guide to Childbirth,* Bantam-Doubleday-Dell, 2003

Gilovich, Thomas, *How We Know What Isn't So: The Fallibility of Human Reason in Everyday Life,* The Free Press, 1991

Goer, Henci, *Obstetric Myths versus Research Realities: A Guide to the Medical Literature,* Bergin and Garvey, 1995

Goer, Henci *The Thinking Woman's Guide to a Better Birth,* Perigree, 1999

Gopnik, Meltzoff, Kuhl, *The Scientist in the Crib: Minds, Brains and How Children Learn,* William Morrow and Co., 1999

Gordon, Thomas, *Parent Effectiveness Training: The Proven Program for Raising Responsible Children,* Three Rivers Press, 2000

Granju, Katie Allison, *Attachment Parenting: Instinctive Care for Your Baby and Young Child,* Pocket Books, 1999

Harper, Barbara, *Gentle Birth Choices: A Guide to Making Informed Decisions about Birthing Centers, Birth Attendants, Waterbirth, Homebirth and Hospital Birth,* Healing Arts Press 1994

Karr-Morse and Wiley, *Ghosts from the Nursery: Tracing the Roots of Violence,* Atlantic Monthly Press, 1977

Katz Rothman, Barbara, *The Tentative Pregnancy: How Amniocentesis Changes the Experience of Motherhood,* W.W. Norton & Co., 1993

Liedloff, Jean, *The Continuum Concept; In Search of Happiness Lost,* Addison-Wesley Publishing Company, 1995

Maushart, Susan, *The Mask of Motherhood: How Becoming a Mother Changes Our Lives and Why We Never Talk About It,* Penguin Books, 2000

McGraw, Phillip, *Life Strategies: Doing What Works, Doing What Matters.* Hyperion, 1999

Miguel Ruiz, Don, *The Four Agreements: A Practical Guide to Personal Freedom,* Amber-Allen, 1997

Mongan, Marie, *HypnoBirthing, A Celebration of Life: A Definitive Guide for Easier, Safer, More Comfortable Birthing,* Rivertree Publishing, 1998

Northrup, Christiane, *Women's Bodies, Women's Wisdom,* Bantam Books, 1998

Pantly, Elizabeth, *The No Cry Sleep Solution: Gentle Ways to Help Your Baby Sleep Through the Night,* Contemporary Books, 2002

Robbins, John, *Reclaiming Our Health: Exploding the Medical Myth and Embracing the Source of Healing,* HJ Kramer, 1996

Schlessinger, Laura, *Parenthood by Proxy: Don't Have Them If You Won't Raise Them,* HarperCollins, 2000

Stewert, David, *The Five Safe Standards for Safe Childbearing,* NAPSAC Intl., 1981

Strong, Thomas, *Expecting Trouble: The Myth of Prenatal Care in America,* New York University Press, 2000

Tamoro, Janet, *So That's What They're For!,* Adams Media Corp., 1995

Wagner, Marsden, *Pursuing the Birth Machine: The Search for Appropriate Birth Technology,* A.C.E. Graphics, 1994

Wolf, Naomi, *MisConceptions: Truth, Lies and the Unexpected on the Journey to Motherhood,* Doubleday, 2001

Williams, Poijula, *The PTSD Workbook: Simple, Effective Ways for Overcoming Traumatic Stress Symptoms,* New Harbinger Publications, Inc. 2002

Web Resources

Every attempt has been make to assure the resources listed below are current, but the internet is an ever changing medium. Please let the author know of any changes found that should be made in future editions.

The Original Mongan Method HypnoBirthing®
http://www.hypnobirthing.com/
The Cochran Library. A Guide to Effective Care...data base.
http://www.update-software.com/Cochrane/default.HTM
The International Cesarean Awareness Network
http://www.ican-online.org/
Safety and Cost Effectiveness of the Midwifery Model of Care
http://www.goodnewsnet.org/safety_issues01/safetyIndex01.htm
The Association of Labor Assistants and Childbirth Educators
http://www.alace.org/
Breastfeeding Online, Dr. Jack Newman
http://users.erols.com/cindyrn/newman.htm
Citizens for Midwifery
http://www.cfmidwifery.org/
Henci Goer Articles
http://www.hencigoer.com/articles/
Lamaze International
http://www.lamaze.org/2000/homestudy.html
Midwifery Today Online
http://www.midwiferytoday.com/
Physicians for Midwifery
http://www.well.com/user/zuni/pfm.html
Alliance for the Improvement of Maternity Services
http://www.aimsusa.org/
Association of Nurse Advocates for Childbirth Solutions
http://www.anacs.org/html/index.php
Coalition for Improving Maternity Services
http://www.motherfriendly.org/index.html
National Women's Health Alliance, Obstetric Drug Information
http://www.nwhalliance.org/obstetric_drugs.htm
Who's having this baby anyway?(Game)
www.babysbirthbenefits.com

About the Author (above with her daughter):

Kim Wildner has been a childbirth professional since 1991. Her passion is birth. When she isn't writing, teaching or lecturing she reads about birth, keeping abreast of the current literature. She also creates birth art through sculpture and other mediums. She has attended births in both home and hospital settings, has studied midwifery in the States and abroad, and has served in every capacity from monitrice to primary midwife.

Wildner has had work published in *Midwifery Today* and *Special Delivery*, the journal of ALACE, the Association of Labor Assistants and Childbirth Educators.

She and her husband of nearly 20 years live in Michigan. They have one gently home-born daughter.

Non-birth related interests include spending time with her family, walking, reading, knitting, beading and counted cross-stitch.

Better Birth Basics Order Form

	Price	#	Total
MOTHER'S INTENTION: HOW BELIEF SHAPES BIRTH $ 19.95			
WOMAN'S WISDOM: FROM THE BEST INTENTIONS TO BETTER BIRTH AN EXPERIENTIAL COMPANION GUIDE TO *MOTHER'S INTENTION* $19.95 (AVAILABLE 2004)			
BETTER BIRTH DECK: *MOTHER'S INTENTION* POCKET PACK $12.95			
HEALTHIER PREGNANCY: *WOMAN'S WISDOM* POCKET PACK $12.95 (AVAILABLE 2004)			
BORN OF WATER, A NOVEL OF A SHIFTING BIRTHING PARADIGM $14.95 (RELEASE TO BE ANNOUNCED)			
BETTER BIRTH RELAXATION & VISUALIZATION CD $14.95			
BETTER BIRTH BASICS SERIES: MOTHER'S INTENTION, BETTER BIRTH DECK & RELAXATION CD $39.95 (AVAILABLE 9/03)			
HEALTHIER PREGNANCY SERIES: WOMAN'S WISDOM, HEALTHIER PREGNANCY DECK & RELAXATION CD $39.95 (AVAILABLE 2004)			
BETTER BIRTH BASICS COMPLETE PACKAGE: MOTHER'S INTENTION, WOMAN'S WISDOM, BOTH DECKS & CD $64.95 (AVAILABLE 2004)			
INFORMATION ABOUT SPEAKING ENGAGEMENTS OR CONSULTING: FREE			
SALES TAX: MI RESIDENTS PLEASE ADD 6% SALES TAX			
SHIPPING AND HANDLING, IN THE US, PLEASE ADD $4.00 FOR FIRST BOOK OR CD AND $2.00 FOR EACH ADDITIONAL ITEM.			
TOTAL AMOUNT ENCLOSED:			

(see other side)

Please mail check or money orders, payable to:

Kim Wildner
P.O. Box 265
Ludington, MI 49431

Name: _____

Address: _____City: _____

State: _____ Zip: _____Telephone: _____

Email: _____

Please allow 6 to 8 weeks from release date for delivery.